Microsoft® PowerPoint® 2010

ILLUSTRATED

Introductory

Microsoft® PowerPoint® 2010

ILLUSTRATED

David W. Beskeen

COURSE TECHNOLOGY
CENGAGE Learning™

Australia • Brazil • Japan • Korea • Mexico • Singapore • Spain • United Kingdom • United States

COURSE TECHNOLOGY
CENGAGE Learning™

Microsoft® PowerPoint® 2010—Illustrated Introductory

David W. Beskeen

Vice President, Publisher: Nicole Jones Pinard

Executive Editor: Marjorie Hunt

Associate Acquisitions Editor: Brandi Shailer

Senior Product Manager: Christina Kling Garrett

Associate Product Manager: Michelle Camisa

Editorial Assistant: Kim Klasner

Director of Marketing: Cheryl Costantini

Senior Marketing Manager: Ryan DeGrote

Marketing Coordinator: Kristen Panciocco

Contributing Authors: Carol Cram, Elizabeth Eisner Reding

Developmental Editors: Rachel Biheller Bunin, Pamela Conrad, Jeanne Herring

Content Project Manager: Lisa Weidenfeld

Copy Editor: Mark Goodin

Proofreader: Harry Johnson

Indexer: BIM Indexing and Proofreading Services

QA Manuscript Reviewers: John Frietas, Serge Palladino, Jeff Schwartz, Danielle Shaw, Marianne Snow, Teresa Storch

Print Buyer: Fola Orekoya

Cover Designer: GEX Publishing Services

Cover Artist: Mark Hunt

Composition: GEX Publishing Services

Credits:
Figure Credit line
C-5 Photo courtesy of Janet Moffat
C-18 Photo courtesy of Jennifer Beskeen
C-21, C-22 Photos courtesy of Barbara Clemens
D-3 Photo courtesy of Donna Goudy
D-4, D-5 Photos courtesy of Janet Moffat
E-12 Photo courtesy of Janet Moffat
G-6 Photos courtesy of Donna Goudy, Janet Moffat, and Karen Beskeen
H-4 Photo courtesy of Donna Goudy
H-6 Photo courtesy of Janet Moffat
H-14, H-15 Photos courtesy of Barbara Hilliard
H-20 Photos courtesy of Justin Beskeen
H-21 Photos courtesy of Barbara Hilliard and Joan Johnson

For product information and technology assistance, contact us at **Cengage Learning Customer & Sales Support, 1-800-354-9706**

For permission to use material from this text or product, submit all requests online at **www.cengage.com/permissions**
Further permissions questions can be emailed to **permissionrequest@cengage.com**

Trademarks:

Some of the product names and company names used in this book have been used for identification purposes only and may be trademarks or registered trademarks of their respective manufacturers and sellers.

Microsoft and the Office logo are either registered trademarks or trademarks of Microsoft Corporation in the United States and/or other countries. Course Technology, Cengage Learning is an independent entity from Microsoft Corporation, and not affiliated with Microsoft in any manner.

The Microsoft Office Specialist Exams, the Exam Objectives, logos, the Microsoft Office Specialist Program, the Microsoft Technology Associate Certification Paths and the VAC Program are the sole property of Microsoft Corporation.

Library of Congress Control Number: 2010932360

ISBN-13: 978-0-538-74716-5
ISBN-10: 0-538-74716-1

Course Technology
20 Channel Center Street
Boston, MA 02210
USA

Cengage Learning is a leading provider of customized learning solutions with office locations around the globe, including Singapore, the United Kingdom, Australia, Mexico, Brazil, and Japan. Locate your local office at: **www.cengage.com/global**

Cengage Learning products are represented in Canada by Nelson Education, Ltd.

To learn more about Course Technology, visit **www.cengage.com/coursetechnology**

To learn more about Cengage Learning, visit **www.cengage.com**

Purchase any of our products at your local college store or at our preferred online store **www.cengagebrain.com**

Printed in the United States of America
2 3 4 5 6 7 8 9 18 17 16 15 14 13 12 11

Brief Contents

Contents

Web Apps

Appendix: PowerPoint

Preface

Welcome to *Microsoft PowerPoint 2010— Illustrated Introductory*. If this is your first experience with the Illustrated series, you'll see that this book has a unique design: each skill is presented on two facing pages, with steps on the left and screens on the right. The layout makes it easy to learn a skill without having to read a lot of text and flip pages to see an illustration.

This book is an ideal learning tool for a wide range of learners—the "rookies" will find the clean design easy to follow and focused with only essential information presented, and the "hotshots" will appreciate being able to move quickly through the lessons to find the information they need without reading a lot of text. The design also makes this a great reference after the course is over! See the illustration on the right to learn more about the pedagogical and design elements of a typical lesson.

What's New In This Edition

- **Fully Updated.** Highlights the new features of Microsoft PowerPoint 2010 including new 3-D motion slide transitions, artistic effects and textures for pictures, organizing slides into sections, co-authoring capabilities, broadcasting a presentation over the Internet, and the new Backstage view. A new appendix covers cloud computing concepts and using Microsoft Office Web Apps.

- **Maps to SAM 2010.** This book is designed to work with SAM (Skills Assessment Manager) 2010. **SAM Assessment** contains performance-based, hands-on SAM exams for each unit of this book, and **SAM Training** provides hands-on training for skills covered in the book. Some exercises are available in **SAM Projects**, which is auto-grading software that provides both students and instructors with immediate, detailed feedback (SAM sold separately.) See page xii for more information on SAM.

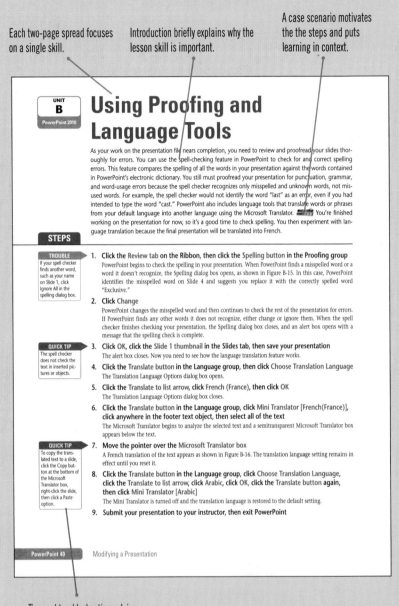

Each two-page spread focuses on a single skill.

Introduction briefly explains why the lesson skill is important.

A case scenario motivates the the steps and puts learning in context.

Tips and troubleshooting advice, right where you need it–next to the step itself.

Assignments

The lessons use Quest Specialty Travel, a fictional adventure travel company, as the case study. The assignments on the light yellow pages at the end of each unit increase in difficulty. Assignments include:

- **Concepts Review** consist of multiple choice, matching, and screen identification questions.

- **Skills Reviews** are hands-on, step-by-step exercises that review the skills covered in each lesson in the unit.

- **Independent Challenges** are case projects requiring critical thinking and application of the unit skills. The Independent Challenges increase in difficulty, with the first one in each unit being the easiest. Independent Challenges 2 and 3 become increasingly open-ended, requiring more independent problem solving.

- **SAM Projects** is live-in-the-application autograding software that provides immediate and detailed feedback reports to students and instructors. Some exercises in this book are available in SAM Projects. (Purchase of a SAM Projects pincode is required).

- **Real Life Independent Challenges** are practical exercises in which students create documents to help them with their every day lives.

- **Advanced Challenge Exercises** set within the Independent Challenges provide optional steps for more advanced students.

- **Visual Workshops** are practical, self-graded capstone projects that require independent problem solving.

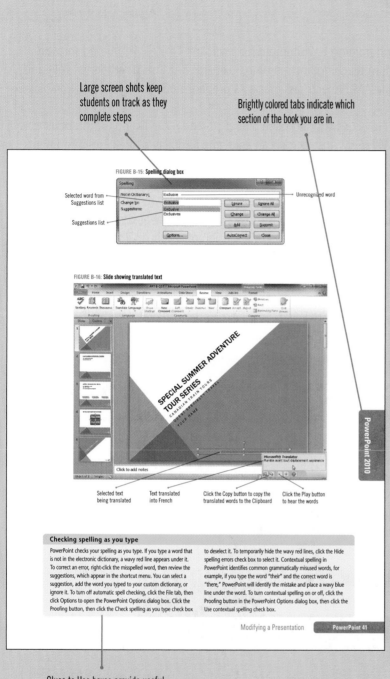

Large screen shots keep students on track as they complete steps

Brightly colored tabs indicate which section of the book you are in.

FIGURE B-15: Spelling dialog box

Selected word from Suggestions list

Suggestions list

Unrecognized word

FIGURE B-16: Slide showing translated text

SPECIAL SUMMER ADVENTURE TOUR SERIES

CANADIAN TRAIN TOURS

QUEST SPECIALTY TRAVEL

YOUR NAME

Selected text being translated

Text translated into French

Click the Copy button to copy the translated words to the Clipboard

Click the Play button to hear the words

Checking spelling as you type

PowerPoint checks your spelling as you type. If you type a word that is not in the electronic dictionary, a wavy red line appears under it. To correct an error, right-click the misspelled word, then review the suggestions, which appear in the shortcut menu. You can select a suggestion, add the word you typed to your custom dictionary, or ignore it. To turn off automatic spell checking, click the File tab, then click Options to open the PowerPoint Options dialog box. Click the Proofing button, then click the Check spelling as you type check box to deselect it. To temporarily hide the wavy red lines, click the Hide spelling errors check box to select it. Contextual spelling in PowerPoint identifies common grammatically misused words, for example, if you type the word "their" and the correct word is "there," PowerPoint will identify the mistake and place a wavy blue line under the word. To turn contextual spelling on or off, click the Proofing button in the PowerPoint Options dialog box, then click the Use contextual spelling check box.

Modifying a Presentation

PowerPoint 41

PowerPoint 2010

Clues to Use boxes provide useful information related to the lesson skill.

xi

About SAM

SAM is the premier proficiency-based assessment and training environment for Microsoft Office. Web-based software along with an inviting user interface provide maximum teaching and learning flexibility. SAM builds students' skills and confidence with a variety of real-life simulations, and SAM Projects' assignments prepare students for today's workplace.

The SAM system includes Assessment, Training, and Projects, featuring page references and remediation for this book as well as Course Technology's Microsoft Office textbooks. With SAM, instructors can enjoy the flexibility of creating assignments based on content from their favorite Microsoft Office books or based on specific course objectives. Instructors appreciate the scheduling and reporting options that have made SAM the market-leading online testing and training software for over a decade. Over 2,000 performance-based questions and matching Training simulations, as well as tens of thousands of objective-based questions from many Course Technology texts, provide instructors with a variety of choices across multiple applications from the introductory level through the comprehensive level. The inclusion of hands-on Projects guarantee that student knowledge will skyrocket from the practice of solving real-world situations using Microsoft Office software.

SAM Assessment

- Content for these hands-on, performance-based tasks includes Word, Excel, Access, PowerPoint, Internet Explorer, Outlook, and Windows. Includes tens of thousands of objective-based questions from many Course Technology texts.

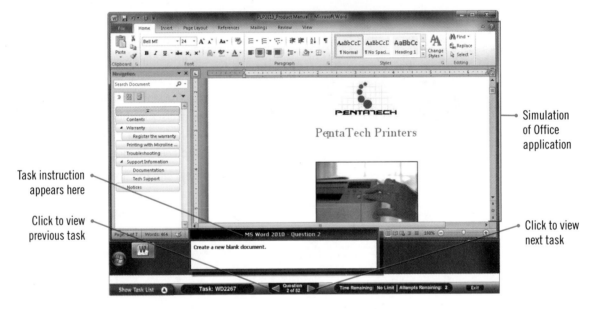

Simulation of Office application

Task instruction appears here

Click to view previous task

Click to view next task

SAM Training

- Observe mode allows the student to watch and listen to a task as it is being completed.
- Practice mode allows the student to follow guided arrows and hear audio prompts to help visual learners know how to complete a task.
- Apply mode allows the student to prove what they've learned by completing a task using helpful instructions.

SAM Projects

- Live-in-the-application assignments in Word, Excel, Access and PowerPoint that help students be sure they know how to effectively communicate, solve a problem or make a decision.
- Students receive detailed feedback on their project within minutes.
- Additionally, teaches proper file management techniques.
- Ensures that academic integrity is not compromised, with unique anti-cheating detection encrypted into the data files.

Instructor Resources

The Instructor Resources CD is Course Technology's way of putting the resources and information needed to teach and learn effectively into your hands. With an integrated array of teaching and learning tools that offer you and your students a broad range of technology-based instructional options, we believe this CD represents the highest quality and most cutting edge resources available to instructors today. The resources available with this book are:

- **Instructor's Manual**—Available as an electronic file, the Instructor's Manual includes detailed lecture topics with teaching tips for each unit.

- **Sample Syllabus**—Prepare and customize your course easily using this sample course outline.

- **PowerPoint Presentations**—Each unit has a corresponding PowerPoint presentation that you can use in lecture, distribute to your students, or customize to suit your course.

- **Figure Files**—The figures in the text are provided on the Instructor Resources CD to help you illustrate key topics or concepts. You can create traditional overhead transparencies by printing the figure files. Or you can create electronic slide shows by using the figures in a presentation program such as PowerPoint.

- **Solutions to Exercises**—Solutions to Exercises contains every file students are asked to create or modify in the lessons and end-of-unit material. Also provided in this section, there is a document outlining the solutions for the end-of-unit Concepts Review, Skills Review, and Independent Challenges. An Annotated Solution File and Grading Rubric accompany each file and can be used together for quick and easy grading.

- **Data Files for Students**—To complete most of the units in this book, your students will need Data Files. You can post the Data Files on a file server for students to copy. The Data Files are available on the Instructor Resources CD-ROM, the Review Pack, and can also be downloaded from cengagebrain.com. For information on how to download the Data Files from cengagebrain.com, see the inside back cover.

Instruct students to use the Data Files List included on the Review Pack and the Instructor Resources CD. This list gives instructions on copying and organizing files.

- **ExamView**—ExamView is a powerful testing software package that allows you to create and administer printed, computer (LAN-based), and Internet exams. ExamView includes hundreds of questions that correspond to the topics covered in this text, enabling students to generate detailed study guides that include page references for further review. The computer-based and Internet testing components allow students to take exams at their computers, and also saves you time by grading each exam automatically.

Content for Online Learning.

Course Technology has partnered with the leading distance learning solution providers and class-management platforms today. To access this material, visit www.cengage.com/webtutor and search for your title. Instructor resources include the following: additional case projects, sample syllabi, PowerPoint presentations, and more. For additional information, please contact your sales representative. For students to access this material, they must have purchased a WebTutor PIN-code specific to this title and your campus platform. The resources for students might include (based on instructor preferences): topic reviews, review questions, practice tests, and more.

Acknowledgements

Instructor Advisory Board

We thank our Instructor Advisory Board who gave us their opinions and guided our decisions as we updated our texts for Microsoft Office 2010. They are as follows:

Terri Helfand, Chaffey Community College

Barbara Comfort, J. Sargeant Reynolds Community College

Brenda Nielsen, Mesa Community College

Sharon Cotman, Thomas Nelson Community College

Marian Meyer, Central New Mexico Community College

Audrey Styer, Morton College

Richard Alexander, Heald College

Xiaodong Qiao, Heald College

Student Advisory Board

We also thank our Student Advisory Board members, who shared their experiences using the book and offered suggestions to make it better: **Latasha Jefferson**, Thomas Nelson Community College, **Gary Williams**, Thomas Nelson Community College, **Stephanie Miller**, J. Sargeant Reynolds Community College, **Sarah Styer**, Morton Community College, **Missy Marino**, Chaffey College

Author Acknowledgements

David W. Beskeen Being a part of the extremely talented and experienced Office Illustrated team makes working on this book that much more enjoyable—many thanks to Rachel Biheller Bunin, Christina Kling Garrett, the production group, the testers, and the rest of the Cengage team! I also want to acknowledge my family, especially my parents Don and Darlene, for all they have done for me...I am forever grateful.

Dedication

This book is dedicated to the memory of Donald W. Beskeen.

Read This Before You Begin

Frequently Asked Questions

What are Data Files?

A Data File is a partially completed PowerPoint presentation or another type of file that you use to complete the steps in the units and exercises to create the final document that you submit to your instructor. Each unit opener page lists the Data Files that you need for that unit.

Where are the Data Files?

Your instructor will provide the Data Files to you or direct you to a location on a network drive from which you can download them. For information on how to download the Data Files from cengagebrain.com, see the inside back cover.

What software was used to write and test this book?

This book was written and tested using a typical installation of Microsoft Office 2010 Professional Plus on a computer with a typical installation of Microsoft Windows 7 Ultimate.

The browser used for any Web-dependent steps is Internet Explorer 8.

Do I need to be connected to the Internet to complete the steps and exercises in this book?

Some of the exercises in this book require that your computer be connected to the Internet. If you are not connected to the Internet, see your instructor for information on how to complete the exercises.

What do I do if my screen is different from the figures shown in this book?

This book was written and tested on computers with monitors set at a resolution of 1024 × 768. If your screen shows more or less information than the figures in the book, your monitor is probably set at a higher or lower resolution. If you don't see something on your screen, you might have to scroll down or up to see the object identified in the figures.

The Ribbon—the blue area at the top of the screen—in Microsoft Office 2010 adapts to different resolutions. If your monitor is set at a lower resolution than 1024 × 768, you might not see all of the buttons shown in the figures. The groups of buttons will always appear, but the entire group might be condensed into a single button that you need to click to access the buttons described in the instructions.

COURSECASTS Learning on the Go. Always Available...Always Relevant.

Our fast-paced world is driven by technology. You know because you are an active participant—always on the go, always keeping up with technological trends, and always learning new ways to embrace technology to power your life. Let CourseCasts, hosted by Ken Baldauf of Florida State University, be your guide into weekly updates in this ever-changing space. These timely, relevant podcasts are produced weekly and are available for download at http://coursecasts.course.com or directly from iTunes (search by CourseCasts). CourseCasts are a perfect solution to getting students (and even instructors) to learn on the go!

What is the Microsoft® Office Specialist Program?

The Microsoft Office Specialist Program enables candidates to show that they have something exceptional to offer—proven expertise in certain Microsoft programs. Recognized by businesses and schools around the world, over 4 million certifications have been obtained in over 100 different countries. The Microsoft Office Specialist Program is the only Microsoft-approved certification program of its kind.

What is the Microsoft Office Specialist Certification?

The Microsoft Office Specialist certification validates through the use of exams that you have obtained specific skill sets within the applicable Microsoft Office programs and other Microsoft programs included in the Microsoft Office Specialist Program. The candidate can choose which exam(s) they want to take according to which skills they want to validate.

The available Microsoft Office Specialist Program exams include*:

- Using Windows Vista®
- Using Microsoft® Office Word 2007
- Using Microsoft® Office Word 2007 – Expert
- Using Microsoft® Office Excel® 2007
- Using Microsoft® Office Excel® 2007 – Expert
- Using Microsoft® Office PowerPoint® 2007
- Using Microsoft® Office Access® 2007
- Using Microsoft® Office Outlook® 2007
- Using Microsoft SharePoint® 2007

The Microsoft Office Specialist Program 2010 exams will include*:

- Microsoft Word 2010
- Microsoft Word 2010 Expert
- Microsoft Excel® 2010
- Microsoft Excel® 2010 Expert
- Microsoft PowerPoint® 2010
- Microsoft Access® 2010
- Microsoft Outlook® 2010
- Microsoft SharePoint® 2010

What does the Microsoft Office Specialist Approved Courseware logo represent?

The logo indicates that this courseware has been approved by Microsoft to cover the course objectives that will be included in the relevant exam. It also means that after utilizing this courseware, you may be better prepared to pass the exams required to become a certified Microsoft Office Specialist.

For more information:

To learn more about Microsoft Office Specialist exams, visit www.microsoft.com/learning/msbc

To learn about other Microsoft approved courseware from Course Technology, visit www.cengage.com/coursetechnology

* The availability of Microsoft Office Specialist certification exams varies by Microsoft program, program version and language. Visit www.microsoft.com/learning for exam availability.

Getting Started with Microsoft Office 2010

Microsoft Office 2010 is a group of software programs designed to help you create documents, collaborate with coworkers, and track and analyze information. Each program is designed so you can work quickly and efficiently to create professional-looking results. You use different Office programs to accomplish specific tasks, such as writing a letter or producing a sales presentation, yet all the programs have a similar look and feel. Once you become familiar with one program, you'll find it easy to transfer your knowledge to the others. This unit introduces you to the most frequently used programs in Office, as well as common features they all share.

OBJECTIVES

Understand the Office 2010 suite

Start and exit an Office program

View the Office 2010 user interface

Create and save a file

Open a file and save it with a new name

View and print your work

Get Help and close a file

Understanding the Office 2010 Suite

Microsoft Office 2010 features an intuitive, context-sensitive user interface, so you can get up to speed faster and use advanced features with greater ease. The programs in Office are bundled together in a group called a **suite** (although you can also purchase them separately). The Office suite is available in several configurations, but all include Word, Excel, and PowerPoint. Other configurations include Access, Outlook, Publisher, and other programs. Each program in Office is best suited for completing specific types of tasks, though there is some overlap in capabilities.

DETAILS

The Office programs covered in this book include:

- **Microsoft Word 2010**

  When you need to create any kind of text-based document, such as a memo, newsletter, or multipage report, Word is the program to use. You can easily make your documents look great by inserting eye-catching graphics and using formatting tools such as themes, which are available in most Office programs. **Themes** are predesigned combinations of color and formatting attributes you can apply to a document. The Word document shown in Figure A-1 was formatted with the Solstice theme.

- **Microsoft Excel 2010**

  Excel is the perfect solution when you need to work with numeric values and make calculations. It puts the power of formulas, functions, charts, and other analytical tools into the hands of every user, so you can analyze sales projections, calculate loan payments, and present your findings in style. The Excel worksheet shown in Figure A-1 tracks personal expenses. Because Excel automatically recalculates results whenever a value changes, the information is always up to date. A chart illustrates how the monthly expenses are broken down.

- **Microsoft PowerPoint 2010**

  Using PowerPoint, it's easy to create powerful presentations complete with graphics, transitions, and even a soundtrack. Using professionally designed themes and clip art, you can quickly and easily create dynamic slide shows such as the one shown in Figure A-1.

- **Microsoft Access 2010**

  Access helps you keep track of large amounts of quantitative data, such as product inventories or employee records. The form shown in Figure A-1 was created for a grocery store inventory database. Employees use the form to enter data about each item. Using Access enables employees to quickly find specific information such as price and quantity without hunting through store shelves and stockrooms.

Microsoft Office has benefits beyond the power of each program, including:

- **Common user interface: Improving business processes**

  Because the Office suite programs have a similar **interface**, or look and feel, your experience using one program's tools makes it easy to learn those in the other programs. In addition, Office documents are **compatible** with one another, meaning that you can easily incorporate, or **integrate**, an Excel chart into a PowerPoint slide, or an Access table into a Word document.

- **Collaboration: Simplifying how people work together**

  Office recognizes the way people do business today, and supports the emphasis on communication and knowledge sharing within companies and across the globe. All Office programs include the capability to incorporate feedback—called **online collaboration**—across the Internet or a company network.

FIGURE A-1: Microsoft Office 2010 documents

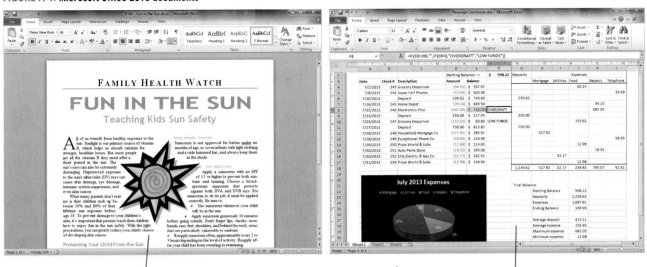

Newsletter created in Word

Checkbook register created in Excel

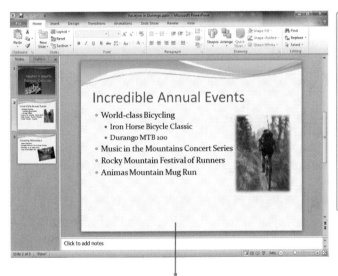

Tourism presentation created in PowerPoint

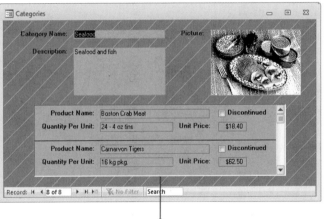

Store inventory form created in Access

Deciding which program to use

Every Office program includes tools that go far beyond what you might expect. For example, although Excel is primarily designed for making calculations, you can use it to create a database. So when you're planning a project, how do you decide which Office program to use? The general rule of thumb is to use the program best suited for your intended task, and make use of supporting tools in the program if you need them. Word is best for creating text-based documents, Excel is best for making mathematical calculations, PowerPoint is best for preparing presentations, and Access is best for managing quantitative data. Although the capabilities of Office are so vast that you *could* create an inventory in Excel or a budget in Word, you'll find greater flexibility and efficiency by using the program designed for the task. And remember, you can always create a file in one program, and then insert it in a document in another program when you need to, such as including sales projections (Excel) in a memo (Word).

Starting and Exiting an Office Program

The first step in using an Office program is to open, or **launch**, it on your computer. The easiest ways to launch a program are to click the Start button on the Windows taskbar or to double-click an icon on your desktop. You can have multiple programs open on your computer simultaneously, and you can move between open programs by clicking the desired program or document button on the taskbar or by using the [Alt][Tab] keyboard shortcut combination. ⬛⬛⬛ When working, you'll often want to open multiple programs in Office and switch among them as you work. Begin by launching a few Office programs now.

1. **Click the Start button ⊛ on the taskbar**

   The Start menu opens. If the taskbar is hidden, you can display it by pointing to the bottom of the screen. Depending on your taskbar property settings, the taskbar may be displayed at all times, or only when you point to that area of the screen. For more information, or to change your taskbar properties, consult your instructor or technical support person.

2. **Click All Programs, scroll down if necessary in the All Programs menu, click Microsoft Office as shown in Figure A-2, then click Microsoft Word 2010**

   Word 2010 starts, and the program window opens on your screen.

3. **Click ⊛ on the taskbar, click All Programs, click Microsoft Office, then click Microsoft Excel 2010**

   Excel 2010 starts, and the program window opens, as shown in Figure A-3. Word is no longer visible, but it remains open. The taskbar displays a button for each open program and document. Because this Excel document is **active**, or in front and available, the Excel button on the taskbar appears slightly lighter.

4. **Point to the Word program button 🗑 on the taskbar, then click 🗑**

   The Word program window is now in front. When the Aero feature is turned on in Windows 7, pointing to a program button on the taskbar displays a thumbnail version of each open window in that program above the program button. Clicking a program button on the taskbar activates that program and the most recently active document. Clicking a thumbnail of a document activates that document.

5. **Click ⊛ on the taskbar, click All Programs, click Microsoft Office, then click Microsoft PowerPoint 2010**

   PowerPoint 2010 starts and becomes the active program.

6. **Click the Excel program button 🗑 on the taskbar**

   Excel is now the active program.

7. **Click ⊛ on the taskbar, click All Programs, click Microsoft Office, then click Microsoft Access 2010**

   Access 2010 starts and becomes the active program. Now all four Office programs are open at the same time.

8. **Click Exit on the navigation bar in the Access program window, as shown in Figure A-4**

   Access closes, leaving Excel active and Word and PowerPoint open.

Using shortcut keys to move between Office programs

As an alternative to the Windows taskbar, you can use a keyboard shortcut to move among open Office programs. The [Alt][Tab] keyboard combination lets you either switch quickly to the next open program or file or choose one from a gallery. To switch immediately to the next open program or file, press [Alt][Tab]. To choose from all open programs and files, press and hold [Alt], then press and release [Tab] without releasing [Alt]. A gallery opens on screen, displaying the filename and a thumbnail image of each open program and file, as well as of the desktop. Each time you press [Tab] while holding [Alt], the selection cycles to the next open file or location. Release [Alt] when the program, file, or location you want to activate is selected.

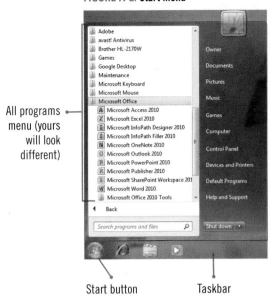

All programs
menu (yours
will look
different)

Start button   Taskbar

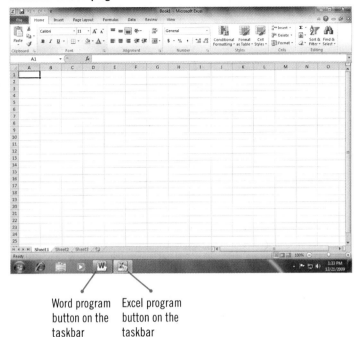

Word program   Excel program
button on the   button on the
taskbar   taskbar

Office 2010

FIGURE A-4: Access program window

File tab

Navigation bar

Exit command

Windows Live and Microsoft Office Web Apps

All Office programs include the capability to incorporate feedback—called online collaboration—across the Internet or a company network. Using **cloud computing** (work done in a virtual environment), you can take advantage of Web programs called Microsoft Office Web Apps, which are simplified versions of the programs found in the Microsoft Office 2010 suite. Because these programs are online, they take up no computer disk space and are accessed using

Windows Live SkyDrive, a free service from Microsoft. Using Windows Live SkyDrive, you and your colleagues can create and store documents in a "cloud" and make the documents available to whomever you grant access. To use Windows Live SkyDrive, you need a free Windows Live ID, which you obtain at the Windows Live Web site. You can find more information in the "Working with Windows Live and Office Web Apps" appendix.

Viewing the Office 2010 User Interface

One of the benefits of using Office is that the programs have much in common, making them easy to learn and making it simple to move from one to another. Individual Office programs have always shared many features, but the innovations in the Office 2010 user interface mean even greater similarity among them all. That means you can also use your knowledge of one program to get up to speed in another. A **user interface** is a collective term for all the ways you interact with a software program. The user interface in Office 2010 provides intuitive ways to choose commands, work with files, and navigate in the program window. ▓▓▓▓ Familiarize yourself with some of the common interface elements in Office by examining the PowerPoint program window.

STEPS

1. **Click the PowerPoint program button 🅿 on the taskbar**

   PowerPoint becomes the active program. Refer to Figure A-5 to identify common elements of the Office user interface. The **document window** occupies most of the screen. In PowerPoint, a blank slide appears in the document window, so you can build your slide show. At the top of every Office program window is a **title bar** that displays the document name and program name. Below the title bar is the **Ribbon**, which displays commands you're likely to need for the current task. Commands are organized onto **tabs**. The tab names appear at the top of the Ribbon, and the active tab appears in front. The Ribbon in every Office program includes tabs specific to the program, but all Office programs include a File tab and Home tab on the left end of the Ribbon.

2. **Click the File tab**

   The File tab opens, displaying **Backstage view**. The navigation bar on the left side of Backstage view contains commands to perform actions common to most Office programs, such as opening a file, saving a file, and closing the current program. Just above the File tab is the **Quick Access toolbar**, which also includes buttons for common Office commands.

3. **Click the File tab again to close Backstage view and return to the document window, then click the Design tab on the Ribbon**

   To display a different tab, you click the tab on the Ribbon. Each tab contains related commands arranged into **groups** to make features easy to find. On the Design tab, the Themes group displays available design themes in a **gallery**, or visual collection of choices you can browse. Many groups contain a **dialog box launcher**, an icon you can click to open a dialog box or task pane from which to choose related commands.

4. **Move the mouse pointer ▷ over the Angles theme in the Themes group as shown in Figure A-6, but do not click the mouse button**

   The Angles theme is temporarily applied to the slide in the document window. However, because you did not click the theme, you did not permanently change the slide. With the **Live Preview** feature, you can point to a choice, see the results right in the document, and then decide if you want to make the change.

5. **Move ▷ away from the Ribbon and towards the slide**

   If you had clicked the Angles theme, it would be applied to this slide. Instead, the slide remains unchanged.

6. **Point to the Zoom slider ▽ on the status bar, then drag ▽ to the right until the Zoom level reads 166%**

   The slide display is enlarged. Zoom tools are located on the status bar. You can drag the slider or click the Zoom In or Zoom Out buttons to zoom in or out on an area of interest. **Zooming in**, or choosing a higher percentage, makes a document appear bigger on screen, but less of it fits on the screen at once; **zooming out**, or choosing a lower percentage, lets you see more of the document but at a reduced size.

7. **Drag ▽ on the status bar to the left until the Zoom level reads 73%**

FIGURE A-5: PowerPoint program window

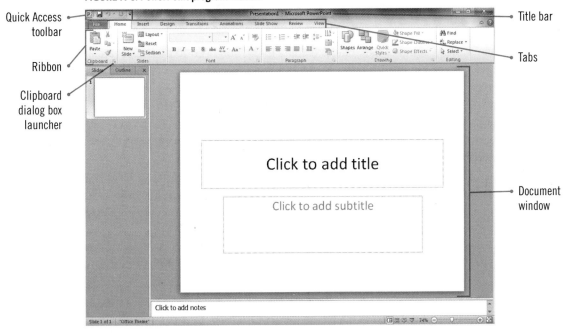

Quick Access toolbar
Ribbon
Clipboard dialog box launcher
Title bar
Tabs
Document window

FIGURE A-6: Viewing a theme with Live Preview

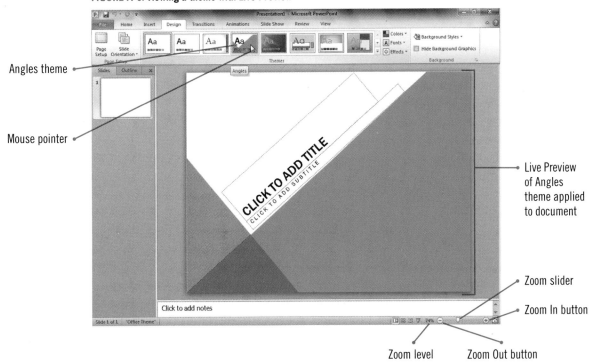

Angles theme
Mouse pointer
Live Preview of Angles theme applied to document
Zoom slider
Zoom In button
Zoom level
Zoom Out button

Using Backstage view

Backstage view in each Microsoft Office program offers "one stop shopping" for many commonly performed tasks, such as opening and saving a file, printing and previewing a document, defining document properties, sharing information, and exiting a program.

Backstage view opens when you click the File tab in any Office program, and while features such as the Ribbon, Mini toolbar, and Live Preview all help you work *in* your documents, the File tab and Backstage view help you work *with* your documents.

Office 2010

Creating and Saving a File

When working in a program, one of the first things you need to do is to create and save a file. A **file** is a stored collection of data. Saving a file enables you to work on a project now, then put it away and work on it again later. In some Office programs, including Word, Excel, and PowerPoint, a new file is automatically created when you start the program, so all you have to do is enter some data and save it. In Access, you must expressly create a file before you enter any data. You should give your files meaningful names and save them in an appropriate location so that they're easy to find. 🖊️🖊️🖊️ Use Word to familiarize yourself with the process of creating and saving a document. First you'll type some notes about a possible location for a corporate meeting, then you'll save the information for later use.

STEPS

1. **Click the** Word program button 🖼️ **on the taskbar**

2. **Type** Locations for Corporate Meeting, **then press [Enter] twice**
   The text appears in the document window, and the **insertion point** blinks on a new blank line. The insertion point indicates where the next typed text will appear.

3. **Type** Las Vegas, NV, **press [Enter], type** Orlando, FL, **press [Enter], type** Boston, MA, **press [Enter] twice, then type your name**
   Compare your document to Figure A-7.

4. **Click the** Save button 🖼️ **on the Quick Access toolbar**
   Because this is the first time you are saving this document, the Save As dialog box opens, as shown in Figure A-8. The Save As dialog box includes options for assigning a filename and storage location. Once you save a file for the first time, clicking 🖼️ saves any changes to the file *without* opening the Save As dialog box, because no additional information is needed. The Address bar in the Save As dialog box displays the default location for saving the file, but you can change it to any location. The File name field contains a suggested name for the document based on text in the file, but you can enter a different name.

5. **Type** OF A-Potential Corporate Meeting Locations
   The text you type replaces the highlighted text. (The "OF A-" in the filename indicates that the file is created in Office Unit A. You will see similar designations throughout this book when files are named. For example, a file named in Excel Unit B would begin with "EX B-" .)

6. **In the Save As dialog box, use the Address bar or Navigation Pane to navigate to the drive and folder where you store your Data Files**
   Many students store files on a flash drive, but you can also store files on your computer, a network drive, or any storage device indicated by your instructor or technical support person.

7. **Click** Save
   The Save As dialog box closes, the new file is saved to the location you specified, then the name of the document appears in the title bar, as shown in Figure A-9. (You may or may not see the file extension ".docx" after the filename.) See Table A-1 for a description of the different types of files you create in Office, and the file extensions associated with each.

TABLE A-1: Common filenames and default file extensions

file created in	is called a	and has the default extension
Word	document	.docx
Excel	workbook	.xlsx
PowerPoint	presentation	.pptx
Access	database	.accdb

FIGURE A-7: Document created in Word

Save button

Your name
should appear
here

Insertion point

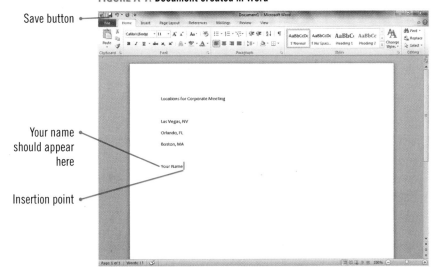

FIGURE A-8: Save As dialog box

Address bar

Navigation
Pane; your
links and
folders
may differ

File name field;
your computer
may not display
file extensions

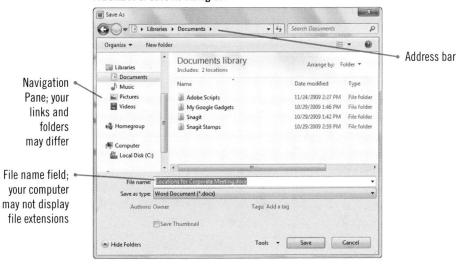

FIGURE A-9: Saved and named Word document

Filename
appears in
title bar

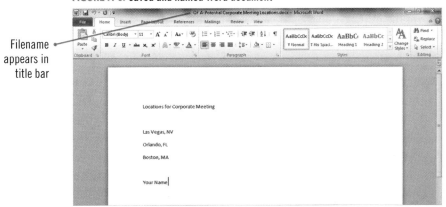

Using the Office Clipboard

You can use the Office Clipboard to cut and copy items from one Office program and paste them into others. The Office Clipboard can store a maximum of 24 items. To access it, open the Office Clipboard task pane by clicking the dialog box launcher 🔲 in the Clipboard group on the Home tab. Each time you copy a selection, it is saved in the Office Clipboard. Each entry in the Office Clipboard includes an icon that tells you the program it was created in. To paste an entry, click in the document where you want it to appear, then click the item in the Office Clipboard. To delete an item from the Office Clipboard, right-click the item, then click Delete.

Opening a File and Saving It with a New Name

In many cases as you work in Office, you start with a blank document, but often you need to use an existing file. It might be a file you or a coworker created earlier as a work in progress, or it could be a complete document that you want to use as the basis for another. For example, you might want to create a budget for this year using the budget you created last year; you could type in all the categories and information from scratch, or you could open last year's budget, save it with a new name, and just make changes to update it for the current year. By opening the existing file and saving it with the Save As command, you create a dupli-cate that you can modify to your heart's content, while the original file remains intact. ██████ Use Excel to open an existing workbook file, and save it with a new name so the original remains unchanged.

STEPS

1. **Click the Excel program button 🖩 on the taskbar, click the File tab, then click Open on the navigation bar**

   The Open dialog box opens, where you can navigate to any drive or folder accessible to your computer to locate a file.

2. **In the Open dialog box, navigate to the drive and folder where you store your Data Files**

   The files available in the current folder are listed, as shown in Figure A-10. This folder contains one file.

3. **Click OFFICE A-1.xlsx, then click Open**

   The dialog box closes, and the file opens in Excel. An Excel file is an electronic spreadsheet, so it looks differ-ent from a Word document or a PowerPoint slide.

4. **Click the File tab, then click Save As on the navigation bar**

   The Save As dialog box opens, and the current filename is highlighted in the File name text box. Using the Save As command enables you to create a copy of the current, existing file with a new name. This action pre-serves the original file and creates a new file that you can modify.

5. **Navigate to the drive and folder where you store your Data Files if necessary, type OF A-Budget for Corporate Meeting in the File name text box, as shown in Figure A-11, then click Save**

   A copy of the existing workbook is created with the new name. The original file, Office A-1.xlsx, closes automatically.

6. **Click cell A19, type your name, then press [Enter], as shown in Figure A-12**

   In Excel, you enter data in cells, which are formed by the intersection of a row and a column. Cell A19 is at the intersection of column A and row 19. When you press [Enter], the cell pointer moves to cell A20.

7. **Click the Save button 🖫 on the Quick Access toolbar**

   Your name appears in the workbook, and your changes to the file are saved.

Working in Compatibility Mode

Not everyone upgrades to the newest version of Office. As a general rule, new software versions are **backward compatible**, meaning that documents saved by an older version can be read by newer soft-ware. To open documents created in older Office versions, Office 2010 includes a feature called Compatibility Mode. When you use Office 2010 to open a file created in an earlier version of Office, "Compatibility Mode" appears in the title bar, letting you know the file was created in an earlier but usable version of the program. If

you are working with someone who may not be using the newest version of the software, you can avoid possible incompatibility prob-lems by saving your file in another, earlier format. To do this in an Office program, click the File tab, click Save As on the navigation bar, click the Save as type list arrow in the Save As dialog box, then click an option on the list. For example, if you're working in Excel, click Excel 97-2003 Workbook format in the Save as type list to save an Excel file so that it can be opened in Excel 97 or Excel 2003.

FIGURE A-10: Open dialog box

Available files in this folder •

Open button

Open list arrow

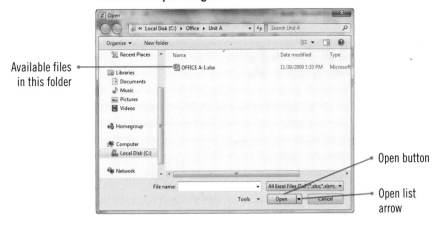

FIGURE A-11: Save As dialog box

New filename •

Save as type list arrow

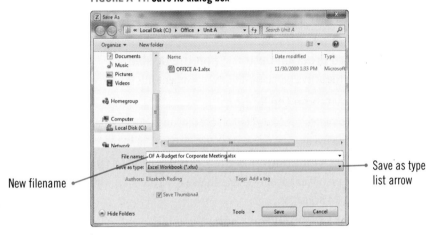

FIGURE A-12: Your name added to the workbook

Address for cell A19 formed by column A and row 19

Cell A19; type your name here

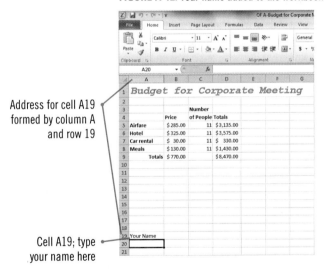

Exploring File Open options

You might have noticed that the Open button on the Open dialog box includes an arrow. In a dialog box, if a button includes an arrow you can click the button to invoke the command, or you can click the arrow to choose from a list of related commands. The Open list arrow includes several related commands, including Open Read-Only and Open as Copy. Clicking Open Read-Only opens a file that you can only save with a new name; you cannot save changes to the original file. Clicking Open as Copy creates a copy of the file already saved and named with the word "Copy" in the title. Like the Save As command, these commands provide additional ways to use copies of existing files while ensuring that original files do not get changed by mistake.

Viewing and Printing Your Work

Each Microsoft Office program lets you switch among various **views** of the document window to show more or fewer details or a different combination of elements that make it easier to complete certain tasks, such as formatting or reading text. Changing your view of a document does not affect the file in any way, it affects only the way it looks on screen. If your computer is connected to a printer or a print server, you can easily print any Office document using the Print button on the Print tab in Backstage view. Printing can be as simple as **previewing** the document to see exactly what a document will look like when it is printed and then clicking the Print button. Or, you can customize the print job by printing only selected pages or making other choices. ▓▓▓▓ Experiment with changing your view of a Word document, and then preview and print your work.

STEPS

1. **Click the Word program button** 🔲 **on the taskbar**

   Word becomes the active program, and the document fills the screen.

2. **Click the View tab on the Ribbon**

   In most Office programs, the View tab on the Ribbon includes groups and commands for changing your view of the current document. You can also change views using the View buttons on the status bar.

3. **Click the Web Layout button in the Document Views group on the View tab**

   The view changes to Web Layout view, as shown in Figure A-13. This view shows how the document will look if you save it as a Web page.

4. **Click the Print Layout button on the View tab**

   You return to Print Layout view, the default view in Word.

5. **Click the File tab, then click Print on the navigation bar**

   The Print tab opens in Backstage view. The preview pane on the right side of the window automatically displays a preview of how your document will look when printed, showing the entire page on screen at once. Compare your screen to Figure A-14. Options in the Settings section enable you to change settings such as margins, orientation, and paper size before printing. To change a setting, click it, and then click the new setting you want. For instance, to change from Letter paper size to Legal, click Letter in the Settings section, then click Legal on the menu that opens. The document preview is updated as you change the settings. You also can use the Settings section to change which pages to print and even the number of pages you print on each sheet of printed paper. If you have multiple printers from which to choose, you can change from one installed printer to another by clicking the current printer in the Printer section, then clicking the name of the installed printer you want to use. The Print section contains the Print button and also enables you to select the number of copies of the document to print.

6. **Click the Print button in the Print section**

   A copy of the document prints, and Backstage view closes.

Customizing the Quick Access toolbar

You can customize the Quick Access toolbar to display your favorite commands. To do so, click the Customize Quick Access Toolbar button 🔽 in the title bar, then click the command you want to add. If you don't see the command in the list, click More Commands to open the Quick Access Toolbar tab of the current program's Options dialog box. In the Options dialog box, use the Choose commands from list to choose a category, click the desired command in the list on the left, click Add to add it to the Quick Access toolbar, then click OK. To remove a button from the toolbar, click the name in the list on the right in the Options dialog box, then click Remove. To add a command to the Quick Access toolbar on the fly, simply right-click the button on the Ribbon, then click Add to Quick Access Toolbar on the shortcut menu. To move the Quick Access toolbar below the Ribbon, click the Customize Quick Access Toolbar button, and then click Show Below the Ribbon.

FIGURE A-13: Web Layout view

Web Layout button

View buttons on status bar

FIGURE A-14: Print tab in Backstage view

Print button

Click to select a different installed printer

Settings section

Preview of document

Creating a screen capture

A **screen capture** is a digital image of your screen, as if you took a picture of it with a camera. For instance, you might want to take a screen capture if an error message occurs and you want Technical Support to see exactly what's on the screen. You can create a screen capture using features found in Windows 7 or Office 2010. Windows 7 comes with the Snipping Tool, a separate program designed to capture whole screens or portions of screens. To open the Snipping Tool, click it on the Start menu or click All Programs, click Accessories, then click Snipping Tool. After opening the Snipping Tool, drag the pointer on the screen to select the area of the screen you want to capture. When you release the mouse button, the screen capture opens in the Snipping Tool window, and you can save, copy, or send it in an e-mail. In Word, Excel, and PowerPoint 2010, you can capture screens or portions of screens and insert them in the current document using the Screenshot button on the Insert tab. And finally, you can create a screen capture by pressing [PrtScn]. (Keyboards differ, but you may find the [PrtScn] button in or near your keyboard's function keys.) Pressing this key places a digital image of your screen in the Windows temporary storage area known as the **Clipboard**. Open the document where you want the screen capture to appear, click the Home tab on the Ribbon (if necessary), then click the Paste button on the Home tab. The screen capture is pasted into the document.

Getting Help and Closing a File

You can get comprehensive help at any time by pressing [F1] in an Office program. You can also get help in the form of a ScreenTip by pointing to almost any icon in the program window. When you're finished working in an Office document, you have a few choices regarding ending your work session. You can close a file or exit a program by using the File tab or by clicking a button on the title bar. Closing a file leaves a program running, while exiting a program closes all the open files in that program as well as the program itself. In all cases, Office reminds you if you try to close a file or exit a program and your document contains unsaved changes. ⬛⬛⬛⬛⬛ Explore the Help system in Microsoft Office, and then close your documents and exit any open programs.

TROUBLE
If the Table of Contents pane doesn't appear on the left in the Help window, click the Show Table of Contents button 🖉 on the Help toolbar to show it.

QUICK TIP
You can also open the Help window by clicking the Microsoft Office Word Help button ⍰ to the right of the tabs on the Ribbon.

QUICK TIP
You can print the entire current topic by clicking the Print button 🖶 on the Help toolbar, then clicking Print in the Print dialog box.

1. **Point to the Zoom button on the View tab of the Ribbon**
   A ScreenTip appears that describes how the Zoom button works and explains where to find other zoom controls.

2. **Press [F1]**
   The Word Help window opens, as shown in Figure A-15, displaying the home page for help in Word on the right and the Table of Contents pane on the left. In both panes of the Help window, each entry is a hyperlink you can click to open a list of related topics. The Help window also includes a toolbar of useful Help commands and a Search field. The connection status at the bottom of the Help window indicates that the connection to Office.com is active. Office.com supplements the help content available on your computer with a wide variety of up-to-date topics, templates, and training. If you are not connected to the Internet, the Help window displays only the help content available on your computer.

3. **Click the Creating documents link in the Table of Contents pane**
   The icon next to Creating documents changes, and a list of subtopics expands beneath the topic.

4. **Click the Create a document link in the subtopics list in the Table of Contents pane**
   The topic opens in the right pane of the Help window, as shown in Figure A-16.

5. **Click Delete a document under "What do you want to do?" in the right pane**
   The link leads to information about deleting a document.

6. **Click the Accessibility link in the Table of Contents pane, click the Accessibility features in Word link, read the information in the right pane, then click the Help window Close button ❌**

7. **Click the File tab, then click Close on the navigation bar; if a dialog box opens asking whether you want to save your changes, click Save**
   The Potential Corporate Meeting Locations document closes, leaving the Word program open.

8. **Click the File tab, then click Exit on the navigation bar**
   Word closes, and the Excel program window is active.

9. **Click the File tab, click Exit on the navigation bar to exit Excel, click the PowerPoint program button 🄿 on the taskbar if necessary, click the File tab, then click Exit on the navigation bar to exit PowerPoint**
   Excel and PowerPoint both close.

FIGURE A-15: Word Help window

Help toolbar

Search field

The colors of your links may differ if the links have been visited previously

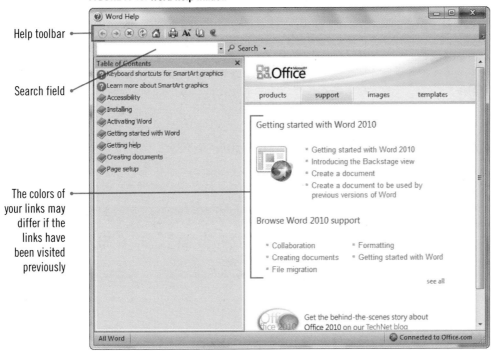

FIGURE A-16: Create a document Help topic

Print button

Icon indicates expanded topic

Create a document link

Create a document topic

Click to read how to perform the action described

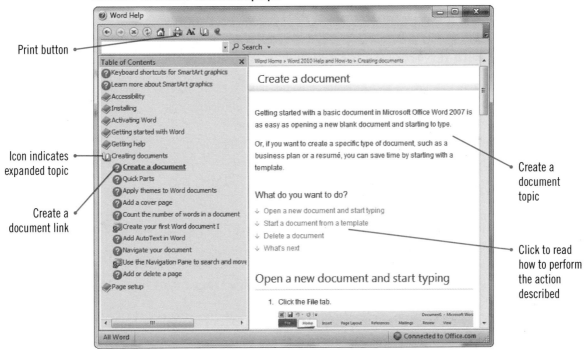

Recovering a document

Each Office program has a built-in recovery feature that allows you to open and save files that were open at the time of an interruption such as a power failure. When you restart the program(s) after an interruption, the Document Recovery task pane opens on the left side of your screen displaying both original and recovered versions of the files that were open. If you're not sure which file to open (original or recovered), it's usually better to open the recovered file because it will contain the latest information. You can, however, open and review all versions of the file that were recovered and save the best one. Each file listed in the Document Recovery task pane displays a list arrow with options that allow you to open the file, save it as is, delete it, or show repairs made to it during recovery.

Practice

For current SAM information, including versions and content details, visit SAM Central (http://www.cengage.com/samcentral). If you have a SAM user profile, you may have access to hands-on instruction, practice, and assessment of the skills covered in this unit. Since various versions of SAM are supported throughout the life of this text, check with your instructor for the correct instructions and URL/Web site for accessing assignments.

Concepts Review

Label the elements of the program window shown in Figure A-17.

FIGURE A-17

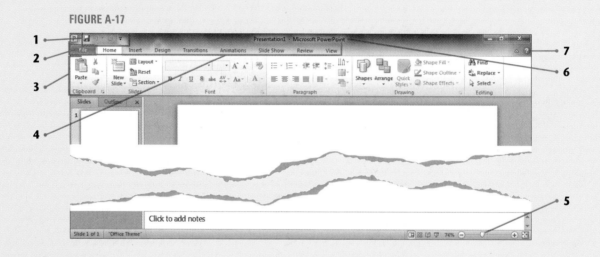

Match each project with the program for which it is best suited.

8. Microsoft Access	a. Corporate convention budget with expense projections
9. Microsoft Excel	b. Business cover letter for a job application
10. Microsoft Word	c. Department store inventory
11. Microsoft PowerPoint	d. Presentation for city council meeting

Independent Challenge 1

You just accepted an administrative position with a local independently owned produce vendor that has recently invested in computers and is now considering purchasing Microsoft Office for the company. You are asked to propose ways Office might help the business. You produce your document in Word.

a. Start Word, then save the document as **OF A-Microsoft Office Document** in the drive and folder where you store your Data Files.

b. Type **Microsoft Word**, press [Enter] twice, type **Microsoft Excel**, press [Enter] twice, type **Microsoft PowerPoint**, press [Enter] twice, type **Microsoft Access**, press [Enter] twice, then type your name.

c. Click the line beneath each program name, type at least two tasks suited to that program (each separated by a comma), then press [Enter].

Advanced Challenge Exercise

- Press the [PrtScn] button to create a screen capture.
- Click after your name, press [Enter] to move to a blank line below your name, then click the Paste button in the Clipboard group on the Home tab.

d. Save the document, then submit your work to your instructor as directed.

e. Exit Word.

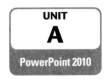

Creating a Presentation in PowerPoint 2010

Microsoft PowerPoint 2010 is a powerful computer software program that enables you to create visually dynamic presentations. With PowerPoint, you can create individual slides and display them as a slide show on your computer, a video projector, or over the Internet. ▓▓▓ Quest Specialty Travel (QST) is an adventure tour company dedicated to providing exclusive and unique cultural travel experiences for its clients. As a sales associate for QST, one of your responsibilities is to research new vacation tours throughout North America, including Canada and Alaska, that QST can sell over the Internet using the company Web site. You have just finished investigating Canadian train travel, and now you need to create a presentation using PowerPoint 2010 that describes the results of your research.

OBJECTIVES

Define presentation software

Plan an effective presentation

Examine the PowerPoint window

Enter slide text

Add a new slide

Apply a design theme

Compare presentation views

Print a PowerPoint presentation

Defining Presentation Software

Presentation software is a computer program you use to organize and present information to others. Whether you are explaining a new product or moderating a meeting, presentation software can help you effectively communicate your ideas. You can use PowerPoint to create presentations, as well as speaker notes for the presenter and handouts for the audience. Table A-1 explains how your information can be presented using PowerPoint. 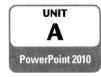 You need to start work on the presentation you will use to present the new Canadian train tours. Because you are only somewhat familiar with PowerPoint, you get to work exploring its capabilities. Figure A-1 shows how a presentation looks printed as handouts. Figure A-2 shows how the same presentation might look printed as notes for a speaker.

DETAILS

You can easily complete the following tasks using PowerPoint:

- **Enter and edit text easily**

  Text editing and formatting commands in PowerPoint are organized by the task you are performing at the time, so you can enter, edit, and format text information simply and efficiently to produce the best results in the least amount of time.

- **Change the appearance of information**

  PowerPoint has many effects that can transform the way text, graphics, and slides appear. By exploring some of these capabilities, you discover how easy it is to change the appearance of your presentation.

- **Organize and arrange information**

  Once you start using PowerPoint, you won't have to spend much time making sure your information is correct and in the right order. With PowerPoint, you can quickly and easily rearrange and modify text, graphics, and slides in your presentation.

- **Incorporate information from other sources**

  Often, when you create presentations, you use information from a variety of sources. With PowerPoint, you can import text, photographs, numerical data, and facts from files created in programs such as Microsoft Word, Corel WordPerfect, Adobe Photoshop, Microsoft Excel, and Microsoft Access. You can also import graphic images from a variety of sources such as the Internet, other computers, a digital camera, or other graphics programs. Always be sure you have permission to use any work that you did not create yourself.

- **Present information in a variety of ways**

  With PowerPoint, you can present information using a variety of methods. For example, you can print handout pages or an outline of your presentation for audience members. You can display your presentation as an on-screen slide show using your computer, or if you are presenting to a large group, you can use a video projector and a large screen. If you want to reach an even wider audience, you can broadcast the presentation over the Internet so people anywhere in the world can use a Web browser to view your presentation.

- **Collaborate on a presentation with others**

  PowerPoint makes it easy to collaborate or share a presentation with colleagues and coworkers using the Internet. You can use your e-mail program to send a presentation as an attachment to a colleague for feedback. If you have a number of people that need to work together on a presentation, you can save the presentation to a shared workspace on the Internet so everyone in your group using a Web browser has access to the presentation.

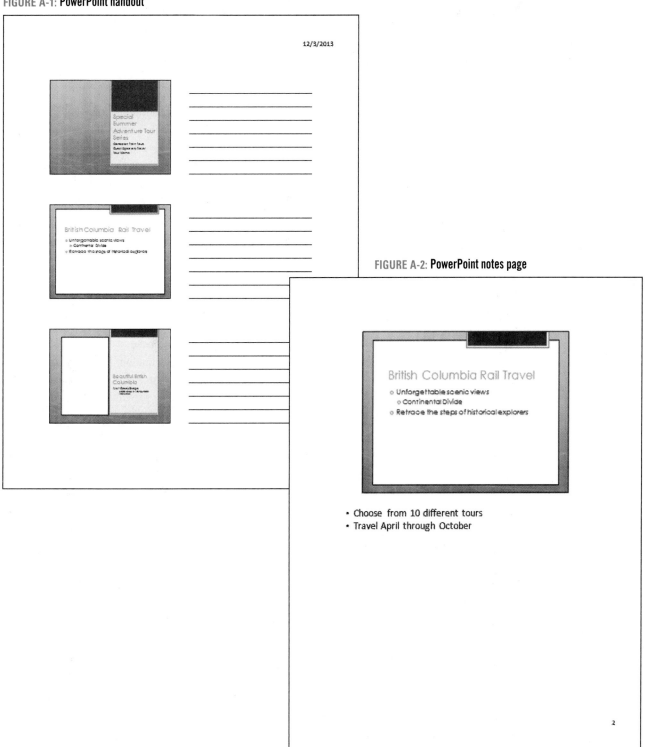

FIGURE A-2: PowerPoint notes page

TABLE A-1: Presenting information using PowerPoint

method	description
On-screen presentations	Run a slide show from your computer or through a video projector to a large screen
Notes	Print a page with the image of a slide and notes about each slide for yourself or your audience
Audience handouts	Print handouts with one, two, three, four, six, or nine slides on a page
Broadcast a slide show	Broadcast a slide show to other viewers who watch using a Web browser
Outline pages	Print a text outline of your presentation to highlight the main points

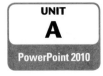
Planning an Effective Presentation

Before you create a presentation, you need to have a general idea of the information you want to communicate. PowerPoint is a powerful and flexible program that gives you the ability to start a presentation simply by entering the text of your message. If you have a specific design or theme you want to use, you can start the presentation by working on the design. In most cases you'll probably enter the text of your presentation into PowerPoint first and then tailor the design to the message and audience. When preparing your presentation, you need to keep in mind not only who you are giving it to, but also where you are giving it. It is important to know what equipment you will need, such as a sound system, computer, or projector. Use the planning guidelines below to help plan an effective presentation. Figure A-3 illustrates a storyboard for a well-planned presentation.

DETAILS

In planning a presentation, it is important to:

- **Determine and outline the message you want to communicate**

  The more time you take developing the message and outline of your presentation, the better your presentation will be in the end. A presentation with a clear message that reads like a story and is illustrated with appropriate visual aids will have the greatest impact on your audience. Start the presentation by giving a general description of Canadian train travel and the types of tours offered by Quest Speciality Travel. See Figure A-3.

- **Identify your audience and delivery location**

  Audience and delivery location are major factors in the type of presentation you create. For example, a presentation you develop for a staff meeting that is held in a conference room would not necessarily need to be as sophisticated or detailed as a presentation that you develop for a large audience held in an auditorium. Room lighting, natural light, screen position, and room layout all affect how the audience responds to your presentation. This presentation will be delivered in a small auditorium to QST's management and sales team.

- **Determine the type of output**

  Output choices for a presentation include black-and-white or color handouts, on-screen slide show, or an online broadcast. Consider the time demands and computer equipment availability as you decide which output types to produce. Because you are speaking in a small auditorium to a large group and have access to a computer and projection equipment, you decide that an on-screen slide show is the best output choice for your presentation.

- **Determine the design**

  Visual appeal, graphics, and presentation design work to communicate your message. You can choose one of the professionally designed themes that come with PowerPoint, modify one of these themes, or create one of your own. You decide to choose one of PowerPoint's design themes to convey the new tour information.

- **Decide what additional materials will be useful in the presentation**

  You need to prepare not only the slides themselves but also supplementary materials, including speaker notes and handouts for the audience. You use speaker notes to help remember key details, and you pass out handouts for the audience to use as a reference during the presentation.

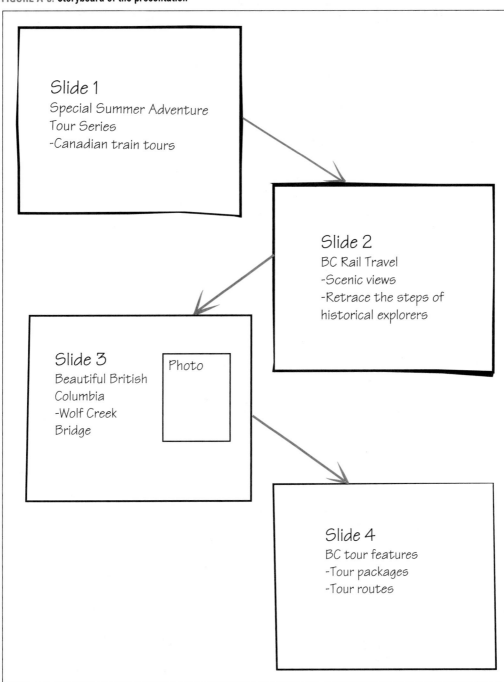

Slide 1
Special Summer Adventure
Tour Series
-Canadian train tours

Slide 2
BC Rail Travel
-Scenic views
-Retrace the steps of
historical explorers

Slide 3
Beautiful British
Columbia
-Wolf Creek
Bridge

Photo

Slide 4
BC tour features
-Tour packages
-Tour routes

PowerPoint 2010

Understanding copyright

Intellectual property is any idea or creation of the human mind. Copyright law is a type of intellectual property law that protects works of authorship, including books, Web pages, computer games, music, artwork, and photographs. Copyright protects the expression of an idea, but not the underlying facts or concepts. In other words, the general subject matter is not protected, but how you express it *is*, such as when several people photograph the same sunset. Copyright attaches to any original work of authorship *as soon* as it is created, you do not have to register it with the Copyright Office or display the copyright symbol, ©.

Fair use is an exception to copyright and permits the public to use copyrighted material for certain purposes without obtaining prior consent from the owner. Determining whether fair use applies to a work depends on its purpose, the nature of the work, how much of the work you want to copy, and the effect on the work's value. Unauthorized use of protected work (such as downloading a photo or a song from the Web) is known as copyright infringement and can lead to legal action.

Examining the PowerPoint Window

When you first start PowerPoint, a blank slide appears in the PowerPoint window. PowerPoint has different **views** that allow you to see your presentation in different forms. By default, the PowerPoint window opens in **Normal view**, which is the primary view that you use to write, edit, and design your presentation. Normal view is divided into three areas called **panes**: the pane on the left contains the Outline and Slides tabs, the large pane is the Slide pane, and the small pane below the Slide pane is the Notes pane. You move around in each pane using the scroll bars. The PowerPoint window and the specific parts of Normal view are described below.

STEPS

TROUBLE
If you have trouble finding Microsoft PowerPoint 2010 on the All Programs menu, check with your instructor or technical support person.

1. **Click the Start button 🌀 on the taskbar, click All Programs, click Microsoft Office, then click Microsoft PowerPoint 2010**

   PowerPoint starts and the PowerPoint window opens, as shown in Figure A-4.

Using Figure A-4 as a guide, examine the elements of the PowerPoint window, then find and compare the elements described below:

- The **Ribbon** is a wide (toolbar-like) band that runs across the entire PowerPoint window that organizes all of PowerPoint's primary commands. Each set of primary commands is identified by a **tab**; for example, the Home tab is selected by default, as shown in Figure A-4. Commands are further arranged into **groups** on the Ribbon based on their function. So, for example, text formatting commands such as Bold, Underline, and Italic are located on the Home tab, in the Font group.

- The **Outline tab** displays the text of your presentation in the form of an outline, without showing graphics or other visual objects. Using this tab, it is easy to move text on or among slides by dragging text to reorder the information.

- The **Slides tab** displays the slides of your presentation as small images, called **thumbnails**. You can quickly navigate through the slides in your presentation by clicking the thumbnails on this tab. You can also add, delete, or rearrange slides using this tab.

- The **Slide pane** displays the current slide in your presentation.

- The **Notes pane** is used to type text that references a slide's content. You can print these notes and refer to them when you make a presentation or print them as handouts and give them to your audience. The Notes pane is not visible to the audience when you show a slide presentation in Slide Show view.

- The **Quick Access toolbar** provides access to common commands such as Save, Undo, and Redo. The Quick Access toolbar is always visible no matter which Ribbon tab you select. This toolbar is fully customizable. Click the Customize Quick Access Toolbar button to add or remove commands.

- The **View Shortcuts** icons on the status bar allow you to switch quickly between PowerPoint views.

- The **status bar**, located at the bottom of the PowerPoint window, shows messages about what you are doing and seeing in PowerPoint, including which slide you are viewing, and the design theme applied to the presentation. In addition, the status bar displays the Zoom slider controls, the Fit slide to current window button 🔲, and information on other functionality such as signatures and permissions.

- The **Zoom slider** is in the lower-right corner of the status bar, use to zoom the slide in and out quickly.

FIGURE A-4: PowerPoint window in Normal view

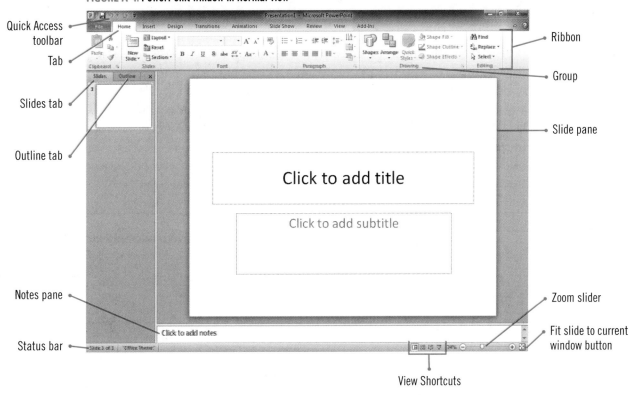

Quick Access toolbar

Tab

Slides tab

Outline tab

Notes pane

Status bar

Ribbon

Group

Slide pane

Zoom slider

Fit slide to current window button

View Shortcuts

Viewing your presentation in grayscale or black and white

Viewing your presentation in grayscale (using shades of gray) or pure black and white is very useful when you are printing a presentation on a black-and-white printer and you want to make sure your presentation prints correctly. To see how your color presentation looks in grayscale or black and white, click the View tab, then click either the Grayscale or Black and White button in the Color/Grayscale group. Depending on which button you select, the Grayscale or the Black and White tab appears, and the Ribbon displays different settings that you can customize. If you don't like the way an individual object looks in black and white or grayscale, you can change its color. Click the object while still in Grayscale or Black and White view, then choose an option in the Change Selected Object group on the Ribbon.

PowerPoint 2010

Entering Slide Text

Each time you start PowerPoint, a new presentation with a blank title slide appears in Normal view. The title slide has two **text placeholders**—boxes with dotted borders—where you enter text. The top text placeholder on the title slide is the **title placeholder**, labeled "Click to add title." The bottom text placeholder on the title slide is the **subtitle text placeholder**, labeled "Click to add subtitle." To enter text in a placeholder, click the placeholder and then type your text. After you enter text in a placeholder, the placeholder becomes a text object. An **object** is any item on a slide that can be modified. Objects are the building blocks that make up a presentation slide. Begin working on your presentation by entering text on the title slide.

STEPS

1. **Move the pointer over the title placeholder labeled Click to add title in the Slide pane**

   The pointer changes to I when you move the pointer over the placeholder. In PowerPoint, the pointer often changes shape, depending on the task you are trying to accomplish.

2. **Click the title placeholder in the Slide pane**

   The **insertion point**, a blinking vertical line, indicates where your text appears when you type in the placeholder. A **selection box** with a dashed line border and **sizing handles** appears around the placeholder, indicating that it is selected and ready to accept text. When a placeholder or object is selected, you can change its shape or size by dragging one of the sizing handles. See Figure A-5.

   > **TROUBLE**
   > If you press a wrong key, press [Backspace] to erase the character.

3. **Type Special Summer Adventure Tour Series**

   PowerPoint wraps and then center-aligns the title text within the title placeholder, which is now a text object. Notice that the text also appears on the slide thumbnail on the Slides tab.

4. **Click the subtitle text placeholder in the Slide pane**

   The subtitle text placeholder is ready to accept text.

5. **Type Canadian Train Tours, then press [Enter]**

   The insertion point moves to the next line in the text object.

6. **Type Quest Specialty Travel, press [Enter], type Adventure Tour Series, press [Enter], then type your name**

   Notice that the AutoFit Options button ≑ appears near the text object. The AutoFit Options button on your screen indicates that PowerPoint has automatically decreased the size of all the text in the text object so that it fits inside the text object.

7. **Click the AutoFit Options button ≑, then click Stop Fitting Text to This Placeholder on the shortcut menu**

   The text in the text object changes back to its original size and no longer fits in the text object.

8. **In the subtitle text object, position I to the right of Series, drag left to select the entire line of text, press [Backspace], then click outside the text object in a blank area of the slide**

   The Adventure Tour Series line of text is deleted and the AutoFit Options button closes, as shown in Figure A-6. Clicking a blank area of the slide deselects all selected objects on the slide.

9. **Click the Save button 🖫 on the Quick Access toolbar to open the Save As dialog box, then save the presentation as PPT A-QST in the drive and folder where you store your Data Files**

   Notice that PowerPoint automatically enters the title of the presentation as the filename in the Save As dialog box.

FIGURE A-5: Title text placeholder ready to accept text

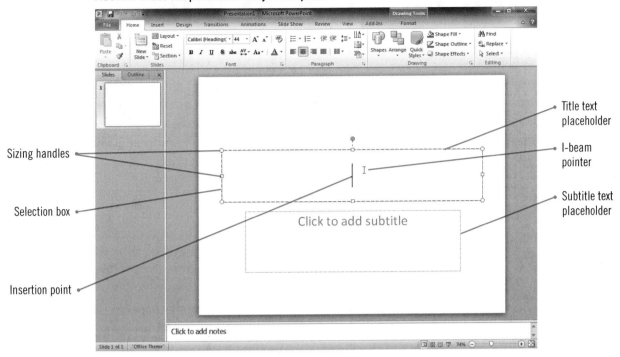

Title text placeholder

I-beam pointer

Subtitle text placeholder

Sizing handles

Selection box

Insertion point

FIGURE A-6: Text on title slide

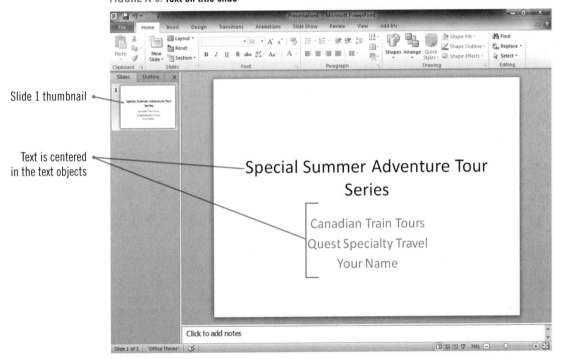

Slide 1 thumbnail

Text is centered in the text objects

Special Summer Adventure Tour Series

Canadian Train Tours
Quest Specialty Travel
Your Name

Saving fonts with your presentation

When you create a presentation, it uses the fonts that are installed on your computer. If you need to open the presentation on another computer, the fonts might look different if that computer has a different set of fonts. To preserve the look of your presentation on any computer, you can save, or embed, the fonts in your presentation. Click the File tab, then click the Options button. The PowerPoint Options dialog box opens. Click Save in the left pane, then click the Embed fonts in the file check box. Click the Embed all characters option button, then click OK to close the dialog box. Click Save on the Quick Access toolbar. Now the presentation looks the same on any computer that opens it. Using this option, however, significantly increases the size of your presentation, so only use it when necessary. You can freely embed any TrueType or OpenType font that comes with Windows. You can embed other TrueType fonts only if they have no license restrictions.

PowerPoint 2010

Adding a New Slide

Ordinarily when you add a new slide to a presentation, you have a pretty good idea of what you want the slide to look like. For example, you may want to add a slide that has a title over bulleted text and a picture. To help you add a slide like this quickly and easily, PowerPoint provides nine standard slide layouts. A **slide layout** contains text and object placeholders that are arranged in a specific way on the slide. You have already worked with the Title Slide layout in the previous lesson. In the event that a standard slide layout does not meet your needs, you can modify an existing slide layout or create a new, custom slide layout. ▰▰▰▰ To continue developing the presentation, you create a slide that defines the new tour series.

STEPS

QUICK TIP

You can easily change the slide lay-out of the current slide by clicking the Layout button in the Slides group.

1. **Click the New Slide button in the Slides group on the Home tab on the Ribbon**

    A new blank slide (now the current slide) appears as the second slide in your presentation, as shown in Figure A-7. The new slide contains a title placeholder and a content placeholder. A **content placeholder** can be used to insert text or objects such as tables, charts, or pictures. Table A-2 describes the content placeholder icons. Notice that the status bar indicates Slide 2 of 2 and that the Slides tab now contains two slide thumbnails.

2. **Type British Columbia Rail Travel, then click the bottom content placeholder**

    The text you type appears in the title placeholder and the insertion point appears at the top of the bottom content placeholder.

3. **Type Unforgettable scenic views, then press [Enter]**

    The insertion point appears directly below the text when you press [Enter] and a new first-level bullet automatically appears.

4. **Press [Tab]**

    The new first-level bullet is indented and becomes a second-level bullet.

QUICK TIP

You can also press [Shift][Tab] to decrease the indent level.

5. **Type Continental Divide, press [Enter], then click the Decrease List Level button ▤ in the Paragraph group**

    The Decrease List Level button changes the second-level bullet into a first-level bullet.

6. **Type Retrace the steps of historical explorers, then click the New Slide list arrow in the Slides group**

    The Office Theme layout gallery opens. Each slide layout is identified by a descriptive name.

7. **Click the Content with Caption slide layout, then type Beautiful British Columbia**

    A new slide with three content placeholders appears as the third slide.

8. **Click the lower-left placeholder, type Wolf Creek Bridge, press [Enter], click the Increase List Level button ▤, then type Established in 1857 by Fraser Ironworks**

    The Increase List Level button moves the insertion point to the right one level. Notice this text placeholder does not use text bullets to identify separate lines of text.

9. **Click a blank area of the slide, then click the Save button ▤ on the Quick Access toolbar**

    The Save button saves all of the changes to the file. Compare your screen with Figure A-8.

FIGURE A-7: New blank slide in Normal view

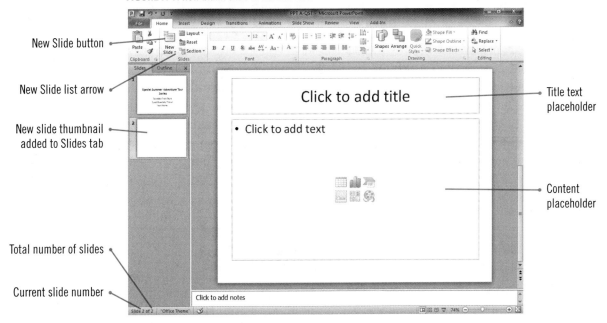

New Slide button

New Slide list arrow

New slide thumbnail
added to Slides tab

Total number of slides

Current slide number

Title text
placeholder

Content
placeholder

FIGURE A-8: New slide with Content with Caption slide layout

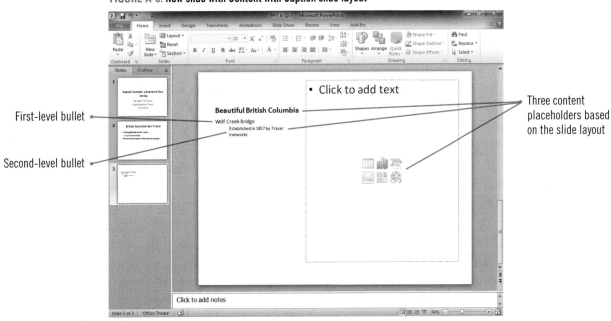

First-level bullet

Second-level bullet

Three content
placeholders based
on the slide layout

TABLE A-2: Content placeholder icons

click this icon	to insert a
	Table
	Graph chart
	SmartArt graphic
	Picture from a file
	Piece of clip art
	Video clip

PowerPoint 2010

Applying a Design Theme

PowerPoint provides a number of design themes to help you quickly create a professional and contemporary looking presentation. A design **theme** includes a set of 12 coordinated colors for fill, line, and shadow, called **theme colors**; a set of fonts for titles and other text, called **theme fonts**; and a set of effects for lines and fills, called **theme effects** to create a cohesive look. In most cases, you would apply one theme to an entire presentation; you can, however, apply multiple themes to the same presentation, or even a different theme on each presentation slide. You can use a design theme as is, or you can alter individual elements of the theme as needed. Unless you need to use a specific design theme, such as a company theme or product design theme, it is faster and easier to use one of the themes supplied with PowerPoint. If you design a custom theme, you can save it to use in the future. ██████ You decide to change the default design theme in the presentation to a new one.

STEPS

1. **Click the Slide 1 thumbnail on the Slides tab**

   Slide 1, the title slide, appears in the Slide pane.

2. **Click the Design tab on the Ribbon, then point to the Adjacency theme in the Themes group as shown in Figure A-9**

   The Design tab appears and a Live Preview of the Adjacency theme is displayed on the slide. A **Live Preview** allows you to see how your changes affect the slides before actually making the change. The Live Preview lasts about 1 minute and then your slide reverts back to its original state. The first (far left) theme thumbnail identifies the current theme applied to the presentation, in this case, the default design theme called the Office Theme. Depending on your monitor resolution and screen size, you can see between five and eleven design themes visible in the Themes group.

3. **Slowly move your pointer ⮕ over the other design themes, then click the Themes group down scroll arrow once**

   A Live Preview of the theme appears on the slide each time you pass your pointer over the theme thumbnails, and a ScreenTip identifies the theme names.

4. **Move ⮕ over the design themes, then click the Couture theme**

   The Couture design theme is applied to all the slides in the presentation. Notice the new slide background color, graphic elements, fonts, and text color. You decide that this theme isn't right for this presentation.

QUICK TIP

One way to apply multiple themes to the same presentation is to click the Slide Sorter button on the status bar, select a slide or a group of slides, then click the theme.

5. **Click the More button ⯆ in the Themes group**

   The All Themes gallery window opens. At the top of the gallery window in the This Presentation section is the current theme applied to the presentation. Notice that just the Couture theme is listed here because when you changed the theme in the last step, you replaced the default theme with the Couture theme. The Built-In section identifies all 40 of the standard themes that come with PowerPoint.

6. **Right-click the Angles theme in the Built-In section, then click Apply to Selected Slides**

   The Angles theme is applied only to Slide 1. You like the Angles theme better and decide to apply it to all slides.

7. **Right-click the Angles theme in the Themes group, then click Apply to All Slides**

   The Angles theme is applied to all three slides. Preview the next slides in the presentation to see how it looks.

8. **Click the Next Slide button ⯆ at the bottom of the vertical scroll bar**

   Compare your screen to Figure A-10.

9. **Click the Previous Slide button ⯅ at the bottom of the vertical scroll bar, then save your changes**

FIGURE A-9: Slide showing a different design theme

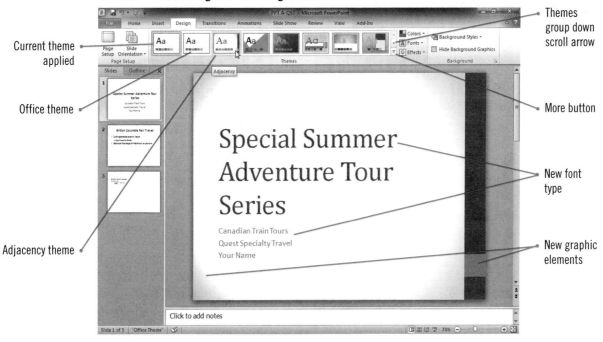

Current theme applied

Office theme

Adjacency theme

Themes group down scroll arrow

More button

New font type

New graphic elements

FIGURE A-10: Presentation with Angles theme applied

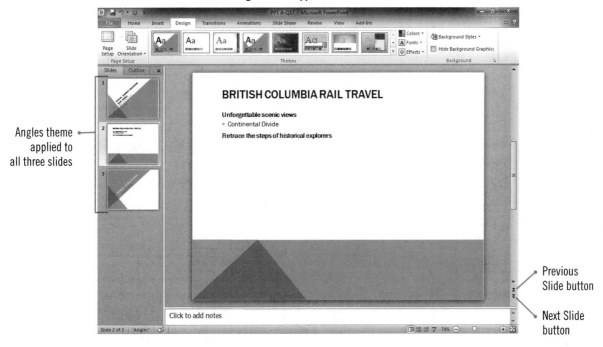

Angles theme applied to all three slides

Previous Slide button

Next Slide button

Customizing themes

You are not limited to using the standard themes PowerPoint provides; you can also modify a theme to create your own custom theme. For example, you might want to incorporate your school's or company's colors on the slide background of the presentation or be able to type using fonts your company uses for brand recognition. To modify an existing theme, you can change the color theme, font theme, or the effects theme and then save it for future use by clicking the More button in the Themes group, then clicking Save Current Theme. You also have the ability to create a new font theme or a new color theme from scratch by clicking the Theme Fonts button or the Theme Colors button and then clicking Create New Theme Fonts or Create New Theme Colors. You work in the Create New Theme Fonts or Create New Theme Colors dialog box to define the custom theme fonts or colors.

Comparing Presentation Views

PowerPoint has five primary views: Normal view, Slide Sorter view, Notes Page view, Slide Show view, and Reading view. Each PowerPoint view displays your presentation in a different way and is used for different purposes. Normal view is the primary editing view where you add text, graphics, and other elements to the slides. Slide Sorter view is primarily used to rearrange slides; however, you can also add slide effects and design themes in this view. You use Notes Page view to type notes that are important for each slide. Slide Show view displays your presentation over the whole computer screen and is designed to show your presentation to an audience. Similar to Slide Show view, Reading view is designed to view your presentation on a computer screen. To move easily among the main PowerPoint views, use the View Shortcuts buttons located on the Status bar next to the Zoom slider. Most PowerPoint views can be accessed using the View tab on the Ribbon. Table A-3 provides a brief description of the PowerPoint views. ◢◣◥◤ Examine each of the PowerPoint views, starting with Normal view.

STEPS

1. **Click the Outline tab, then click the small slide icon ▣ next to Slide 2 in the Outline tab**

   The text for Slide 2 is selected in the Outline tab, and Slide 2 appears in the Slide pane, as shown in Figure A-11. Notice that the status bar identifies the number of the slide you are viewing, the total number of slides in the presentation, and the name of the applied design theme.

2. **Click the Slides tab, then click the Slide 1 thumbnail**

   Slide 1 appears in the Slide pane. Thumbnails of the slides in your presentation appear again on the Slides tab. Since the Slides tab is by default narrower than the Outline tab, the Slide pane enlarges. The scroll box in the vertical scroll bar moves back up the scroll bar.

   QUICK TIP

   You can also switch between views using the commands in the Presentation Views group on the View tab.

3. **Click the Slide Sorter button ▦ on the status bar**

   A thumbnail of each slide in the presentation appears in the window. You can examine the flow of your slides and drag any slide or group of slides to rearrange the order of the slides in the presentation.

4. **Double-click the Slide 1 thumbnail, then click the Reading View button 📖 on the status bar**

   The first slide fills the screen as shown in Figure A-12. Use Reading view to review your presentation or to show your presentation to someone directly on your computer. The status bar controls at the bottom of the window make it easy to move between slides in this view.

5. **Click the Slide Show button 🖵 on the status bar**

   The first slide fills the entire screen now without the title bar and status bar. In this view, you can practice running through your slides as they would appear in a slide show.

   QUICK TIP

   You can also press [Enter], [Spacebar], [Page Up], [Page Down], or the arrow keys to advance the slide show.

6. **Click the left mouse button to advance through the slides one at a time until you see a black slide, then click once more to return to Normal view**

   The black slide at the end of the slide show indicates that the slide show is finished. At the end of a slide show you automatically return to the slide and PowerPoint view you were in before you ran the slide show, in this case Slide 1 in Normal view.

7. **Click the View tab on the Ribbon, then click the Notes Page button in the Presentation Views group**

   Notes Page view appears, showing a reduced image of the current slide above a large text placeholder. You can enter text in this placeholder and then print the notes page for your own use.

8. **Click the Normal button in the Presentation Views group**

FIGURE A-11: Normal view with the outline tab displayed

Outline tab

Slides tab

Slide icon

Design theme name

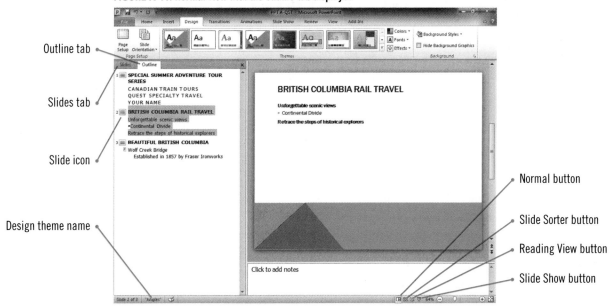

Normal button

Slide Sorter button

Reading View button

Slide Show button

FIGURE A-12: Reading view

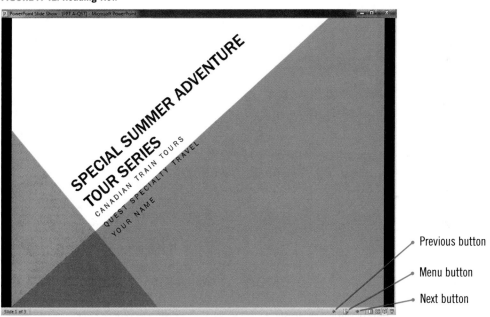

Previous button

Menu button

Next button

TABLE A-3: PowerPoint views

view name	button	button name	description
Normal		Normal	Displays the Outline and Slides tabs, the Slide pane, and the Notes pane at the same time; use this view to work on your presentation's content, layout, and notes concurrently
Slide Sorter		Slide Sorter	Displays thumbnails of all slides; use this view to rearrange and add special effects to your slides
Slide Show		Slide Show	Displays your presentation on the whole computer screen
Reading View		Reading View	Displays your presentation in a large window on your computer screen
Notes Page	(no View Shortcuts button)		Displays a reduced image of the current slide above a large text box where you can enter or view notes

Printing a PowerPoint Presentation

You print your presentation when you want to review your work or when you have completed it and want a hard copy. Reviewing your presentation at different stages of development gives you a better perspective of the overall flow and feel of the presentation. You can also preview your presentation to see exactly how each slide looks before you print the presentation. When you are finished working on your presentation, even if it is not yet complete, you can close the presentation file and exit PowerPoint. You are done working on the tour presentation for now. You save and preview the presentation, then you print the slides and notes pages of the presentation so you can review them later. Before leaving for the day, you close the file and exit PowerPoint.

1. **Click the Save button 🖫 on the Quick Access toolbar, click the File tab on the Ribbon, then click Print**

   The Print window opens as shown in Figure A-13. Notice the preview pane on the right side of the window that automatically displays the first slide of the presentation.

QUICK TIP

To quickly print the presentation with the current Print options, add the Quick Print button to the Quick Access toolbar.

---

2. **Click the Next Page button ▶ at the bottom of the preview pane, then click ▶ again**

   Each slide in the presentation appears in the preview pane.

3. **Click the Print button**

   Each slide in the presentation prints.

4. **Click the File tab on the Ribbon, click Print, then click the Full Page Slides button in the Settings section**

   The Print Layout gallery opens. In this gallery you can specify what you want to print (slides, handouts, notes pages, or outline), as well as other print options. To save paper when you are reviewing your slides, you can print in handout format, which lets you print up to nine slides per page. The options you choose in the Print window remain there until you change them or close the presentation.

QUICK TIP

To print slides appropriate in size for overhead transparencies, click the Design tab, click the Page Setup button in the Page Setup group, click the Slides sized for list arrow, then click Overhead.

---

5. **Click 3 Slides, click the Color button in the Settings section, then click Pure Black and White**

   PowerPoint removes the color and displays the slides as thumbnails next to blank lines as shown in Figure A-14. Using the Handouts with three slides per page printing option is a great way to print your presentation when you want to provide a way for audience members to take notes. Printing pure black-and-white prints without any gray tones can save printer toner.

6. **Click the Print button**

   The presentation prints one page showing the all the slides of the presentation as thumbnails next to blank lines.

7. **Click the File tab on the Ribbon, then click Close**

   If you have made changes to your presentation, a Microsoft PowerPoint alert box opens asking you if you want to save changes you have made to your presentation file.

8. **Click Save, if necessary, to close the alert box**

   Your presentation closes.

9. **Click the File tab on the Ribbon, then click Exit**

   The PowerPoint program closes, and you return to the Windows desktop.

FIGURE A-13: Print window

Current printer

Current print settings

Click to change the print range

Click to select a print layout

Previous button

Point here for additional information on an item

Preview pane

Next button

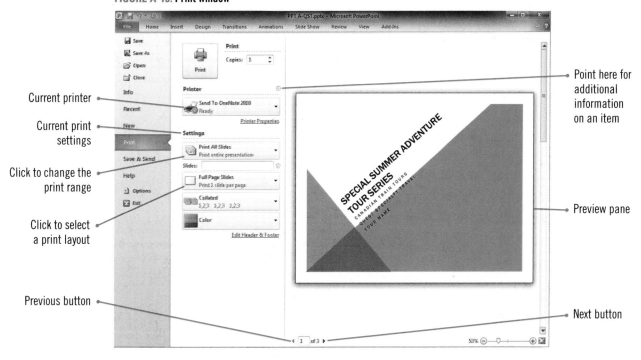

FIGURE A-14: Print window with changed settings

Print button

Your printer name may be different

Preview shows presentation in black and white

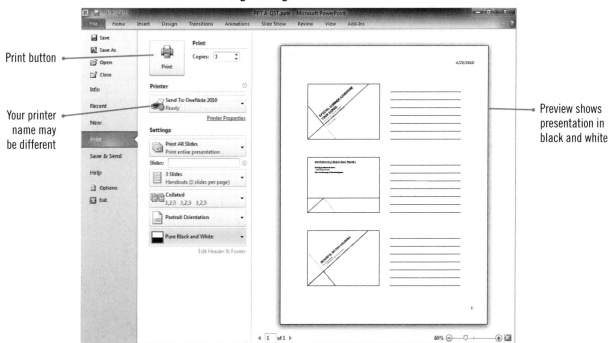

Windows Live and Microsoft Office Web Apps

All Office programs include the capability to incorporate feedback—called online collaboration—across the Internet or a company network. Using **cloud computing** (work done in a virtual environment), you can take advantage of Web programs called Microsoft Office Web Apps, which are simplified versions of the programs found in the Microsoft Office 2010 suite. Because these programs are online, they take up no computer disk space and are accessed using Windows Live SkyDrive, a free service from Microsoft. Using Windows Live SkyDrive, you and your colleagues can create and store documents in a "cloud" and make the documents available to whomever you grant access. To use Windows Live SkyDrive, you need a free Windows Live ID, which you obtain at the Windows Live Web site. You can find more information in the "Working with Windows Live and Microsoft Office Web Apps" appendix.

Practice

Concepts Review

For current SAM information, including versions and content details, visit SAM Central (http://www.cengage.com/samcentral). If you have a SAM user profile, you may have access to hands-on instruction, practice, and assessment of the skills covered in this unit. Since various versions of SAM are supported throughout the life of this text, check with your instructor for the correct instructions and URL/Web site for accessing assignments.

Label each element of the PowerPoint window shown in Figure A-15.

FIGURE A-15

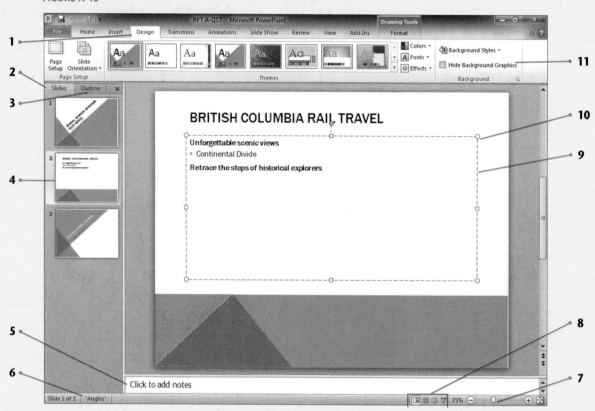

Match each term with the statement that best describes it.

12. Reading view
13. Notes pane
14. Slide Show view
15. Slide Layout
16. Ribbon
17. Zoom slider

a. A view that displays a presentation over an entire computer screen and that is used to show to an audience

b. Allows you to change the size of the slide in the window

c. A view that is used to review a presentation or to show someone a presentation directly on a computer screen

d. Arranges placeholders in a specific way on the slide

e. Used to type text that references slide content

f. Used to organize all of the commands in PowerPoint

Select the best answer from the list of choices.

18. Which statement about incorporating information is *not* correct?

- **a.** You can import text and numerical data into PowerPoint.
- **b.** You can open a PowerPoint presentation in another program to incorporate data.
- **c.** Images from Adobe Photoshop can be inserted into a presentation.
- **d.** Graphic images from a digital camera can be inserted into PowerPoint.

19. Finish the following sentence: "Copyright protects the expression of an idea,...":

- **a.** But not the underlying facts or concepts.
- **b.** Including all general subject matter.
- **c.** Only if you have it regestered with the Copyright Office.
- **d.** Under the Fair Use policy.

20. Which of the following is/are located on the status bar and allow you to quickly switch between views?

- **a.** Fit slide to current window button
- **b.** Switch view button
- **c.** Zoom Slider
- **d.** View Shortcuts

21. What is the blinking vertical line that appears when you type text called?

- **a.** Text handle
- **b.** Placeholder
- **c.** Text insertion line
- **d.** Insertion point

22. The view that fills the entire screen with each slide in the presentation without the title bar is called:

- **a.** Slide Show view.
- **b.** Fit to window view.
- **c.** Reading view.
- **d.** Normal view.

23. Other than the Slide pane, where else can you enter slide text?

- **a.** Reading pane
- **b.** Notes Page view
- **c.** Outline tab
- **d.** Slides tab

24. What does the slide layout do in a presentation?

- **a.** The slide layout puts all your slides in order.
- **b.** A slide layout automatically applies all the objects you can use on a slide.
- **c.** A slide layout defines how all the elements on a slide are arranged.
- **d.** The slide layout enables you to apply a template to the presentation.

25. Which of the following is not included in a design theme?

- **a.** Effects
- **b.** Pictures
- **c.** Colors
- **d.** Fonts

Skills Review

1. Examine the PowerPoint window.

- **a.** Start PowerPoint, if necessary.
- **b.** Identify as many elements of the PowerPoint window as you can without referring to the unit material.
- **c.** Be able to describe the purpose or function of each element.
- **d.** For any elements you cannot identify, refer to the unit.

2. Enter slide text.

- **a.** In the Slide pane in Normal view, enter the text **Alutiiq Indian Lands Protection Proposal** in the title placeholder. Refer to Figure A-16 as you complete the slide.
- **b.** In the subtitle text placeholder, enter **Karluk Lake on Kodiak Island**.

FIGURE A-16

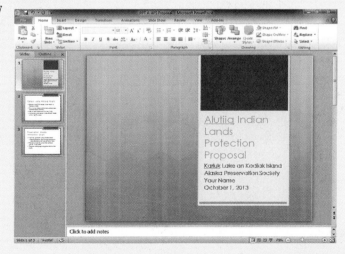

Skills Review (continued)

    c. On the next line of the placeholder, enter **Alaska Preservation Society**.

    d. On the next line of the placeholder, enter your name.

    e. On the next line of the placeholder, enter **October 1, 2013**. Let PowerPoint AutoFit the text in the text object.

    f. Deselect the text object.

    g. Save the presentation using the filename **PPT A-APS Proposal** to the drive and folder where you store your Data Files.

3. Add a new slide.

    a. Create a new slide.

    b. Using Figure A-17, enter text on the slide.

    c. Create another new slide.

    d. Using Figure A-18, enter text on the slide.

    e. Save your changes.

4. Apply a design theme.

    a. Click the Design tab.

    b. Click the Themes group More button, then point to all of the themes.

    c. Locate the Grid theme, then apply it to the selected slide.

    d. Move to Slide 1.

    e. Locate the Austin theme, then apply it to Slide 1.

    f. Apply the Austin theme to all of the slides in the presentation.

    g. Use the Next Slide button to move to Slide 3, then save your changes.

5. Compare presentation views.

    a. Click the View tab.

    b. Click the Slide Sorter button in the Presentation Views group.

    c. Click the Notes Page button in the Presentation Views group, then click the Previous Slide button twice.

    d. Click the Reading View button in the Presentation Views group, then click the Next button on the status bar.

    e. Click the Normal button on the status bar, then click the Slide Show button.

    f. Advance the slides until a black screen appears, then click to end the presentation.

    g. Save your changes.

6. Print a presentation.

    a. Print all the slides as handouts, 4 Slides Horizontal, in color.

    b. Print the presentation outline.

    c. Close the file, saving your changes.

    d. Exit PowerPoint.

FIGURE A-17

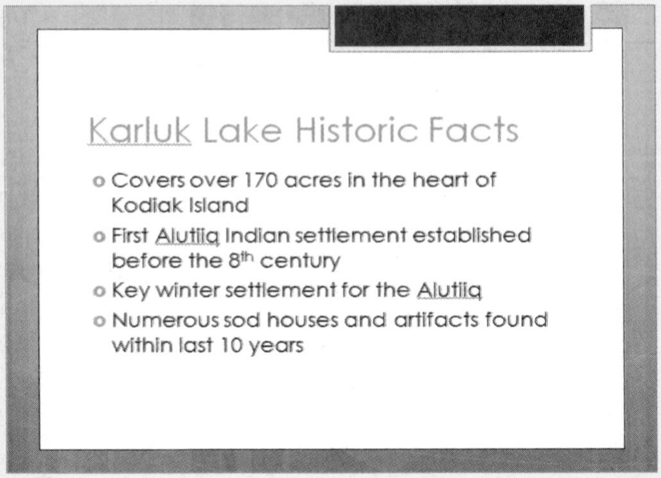

Karluk Lake Historic Facts

- Covers over 170 acres in the heart of Kodiak Island
- First Alutiiq Indian settlement established before the 8th century
- Key winter settlement for the Alutiiq
- Numerous sod houses and artifacts found within last 10 years

FIGURE A-18

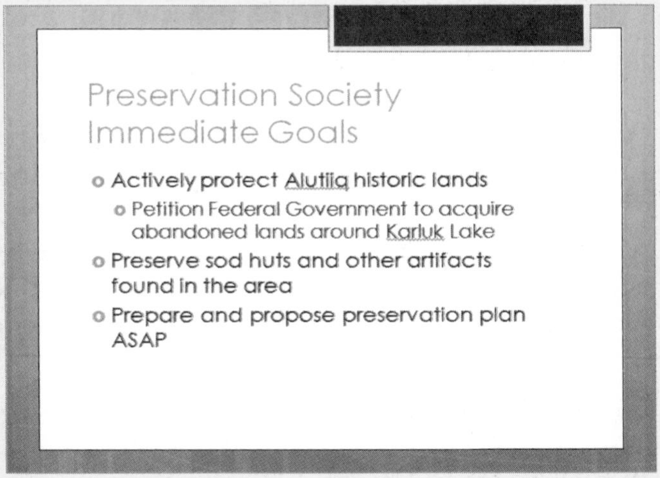

Preservation Society Immediate Goals

- Actively protect Alutiiq historic lands
  - Petition Federal Government to acquire abandoned lands around Karluk Lake
- Preserve sod huts and other artifacts found in the area
- Prepare and propose preservation plan ASAP

Independent Challenge 1

You work for BioCare Service Industries, a business that offers environmental hazard cleanup and project management. One of your jobs at the company is to go on new sales calls with your boss. Your boss has asked you to create a sales presentation that describes and compares the services BioCare Industries offers.

If you have a SAM 2010 user profile, an autogradable SAM version of this assignment may be available at http://www.cengage.com/sam2010. Check with your instructor to confirm that this assignment is available in SAM. To use the SAM version of this assignment, log into the SAM 2010 Web site and download the instruction and start files.

a. Start PowerPoint.

b. In the title placeholder on Slide 1, type **BioCare Service Industries**.

c. In the subtitle placeholder, type your name, press [Enter], then type today's date.

d. Apply the Thatch design theme to the presentation.

e. Save your presentation with the filename **PPT A-BioCare** to the drive and folder where you store your Data Files.

f. Use Figures A-19 and A-20 to add two more slides to your presentation. (*Hint*: Slide 2 uses the Comparison layout.)

g. Use the commands on the View tab to switch between all of PowerPoint's views.

h. Print the presentation using handouts, 3 Slides, in black and white.

i. Save and close the file, then exit PowerPoint.

FIGURE A-19

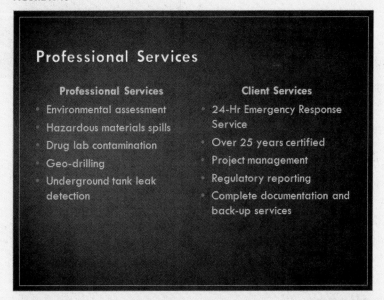

FIGURE A-20

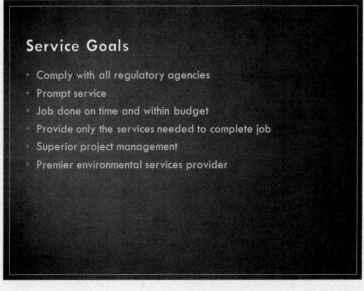

PowerPoint 2010

Independent Challenge 2

You have recently been promoted to sales manager at PowerCraft Sports, which manufactures personal aircraft, including different types of ultralite and composite airplanes. Part of your job is to present company sales figures at a yearly sales meeting. Use the following information as the basis for units sold nationally in your presentation: 283 Aircruiser, 105 Aero Twin, 89 UltraFlight, 73 Tomahawk V, and 47 Vision II. Assume that PowerCraft Sports has six sales regions throughout the country: Northwest, West, South, Midwest, Mid Atlantic, and Northeast. Also, assume overall sales rose 5% over last year, and gross sales reached $49 million. The presentation should have at least five slides.

a. Spend some time planning the slides of your presentation. What is the best way to show the information provided? What other information could you add that might be useful for this presentation?

b. Start PowerPoint.

c. Give the presentation an appropriate title on the title slide, and enter today's date and your name in the subtitle placeholder.

d. Add slides and enter appropriate slide text.

e. On the last slide of the presentation, include the following information:

PowerCraft Sports

PO Box 7373

Wrightsville, NC 19698-7373

f. Apply a design theme. A typical slide might look like the one shown in Figure A-21.

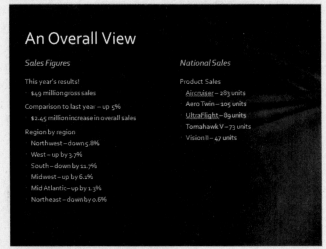

Advanced Challenge Exercise

- Open the Notes Page view.
- Add notes to three slides.
- Print the Notes Page view for the presentation.

g. Switch views. Run through the slide show at least once.

h. Save your presentation with the filename **PPT A-PowerCraft Sports** where you store your Data Files.

i. Close the presentation and exit PowerPoint.

Independent Challenge 3

You work for Baja Central, an emerging company that exports goods from Mexico. The company wants to expand its business globally. The Internet marketing director has asked you to plan and create a PowerPoint presentation that he will use to convey an expanded Internet service that will target Western countries. This new Internet service will allow customers to purchase all kinds of Mexican-made goods. Sample items for sale include silver and turquoise jewelry, hand crafts, folk art, terra cotta kitchenware, wood decorative items, and leather goods. Your presentation should contain product information and pricing. Use the Internet, if possible, to research information that will help you formulate your ideas. The presentation should have at least five slides.

a. Spend some time planning the slides of your presentation. What information would a consumer need to have to purchase items on this Web site?

b. Start PowerPoint.

c. Give the presentation an appropriate title on the title slide, and enter today's date and your name in the subtitle placeholder.

d. Add slides and enter appropriate slide text.

Independent Challenge 3 (continued)

e. On the last slide of the presentation, type the following information:

Baja Central Ltd.

Adolfo P Limon "T"

Oaxaca, Oax

ZC 98000

Tel: 50-001-660-44

info@bjacenltd.com

f. Apply a design theme. A typical slide might look like the one shown in Figure A-22.

g. Switch views. Run through the slide show at least once.

h. Save your presentation with the filename **PPT A-Baja** where you store your Data Files.

i. Close the presentation and exit PowerPoint.

FIGURE A-22

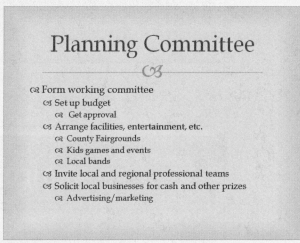

Real Life Independent Challenge

Every year your college holds a large fund-raising event to support a local charity. You are a member of the Student Council Advisory Board (SCAB), which is in charge of deciding which charity gets help. This year the board decided to support the city food bank by hosting a chili cook-off competition. The competition needs to include local and professional cooking teams from around the region. You have been chosen to present the charity proposal in a meeting of the College Events Council.

FIGURE A-23

a. Spend some time planning the slides of your presentation. Assume the following: the competition is a 2-day event; event advertising will be city- and regionwide; local music groups will also be invited; there will be a kids section with events and games; the event will be held at the county fairgrounds. Use the Internet, if possible, to research information that will help you formulate your ideas.

b. Start PowerPoint.

c. Give the presentation an appropriate title on the title slide and enter your school's name, your name, and today's date in the subtitle placeholder.

d. Add slides and enter appropriate slide text. You must create at least three slides. Typical slides might look like the ones shown in Figure A-23 and Figure A-24.

e. View the presentation.

f. Save your presentation with the filename **PPT A-Chili Cookoff** where you store your Data Files.

g. Close the presentation and exit PowerPoint.

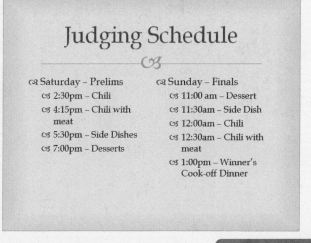

FIGURE A-24

Visual Workshop

Create the presentation shown in Figures A-25 and A-26. Make sure you include your name on the title slide. Save the presentation as **PPT A-Landscape Industries** where you store your Data Files. Print the slides.

FIGURE A-25

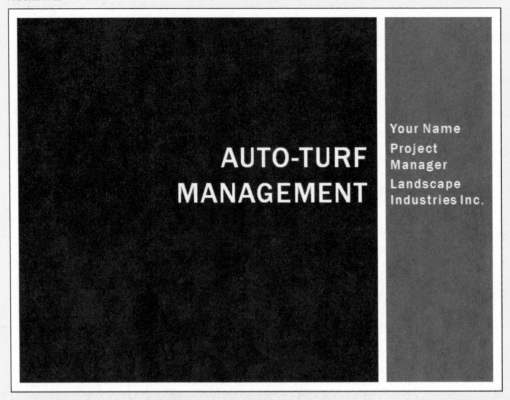

FIGURE A-26

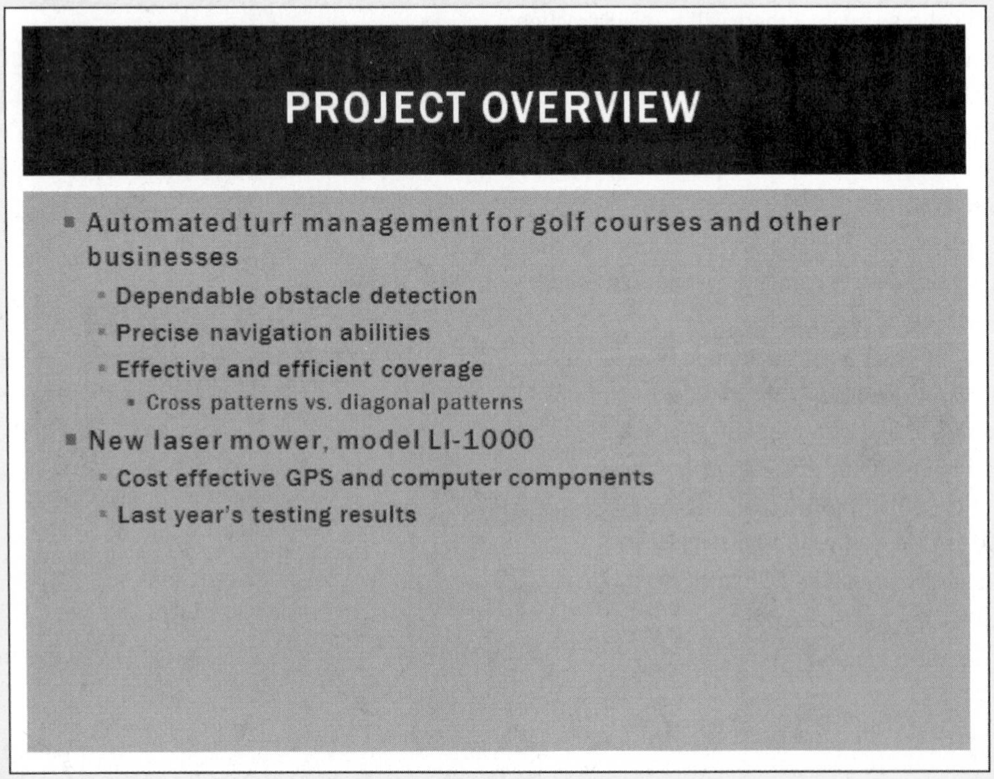

Modifying a Presentation

Files You Will Need:

PPT B-1.pptx
PPT B-2.pptx
PPT B-3.pptx
PPT B-4.pptx
PPT B-5.pptx

In the previous unit you learned how to enter slide text, add a new slide, and apply a design theme. Now, you are ready to take the next step in creating professional-looking presentations by learning to format text and work with drawn objects. In this unit, you'll enter text in the Outline tab, format text, draw and modify objects, add slide footer information, and check the spelling in the presentation. You continue working on your Canadian Train tour presentation.

OBJECTIVES

Enter text in the Outline tab

Format text

Convert text to SmartArt

Insert and modify shapes

Edit and duplicate shapes

Align and group objects

Add slide headers and footers

Use proofing and language tools

Entering Text in the Outline Tab

You can enter presentation text by typing directly on the slide in the Slide pane, or, if you'd rather focus on the presentation text without worrying about the layout, you can enter text in the Outline tab. The outline is organized so that the headings, or slide titles, appear at the top of the outline. Beneath the title, each subpoint, or each line of bulleted text, appears as one or more indented lines under the title. Each indent in the outline creates another level of bulleted text on the slide. ░░░░ You switch to the Outline tab to enter text for two more slides for your presentation.

To open a PowerPoint 97-2003 presentation in PowerPoint 2010, open the presentation, click the File tab, click the Convert button, name the presentation file in the Save As dialog box, then click Save.

1. **Start PowerPoint, open the presentation PPT B-1.pptx from the drive and folder where you store your Data Files, then save it as PPT B-QST.pptx**

   A presentation with the new name appears in the PowerPoint window.

2. **Click the Slide 2 thumbnail in the Slides tab, then click the Outline tab**

   The Outline tab enlarges to display the text that is on the slides. The slide icon and the text for Slide 2 are highlighted, indicating that it is selected.

3. **On the Home tab on the Ribbon, click the New Slide list arrow in the Slides group, then click Title and Content**

   A new slide, Slide 3, with the Title and Content layout appears as the current slide below Slide 2. A blinking insertion point appears next to the new slide in the Outline tab. Text that you enter next to a slide icon becomes the title for that slide.

4. **Type Canadian Rockies Tours, press [Enter], then press [Tab]**

   When you first press [Enter] you create a new slide, but because you want to enter bulleted text on Slide 3 you press [Tab] so that the text you type is entered as bullet text on Slide 3. See Figure B-1. Notice the text you type is in all uppercase letters because that is how the font is set in the design theme.

5. **Type British Columbia Railways Inc., press [Enter], type Based in Vancouver BC, then press [Enter]**

   Each time you press [Enter], the insertion point moves down one line.

6. **Press [Shift][Tab]**

   Because you are working in the Outline tab, a new slide, Slide 4, is created when you press [Shift][Tab].

Press [Ctrl][Enter] while the cursor is in the text object to create a new slide with the same layout as the previous slide.

7. **Type BC Railways Service Packages, press [Ctrl][Enter], type Royal Package, press [Enter], type Exclusve Package, make sure you misspell the word "Exclusve," press [Enter] type Deluxe Package, press [Enter], then type Classic Package**

   Pressing [Ctrl][Enter] while the cursor is in the title text object moves the cursor into the content placeholder.

8. **Position the pointer on the Slide 3 icon in the Outline tab**

   The pointer changes to ✛. Slide 3, Canadian Rockies Tours slide, is out of order.

9. **Drag the Slide 3 icon up until a horizontal indicator line appears above the Slide 2 icon, then release the mouse button**

   The third slide moves up and switches places with the second slide as shown in Figure B-2.

10. **Click the Slides tab, then save your work**

    The Outline tab closes and the Slides tab is now visible in the window.

FIGURE B-1: Outline tab showing new slide

Outline tab

New slide

New slide title

New slide with Title and Content layout

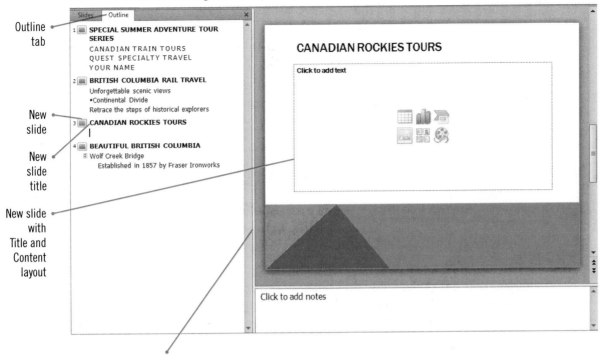

Drag the pane divider to change the width of the Outline tab

FIGURE B-2: Outline tab showing moved slide

Move pointer

Moved slide

Make sure you misspell this word

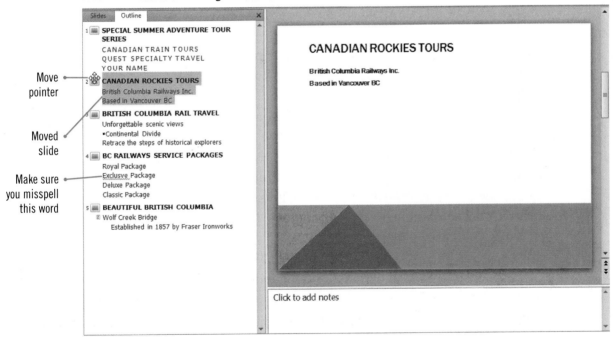

Setting permissions

In PowerPoint, you can set specific access permissions for people who review or edit your work, so you have better control over your content. For example, you may want to give a user permission to edit or change your presentation but not allow them to print it. You can also restrict a user by permitting them to view the presentation, without the ability to edit or print the presentation, or you can give the user full access or control of the presentation. To use this feature, you first have to have access to an Information Rights Management Service from Microsoft or another rights management company. Then, to set user access permissions, click the File tab, click Info, click the Protect Presentation button, point to Restrict Permission by People, then click an appropriate option.

Formatting Text

Once you have entered and edited the text in your presentation, you can modify the way the text looks to emphasize your message. Important text should be highlighted in some way to distinguish it from other text or objects on the slide. For example, if you have two text objects on the same slide, you could draw attention to one text object by changing its color, font, or size. ███████ You decide to format the text on Slide 2 of the presentation.

STEPS

QUICK TIP
To show or hide the Mini toolbar, click the File tab on the Ribbon, then click Options.

1. **Click the Slide 2 thumbnail in the Slides tab, then double-click Canadian in the title text object**

   The word "Canadian" is selected, and a small semitransparent Mini toolbar appears above the text. The **Mini toolbar** contains basic text-formatting commands, such as bold and italic, and appears when you select text using the mouse. This toolbar makes it quick and easy to format text, especially when the Home tab is not open.

2. **Move the pointer over the Mini toolbar, click the Font Color list arrow ▲ ⋅, then click the Purple color box under Standard Colors**

   The text changes color to purple as shown in Figure B-3. As soon as you move the pointer over the Mini toolbar, the toolbar becomes clearly visible. When you click the Font Color list arrow, the Font Color gallery appears showing the Theme Colors and Standard Colors. Notice that the Font Color button on the Mini toolbar and the Font Color button in the Font group on the Home tab change color to reflect the new color choice.

QUICK TIP
To select an unselected text object, press [Shift], click the text object, then release [Shift].

3. **Move the pointer over the title text object border until the pointer changes to ⁺₊, then click the border**

   The entire title text object is selected, and changes you make now affect all of the text in the text object. When the whole text object is selected, you can change its size, shape, or other attributes. Changing the color of the text helps emphasize it.

4. **Click the Font Color button ▲ ⋅ in the Font group**

   All of the text in the title text object changes to the purple color.

5. **Click the Font list arrow in the Font group**

   A list of available fonts opens with Franklin Gothic Medium, the current font used in the title text object, selected at the top of the list in the Theme Fonts section.

6. **Click Algerian in the All Fonts section**

   The Algerian font replaces the original font in the title text object. Notice that as you move the pointer over the font names in the font list the text on the slide displays a Live Preview of the different font choices.

7. **Click the Underline button U in the Font group, then click the Increase Font Size button A˙ in the Font group**

   All of the text now displays an underline and increases in size to 32.

8. **Click the Character Spacing button ᴬⱽ⋅ in the Font group, then click Loose**

   The spacing between the letters in the title text box increases slightly. Compare your screen to Figure B-4.

9. **Click a blank area of the slide outside the text object to deselect it, then save your work**

FIGURE B-3: Selected word with Mini toolbar open

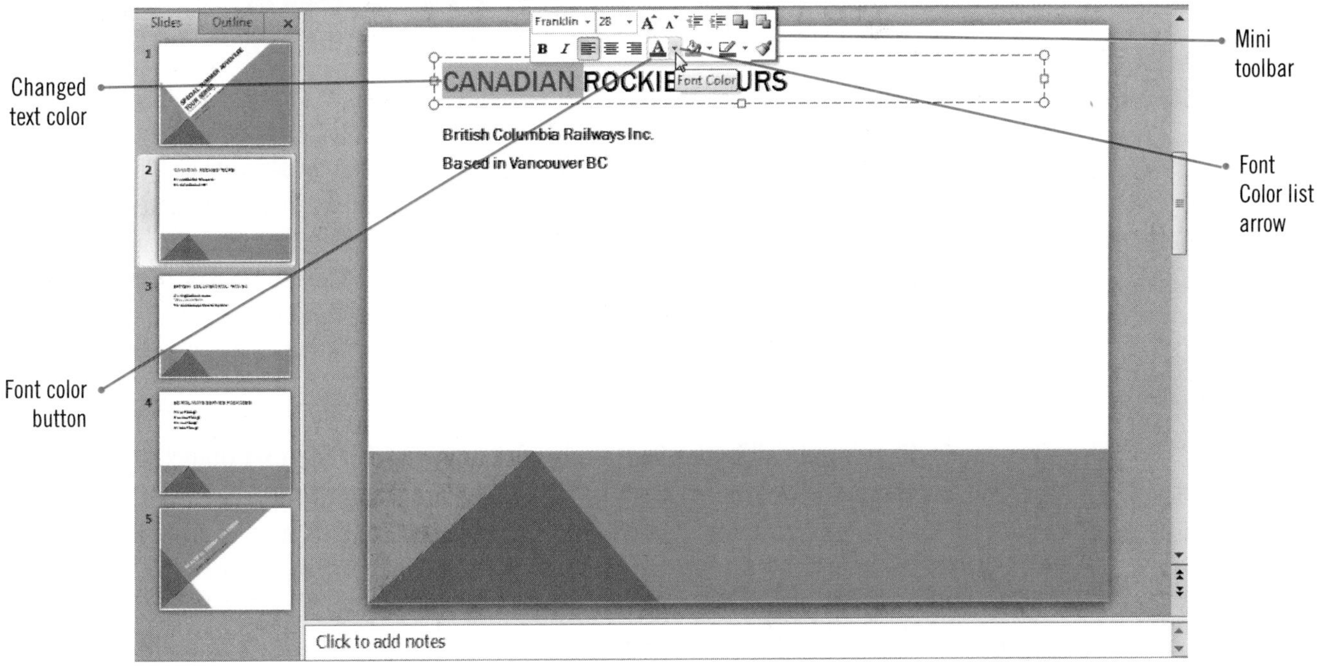

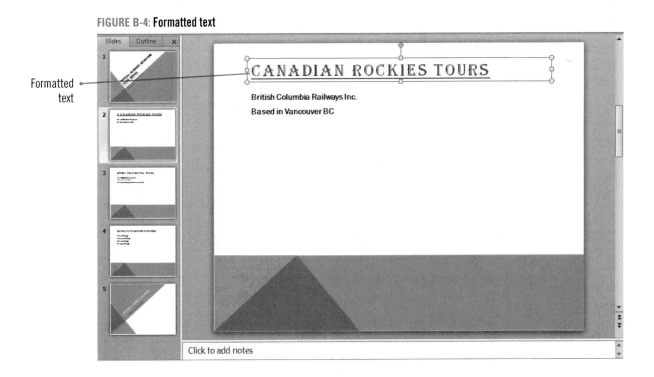

Changed text color
Font color button
Mini toolbar
Font Color list arrow
Slides
Outline
Franklin
28
Font Color
CANADIAN ROCKIE
URS
British Columbia Railways Inc.
Based in Vancouver BC
Click to add notes

FIGURE B-4: Formatted text

Formatted text
Slides
Outline
CANADIAN ROCKIES TOURS
British Columbia Railways Inc.
Based in Vancouver BC
Click to add notes

Replacing text and fonts

As you review your presentation, you may decide to replace certain text or fonts throughout the entire presentation using the Replace command. Text can be a word, phrase, or sentence. To replace specific text, click the Home tab on the Ribbon, then click the Replace button in the Editing group. In the Replace dialog box, enter the text you want to replace then enter the text you want to use as its replacement. You can also use the Replace command to replace one font for another. Simply click the Replace button list arrow in the Editing group, then click Replace Fonts to open the Replace Font dialog box.

Converting Text to SmartArt

Sometimes when you are working with text it just doesn't capture your attention, no matter how you dress it up with color or other formatting attributes. The ability to convert text to a SmartArt graphic increases your ability to create dynamic-looking text. A **SmartArt** graphic is a professional-quality diagram that visually illustrates text. There are eight categories, or types, of SmartArt graphics that incorporate graphics to illustrate text differently. For example, you can show steps in a process or timeline, show proportional relationships, or show how parts relate to a whole. You can create a SmartArt graphic from scratch or create one by converting existing text you have entered on a slide with a few simple clicks of the mouse. ▰▰▰▰ You want the presentation to appear visually dynamic so you convert the text on Slide 4 to a SmartArt graphic.

STEPS

1. **Click the Slide 4 thumbnail in the Slides tab, click anywhere in the text object, then click the Convert to SmartArt Graphic button ▦▾ in the Paragraph group**

   A gallery of SmartArt graphic layouts opens. As with many features in PowerPoint, you can preview how your text will look prior to applying the SmartArt graphic layout by using PowerPoint's Live Preview feature. You can review each SmartArt graphic layout and see how it changes the appearance of text.

2. **Move the pointer over the SmartArt graphic layouts in the gallery**

   Notice how the text becomes part of the graphic and the color and font changes each time you move the pointer over a different graphic layout. SmartArt graphic names appear as ScreenTips.

TROUBLE

If the text pane does not open as shown in Figure B-5, click the Text pane button in the Create Graphic group.

3. **Click the Pyramid List layout in the SmartArt graphics gallery**

   A SmartArt graphic appears on the slide in place of the text object, and a new SmartArt Tools Design tab opens on the Ribbon as shown in Figure B-5. A SmartArt graphic consists of two parts: the SmartArt graphic itself and a Text pane where you type and edit text.

4. **Click each bullet point in the Text pane, then click the Text pane Close button**

   Notice that each time you select a bullet point in the text pane, a selection box appears around the text objects in the SmartArt graphic. The text pane closes.

QUICK TIP

Text objects in the SmartArt graphic can be moved and edited like any other text object in PowerPoint.

5. **Click the More button ▾ in the Layouts group, click More Layouts, click the Basic Matrix layout in the Matrix section, then click OK**

   The SmartArt graphic changes to the new graphic layout. You can radically change how the SmartArt graphic looks by applying a SmartArt Style. A **SmartArt Style** is a preset combination of simple and 3-D formatting options that follows the presentation theme.

6. **Move the pointer slowly over the styles in the SmartArt Styles group, then click the More button ▾ in the SmartArt Styles group**

   A Live Preview of each style is displayed on the SmartArt graphic. The SmartArt styles are organized into sections; the top group offers suggestions for the best match for the document.

QUICK TIP

Click the Convert button in the Reset group then click Convert to Text to revert the SmartArt graphic to a standard text object.

7. **Move the pointer over all the styles in the gallery, then click Intense Effect**

   Notice how the new Intense Effect style adds a bevel and top-left corner lighting to the text boxes.

8. **Click a blank area of the slide outside the SmartArt graphic object to deselect it, then save your work**

   Compare your screen to Figure B-6.

FIGURE B-5: Text converted to a SmartArt graphic

Text pane button

Text pane Close button

Text pane

More button

SmartArt Tools Design tab

SmartArt graphic

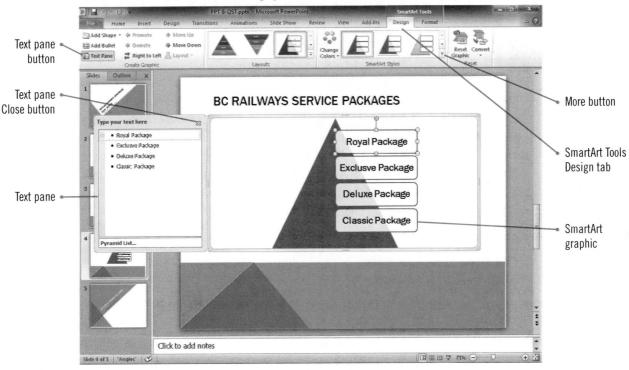

FIGURE B-6: Final SmartArt graphic

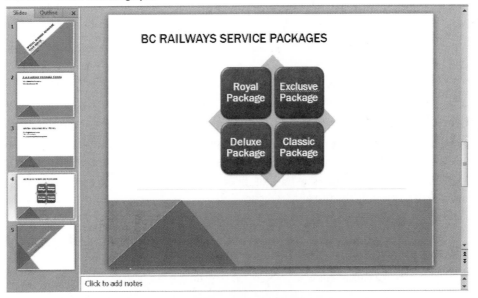

Choosing SmartArt graphics

When choosing a SmartArt graphic to use on your slide, remember that you want the SmartArt graphic to communicate the message of the text effectively; not every SmartArt graphic layout achieves that goal. You must consider the type of text you want to illustrate. For example, does the text show steps in a process, does it show a continual process, or does it show nonsequential information? The answer to this question will dictate the type of SmartArt graphic layout you should choose. Also, the amount of text you want to illustrate will have an effect on the SmartArt graphic layout you choose. Most of the time key points will be the text you use in a SmartArt graphic. Finally, some SmartArt graphic layouts are limited by the number of shapes that they can accommodate, so be sure to choose a graphic layout that can illustrate your text appropriately. Experiment with the SmartArt graphic layouts until you find the right one, and have fun in the process!

PowerPoint 2010

Inserting and Modifying Shapes

In PowerPoint you can insert many different types of shapes including lines, geometric figures, arrows, stars, callouts, and banners to enhance your presentation. You can create single shapes or combine several shapes together to make a more complex figure. You can modify many aspects of a shape including its fill color, line color, and line style, as well as add other effects like shadow and 3-D effects. Instead of changing individual attributes, you can apply a Quick Style to a shape. A **Quick Style** is a set of formatting options, including line style, fill color, and effects. ▒▒▒▒▒ You decide to draw some shapes on Slide 3 of your presentation that identify the different train routes offered by British Columbia Railways.

STEPS

1. **Click the** Slide 3 thumbnail **in the Slides tab**

   Slide 3 appears in the Slide pane.

2. **Press and hold** [Shift], **click the** text object, **then release** [Shift]

   The text object is selected. If you click a text object without pressing [Shift], a dotted selection box appears, indicating that the object is active and ready to accept text, but the text object itself is not selected.

3. **Position the pointer over the** bottom-middle sizing handle, **notice the pointer change to ↕, then drag the** sizing handle **up until the text object looks like Figure B-7**

   The text object decreases in size. When you position the pointer over a sizing handle, it changes to ↕. The pointer points in different directions depending on which sizing handle it is positioned over. When you drag a sizing handle, the pointer changes to ╈, and a faint gray outline appears, representing the size of the text object.

4. **Click the** Shapes button **in the Drawing group or click the** More button ⊽ **in the Drawing group**

   A gallery of shapes organized by type opens. Notice that there is a section at the top of the gallery where all of the recently used shapes are placed. ScreenTips help you identify the shapes.

5. **Click the** Snip Diagonal Corner Rectangle shape ▢ **in the Rectangles section, position ╈ in the blank area of the slide below the text object, drag down and to the right to create the shape, as shown in Figure B-8, then release the mouse button**

   A rectangle shape appears on the slide, filled with the default color. To change the style of the shape, apply a Quick Style from the Shape Styles group.

6. **Click the** Drawing Tools Format tab, **click the** More button ⊽ **in the Shape Styles group, move the pointer over the styles in the gallery to review the effects on the shape, then click** Subtle Effect — Olive Green, Accent 4

   A light green Quick Style with coordinated gradient fill, line, and shadow color is applied to the shape.

7. **Click the** Shape Outline button **in the Shape Styles group, point to** Weight, **then move the pointer over the line weight options to review the effect on the shape**

   The outline line weight changes every time you move the pointer over a different effect.

8. **Click 2 ¼ pt, click in a blank area of the slide, then save your work**

FIGURE B-7: Resized text object

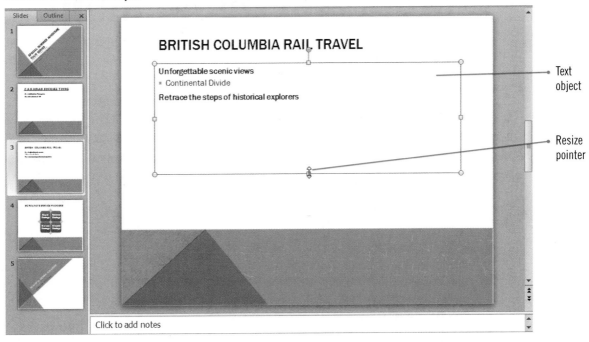

FIGURE B-8: Slide showing Snip Diagonal Corner Rectangle shape

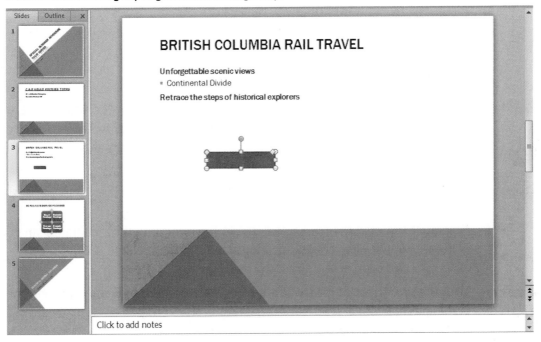

Changing the size and position of shapes

Usually when you resize a shape you can simply drag one of the sizing handles around the outside of the shape, but sometimes you may need to resize a shape more precisely. When you select a shape, the Drawing Tools Format tab appears on the Ribbon, offering you many different formatting options including some sizing commands located in the Size group. The Width and Height commands in the Size group allow you to change the width and height of a shape. You also have the option to open the Size and Position dialog box, which allows you to change the size of a shape, as well as the rotation, scale, and position of a shape on the slide.

Editing and Duplicating Shapes

Once you have created a shape you still have the ability to refine the aspects of the object. PowerPoint allows you to adjust various aspects of shapes to help change the look of them. For example, if you create a shape with an arrowhead but the head of the arrow does not look quite like you want it to look, you can change it. You can also add text to most PowerPoint shapes, and you can move or copy shapes. ▰▰▰▰ You want three identical rectangles on Slide 3. You first change the shape of the rectangle you've already created, and then you make copies of it.

STEPS

1. **Click the rectangle shape on Slide 3 to select it**

   In addition to sizing handles, two other types of handles appear on the selected object. You use the **adjustment handle**—a small yellow diamond—to change the appearance of an object. The adjustment handle appears next to the most prominent feature of the object, like the diagonal sides of the rectangle in this case. You use the **rotate handle**—a small green circle—to manually rotate the object.

2. **Drag the left-middle sizing handle on the rectangle shape to the right approximately 1/4", then release the mouse button**

   QUICK TIP
   You can easily display or hide gridlines by clicking the Gridlines check box in the Show group on the View tab.

3. **Position the pointer over the middle of the selected rectangle shape so that it changes to ✛, then drag the rectangle shape so that the rectangle aligns with the left edge of the text in the text object as shown in Figure B-9**

   A semitransparent copy of the shape appears as you move the rectangle shape to help you position it. PowerPoint uses gridlines to align objects; it forces objects to "snap" to the grid. To turn the snap-to-grid feature off while dragging objects, press and hold [Alt]. Make any needed adjustments to the rectangle shape position so it looks similar to Figure B-9.

   TROUBLE
   To make precise adjustments, press and hold [Alt], then drag the adjustment handle.

4. **Position the pointer over the right adjustment handle on the rectangle shape so that it changes to ▷, then drag the adjustment handle all the way to the left**

   The rectangle shape appearance changes.

5. **Position ✛ over the rectangle shape, then press and hold [Ctrl]**

   The pointer changes to ▨, indicating that PowerPoint makes a copy of the rectangle shape when you drag the mouse.

6. **Holding [Ctrl], drag the rectangle shape to the right until the rectangle shape copy is in a blank area of the slide, release the mouse button, then release [Ctrl]**

   An identical copy of the rectangle shape appears on the slide.

   QUICK TIP
   All shape objects use the dotted alignment line to help you align shapes to an object's top, bottom, or side.

7. **With the second rectangle shape still selected, repeat Steps 5 and 6 to create a third rectangle shape, then type Northern Route**

   A dotted line appears through the center of the shapes identifying the centerline of the shapes and helps you align the shapes. The text appears in the selected rectangle shape. The text is now part of the shape, so if you move or rotate the shape, the text moves with it. Compare your screen with Figure B-10.

8. **Click the middle rectangle shape, type Western Pass, click the left rectangle shape, type Explorer's Trail, then click in a blank area of the slide**

   Clicking a blank area of the slide deselects all objects that are selected.

9. **Save your work**

FIGURE B-9: Slide showing resized shape

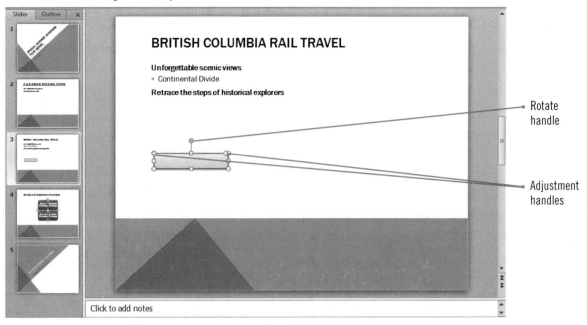

Rotate handle

Adjustment handles

FIGURE B-10: Slide showing duplicated shapes

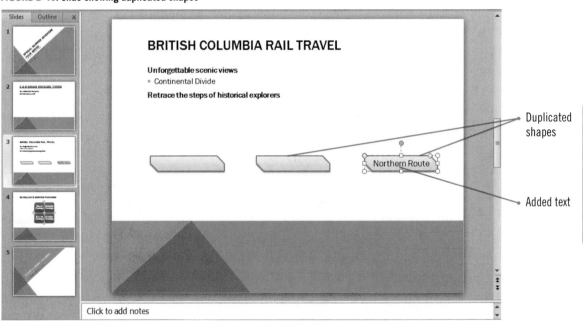

Duplicated shapes

Added text

Understanding PowerPoint objects

Every object on a slide, whether it is a text object, a shape, a chart, a picture, or any other object, is stacked on the slide in the order it was created. So, for example, if you add three shapes to a slide, the first shape you create is on the bottom of the stack, and the last shape you create is on the top of the stack. Each object on a slide can be moved up or down in the stack depending on how you want the objects to look on the slide. To move an object to the front of the stack, select the object, then click the Bring Forward button in the Arrange group on the Drawing Tools Format tab. To move an object to the back of the stack, click the Send Backward button in the Arrange group on the Drawing Tools Format tab. You can also open the Selection and Visibility pane by clicking the Selection Pane button in the Arrange group to view and rearrange all of the objects on the slide.

Aligning and Grouping Objects

After you are finished creating and modifying your objects, you can position them accurately on the slide to achieve the look you want. Using the Align commands in the Arrange group, you can align objects relative to each other by snapping them to a grid of evenly spaced vertical and horizontal lines. The Group command **groups** objects into one object, which secures their relative position to each other and makes it easy to edit and move them. The Distribute commands found with the Align commands evenly space objects horizontally or vertically relative to each other or the slide. You are ready to position and group the arrow shapes on Slide 3 to make the slide look consistent and planned.

STEPS

QUICK TIP
To add a new guide to the slide, press [Ctrl], then drag an existing guide. The original guide remains in place as you move the new guide. Drag a guide off the slide to delete it.

1. **Right-click a blank area of the slide, then click Grid and Guides on the shortcut menu**
   The Grid and Guides dialog box opens.

2. **Click the Display drawing guides on screen check box, then click OK**
   The PowerPoint guides appear as dotted lines on the slide and intersect at the center of the slide. They help you position a rectangle shape.

3. **Position ⬚ over the horizontal guide in a blank area of the slide, press and hold the mouse button until the pointer changes to a measurement guide, then drag the guide down until the guide position box reads 1.25**

4. **Position ⬚ over the Explorer's Trail rectangle shape (not over the text in the shape), then drag the shape so that the bottom edge of the shape touches the horizontal guide as shown in Figure B-11**
   The rectangle shape attaches or "snaps" to the horizontal guide.

5. **With the Explorer's Trail shape selected, press and hold [Shift], click the other two rectangle shapes, then release [Shift]**
   All three shapes are now selected.

6. **Click the Drawing Tools Format tab on the Ribbon, click the Align button in the Arrange group, then click Align Bottom**
   The shapes are now aligned horizontally along their bottom edges. The higher shapes move down and align with the bottom shape.

7. **Click the Align button, then click Distribute Horizontally**
   The shapes are now distributed equally between themselves.

QUICK TIP
Rulers can help you align objects. To display the rulers, position the pointer in a blank area of the slide, right-click, then click Ruler on the shortcut menu.

8. **Click the Group button in the Arrange group, click Group, then press [Left Arrow] or [Right Arrow] until the Rotate handle is on or very near the vertical grid line as shown in Figure B-12**
   The objects group to form one object without losing their individual attributes. Notice that the sizing handles and rotate handle now appear on the outer edge of the grouped object, not around each individual object.

9. **Drag the horizontal guide up until the guide position box reads 0.00, click the View tab on the Ribbon, then click the Guides check box in the Show group**
   The guides are no longer displayed on the slide

10. **Click a blank area of the slide, then save your work**

FIGURE B-11: Repositioned shape

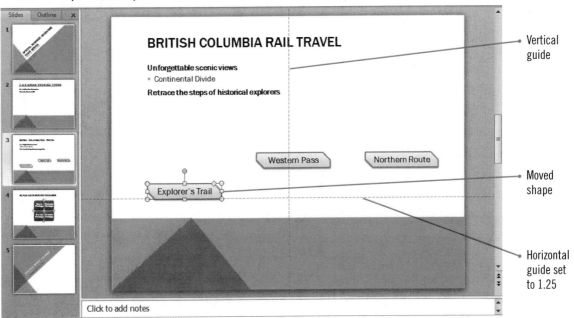

FIGURE B-12: Aligned and grouped shapes

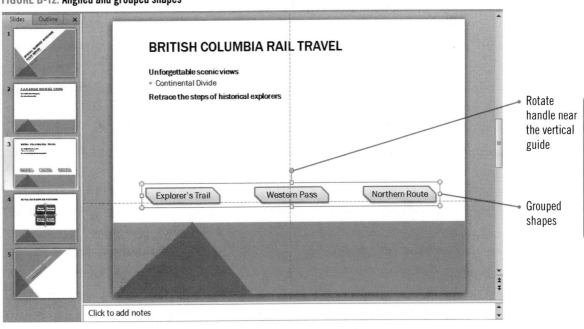

Distributing objects

There are two ways to **distribute** objects in PowerPoint: relative to each other and relative to the slide edge. If you choose to distribute objects relative to each other, PowerPoint evenly divides the empty space between all of the selected objects. When distributing objects in relation to the slide, PowerPoint evenly splits the empty space from slide edge to slide edge between the selected objects. To distribute objects relative to each other, click the Align button in the Arrange group on the Drawing Tools Format tab, then click Align Selected Objects. To distribute objects relative to the slide, click the Align button in the Arrange group on the Drawing Tools Format tab, then click Align to Slide.

Adding Slide Headers and Footers

Header and footer text, such as a company, school or product name, the slide number, and the date, can give your slides a polished look and make it easier for your audience to follow your presentation. On slides, you can add text to the footer; however, notes or handouts can include both header and footer text. Footer information that you apply to the slides of your presentation is visible in the PowerPoint views and when you print the slides. Notes and handouts header and footer text is visible when you print notes pages, handouts, and the outline. ▰▰▰ You add footer text to the slides of the Canadian train tour presentation to make it easier for the audience to follow.

STEPS

1. **Click the Insert tab on the Ribbon, then click the Header & Footer button in the Text group**

   The Header and Footer dialog box opens, as shown in Figure B-13. The Header and Footer dialog box has two tabs: a Slide tab and a Notes and Handouts tab. The Slide tab is selected. There are three types of footer text, Date and time, Slide number, and Footer. The rectangles at the bottom of the Preview box identify the default position and status of the three types of footer text placeholders on the slides.

2. **Click the Date and time check box to select it**

   The date and time suboptions are now available to select. The Update automatically date and time option button is selected by default. This option updates the date and time every time you open or print the file.

3. **Click the Update automatically list arrow, then click the eighth option in the list**

   The time is added to the date.

4. **Click the Slide number check box, click the Footer check box, then type your name**

   The Preview box now shows that all three footer placeholders are selected.

5. **Click the Don't show on title slide check box**

   Selecting this check box prevents the footer information you entered in the Header and Footer dialog box from appearing on the title slide.

6. **Click Apply to All**

   The dialog box closes and the footer information is applied to all of the slides in your presentation except the title slide. Compare your screen to Figure B-14.

7. **Click the Slide 1 thumbnail in the Slides tab, then click the Header & Footer button in the Text group**

   The Header and Footer dialog box opens again.

8. **Click the Don't show on title slide check box to deselect it, click the Footer check box, then select the text in the Footer text box**

9. **Type World's foremost traveling experience, click Apply, then save your work**

   Only the text in the Footer text box appears on the title slide. Clicking Apply applies the footer information to just the current slide.

FIGURE B-13: Header and Footer dialog box

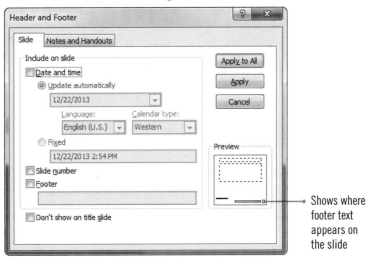

Shows where footer text appears on the slide

FIGURE B-14: Slide showing footer information

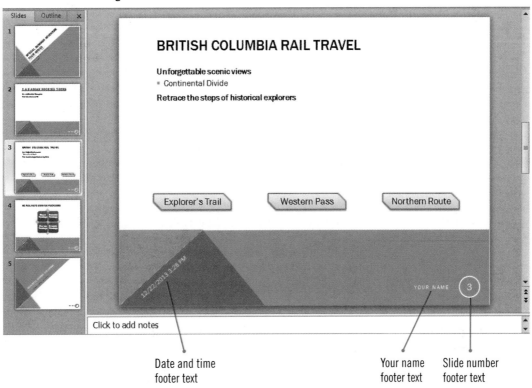

Date and time footer text

Your name footer text

Slide number footer text

Entering and printing notes

You can add notes to your slides when there are certain facts you want to remember during a presentation or when there is information you want to hand out to your audience. Notes do not appear on the slides when you run a slide show. Use the Notes pane in Normal view or Notes Page view to enter notes for your slides. To enter text notes on a slide, click in the Notes pane, then type. If you want to insert graphics as notes, you must use Notes Page view. To open Notes Page view, click the View tab on the Ribbon, then click the Notes Page button in the Presentation Views group. You can print your notes by clicking the File tab to open Backstage view then clicking Print. Click the Full Page Slides list arrow in the Settings section (this button retains the last setting for what was printed previously so it might differ) to open the gallery, and then click Notes Pages. Once you verify your print settings, click the Print button. Notes pages can be a good handout to give your audience to use during the presentation. If you don't enter any notes in the Notes pane, and print the notes pages, the slides print as thumbnails with blank lines to the right of the thumbnails to hand write notes.

Using Proofing and Language Tools

As your work on the presentation file nears completion, you need to review and proofread your slides thoroughly for errors. You can use the spell-checking feature in PowerPoint to check for and correct spelling errors. This feature compares the spelling of all the words in your presentation against the words contained in PowerPoint's electronic dictionary. You still must proofread your presentation for punctuation, grammar, and word-usage errors because the spell checker recognizes only misspelled and unknown words, not misused words. For example, the spell checker would not identify the word "last" as an error, even if you had intended to type the word "cast." PowerPoint also includes language tools that translate words or phrases from your default language into another language using the Microsoft Translator. ▓▓▓▓ You're finished working on the presentation for now, so it's a good time to check spelling. You then experiment with language translation because the final presentation will be translated into French.

STEPS

1. **Click the Review tab on the Ribbon, then click the Spelling button in the Proofing group**

   PowerPoint begins to check the spelling in your presentation. When PowerPoint finds a misspelled word or a word it doesn't recognize, the Spelling dialog box opens, as shown in Figure B-15. In this case, PowerPoint identifies the misspelled word on Slide 4 and suggests you replace it with the correctly spelled word "Exclusive."

2. **Click Change**

   PowerPoint changes the misspelled word and then continues to check the rest of the presentation for errors. If PowerPoint finds any other words it does not recognize, either change or ignore them. When the spell checker finishes checking your presentation, the Spelling dialog box closes, and an alert box opens with a message that the spelling check is complete.

3. **Click OK, click the Slide 1 thumbnail in the Slides tab, then save your presentation**

   The alert box closes. Now you need to see how the language translation feature works.

4. **Click the Translate button in the Language group, then click Choose Translation Language**

   The Translation Language Options dialog box opens.

5. **Click the Translate to list arrow, click French (France), then click OK**

   The Translation Language Options dialog box closes.

6. **Click the Translate button in the Language group, click Mini Translator [French(France)], click anywhere in the footer text object, then select all of the text**

   The Microsoft Translator begins to analyze the selected text and a semitransparent Microsoft Translator box appears below the text.

7. **Move the pointer over the Microsoft Translator box**

   A French translation of the text appears as shown in Figure B-16. The translation language setting remains in effect until you reset it.

8. **Click the Translate button in the Language group, click Choose Translation Language, click the Translate to list arrow, click Arabic, click OK, click the Translate button again, then click Mini Translator [Arabic]**

   The Mini Translator is turned off and the translation language is restored to the default setting.

9. **Submit your presentation to your instructor, then exit PowerPoint**

FIGURE B-15: Spelling dialog box

Selected word from Suggestions list

Suggestions list

Unrecognized word

FIGURE B-16: Slide showing translated text

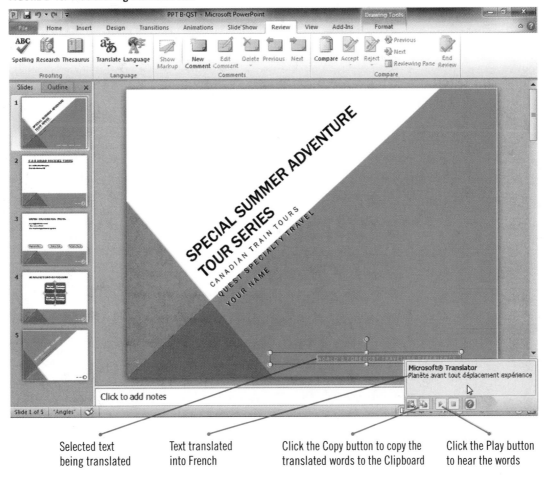

Selected text being translated

Text translated into French

Click the Copy button to copy the translated words to the Clipboard

Click the Play button to hear the words

Checking spelling as you type

PowerPoint checks your spelling as you type. If you type a word that is not in the electronic dictionary, a wavy red line appears under it. To correct an error, right-click the misspelled word, then review the suggestions, which appear in the shortcut menu. You can select a suggestion, add the word you typed to your custom dictionary, or ignore it. To turn off automatic spell checking, click the File tab, then click Options to open the PowerPoint Options dialog box. Click the Proofing button, then click the Check spelling as you type check box

to deselect it. To temporarily hide the wavy red lines, click the Hide spelling errors check box to select it. Contextual spelling in PowerPoint identifies common grammatically misused words, for example, if you type the word "their" and the correct word is "there," PowerPoint will identify the mistake and place a wavy blue line under the word. To turn contextual spelling on or off, click the Proofing button in the PowerPoint Options dialog box, then click the Use contextual spelling check box.

Practice

For current SAM information, including versions and content details, visit SAM Central (http://www.cengage.com/samcentral). If you have a SAM user profile, you may have access to hands-on instruction, practice, and assessment of the skills covered in this unit. Since various versions of SAM are supported throughout the life of this text, check with your instructor for the correct instructions and URL/Web site for accessing assignments.

Concepts Review

Label each element of the PowerPoint window shown in Figure B-17.

FIGURE B-17

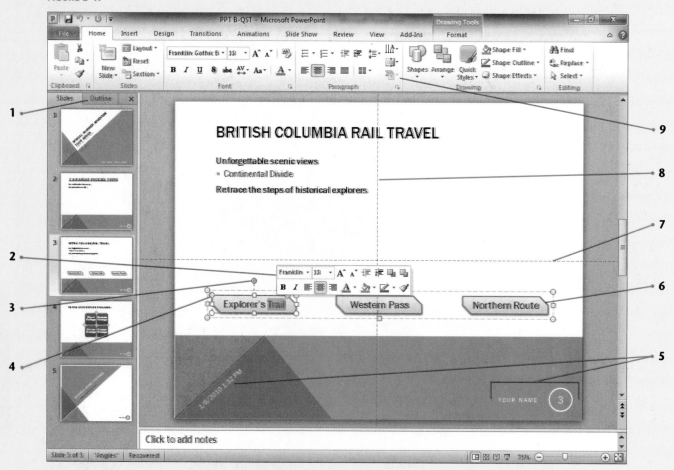

Match each term with the statement that best describes it.

10. **Quick Style**	**a.** Use to space objects evenly
11. **Rotate handle**	**b.** A diagram that visually illustrates text
12. **Distribute**	**c.** Use to manually turn an object
13. **Mini toolbar**	**d.** Combines multiple objects into one object
14. **SmartArt graphic**	**e.** Use to format selected text
15. **Group**	**f.** A preset combination of formatting options that you apply to an object

Select the best answer from the list of choices.

16. Which of the following statements is *not* true about the Outline tab?

  a. Each line of indented text creates a new slide title.

  b. You can enter text directly.

  c. It is organized using headings and subpoints.

  d. Headings are the same as slide titles.

17. What appears just above text when it is selected?

  a. QuickStyles   **c.** Mini toolbar

  b. Option button   **d.** AutoFit Options button

18. What does the adjustment handle do to a shape?

  a. Changes the appearance of a shape   **c.** Changes the size of a shape

  b. Changes the style of a shape   **d.** Changes the shape to another design

19. A professional-quality diagram that visually illustrates text best describes which of the following?

  a. A shape   **c.** A slide layout

  b. A SmartArt graphic   **d.** A QuickStyle object

20. Which of the following is not *true* about checking spelling in PowerPoint?

  a. The spell checker identifies unknown words as misspelled.

  b. Spelling is checked as you type.

  c. You can fix a misspelled word by right-clicking it and selecting a correct word.

  d. All misused words are automatically corrected.

21. What is *not* true about grouped objects?

  a. Grouped objects have one rotate handle.

  b. Sizing handles appear around the grouped object.

  c. Each object has individual sizing handles and a rotate handle.

  d. Grouped objects act as one object.

22. What do objects snap to when you move them?

  a. Slide edges   **c.** Drawing lines

  b. Hidden grid   **d.** Anchor points

Skills Review

1. Enter text in the Outline tab.

  a. Open the presentation PPT B-2.pptx from the drive and folder where you store your Data Files, then save it as **PPT B-PoolClean Pro**. The completed presentation is shown in Figure B-18.

  b. Create a new slide after Slide 2 with the Title and Content layout.

  c. Open the Outline tab, then type **Major Marketing Avenues**.

  d. Press [Enter], press [Tab], type **Online Forums**, press [Enter], type **Instant Messengers**, press [Enter], then type **Online Classifieds**.

  e. Move Slide 3 above Slide 2.

  f. Switch back to the Slides tab.

  g. Save your changes.

2. Format text.

  a. Go to Slide 1.

  b. Select the name **D.T. Wittenger**, then move the pointer over the Mini toolbar.

  c. Click the Font Color list arrow, then click Dark Blue, Text 2 under Theme Colors.

FIGURE B-18

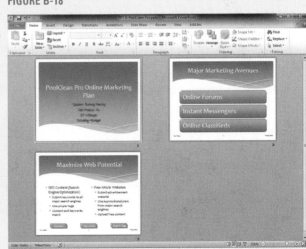

Skills Review (continued)

   d. Select the text object, then change all of the text to the color Dark Blue, Text 2.

   e. Click the Font Size list arrow, then click 24.

   f. Click the Italic button.

   g. Click the Character Spacing button, then click Tight.

   h. Save your changes.

3. Convert text to SmartArt.

   a. Click the text object on Slide 2.

   b. Click the Convert to SmartArt Graphic button, then apply the Vertical Block List graphic layout to the text object.

   c. Click the More button in the Layouts group, click More Layouts, click List in the Choose a SmartArt Graphic dialog box, then click Vertical Bullet List.

   d. Click the More button in the SmartArt Styles group, then apply the Intense Effect style to the graphic.

   e. Close the text pane if necessary, then click outside the SmartArt graphic in an empty part of the slide.

   f. Save your changes.

4. Insert and modify shapes.

   a. Go to Slide 3.

   b. Press [Shift], click both text objects, release [Shift], then drag the bottom-middle sizing handle up to decrease the size of the text objects.

   c. Click the Shapes button in the Drawing group, then insert the Round Diagonal Corner Rectangle shape from the Shapes gallery similar to the one in Figure B-19.

   d. On the Drawing Tools Format tab, click the More button in the Shape Styles group, then click Light 1 Outline, Colored Fill – Green, Accent 3.

FIGURE B-19

   e. Click the Shape Effects button in the Shape Styles group, point to Shadow, then click Offset Diagonal Bottom Right.

   f. Click the Shape Outline button in the Shape Styles group, then click Black, Text 1, Lighter 25%.

   g. Click a blank area of the slide, then save your changes.

5. Edit and duplicate shapes.

   a. Select the rectangle shape, then drag the left adjustment handle all the way to the right.

   b. Drag the rectangle shape so it lines up with the text in the left text object about ½ inch from the bottom of the slide.

   c. Click the Rotate button in the Arrange group, then click Flip Horizontal.

   d. Using [Ctrl] make two copies of the rectangle shape.

   e. Type **Search Tags** in the right rectangle shape, type **Keywords** in the middle rectangle shape, then type **Content** in the left rectangle shape.

   f. Click a blank area of the slide, then save your changes.

6. Align and group objects.

   a. Select the right rectangle shape, press [Shift], then move it to so it lines up with the right edge of the text in the right text object.

   b. Select all three rectangle shapes.

   c. Click the Drawing Tools Format tab if necessary, click the Align button, then click Align Bottom.

   d. Click the Align button in the Arrange group, then click Distribute Horizontally.

   e. Group all three rectangles together, then display the drawing guides on the screen.

Skills Review (continued)

f. Move the horizontal guide down until 3.17 appears, then press [Up Arrow] or press [Down Arrow] until the bottom of the rectangle shapes are on or near the horizontal guide. Compare your screen to Figure B-20.

g. Remove the drawing guides from your screen, then save your work.

7. **Add slide headers and footers.**

a. Open the Header and Footer dialog box.

b. On the Slide tab, click the Date and time check box to select it, click the Fixed option button, then type today's date in the Fixed text box.

c. Add the slide number to the footer.

d. Type your name in the Footer text box.

e. Apply the footer to all of the slides except the title slide.

f. Open the Header and Footer dialog box again, then click the Notes and Handouts tab.

g. Type today's date in the Fixed text box.

h. Type the name of your class in the Header text box, then click the Page number check box.

i. Type your name in the Footer text box.

j. Apply the header and footer information to all the notes and handouts.

k. Save your changes.

FIGURE B-20

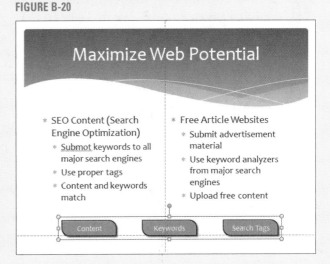

8. **Use proofing and language tools.**

a. Check the spelling of the document, and change any misspelled words. Ignore any words that are correctly spelled but that the spell checker doesn't recognize. There is at least one misspelled word in the presentation.

b. Move to Slide 3, then set the Mini Translator language to Russian.

c. View the Russian translation of two or three individual words and a phrase on Slide 3.

d. Choose one other language (or as many as you want), translate words or phrases on the slide, reset the default language to Arabic, then turn off the Mini Translator.

e. Save your changes, submit your presentation to your instructor, close the presentation, then exit PowerPoint.

Independent Challenge 1

You are the Director of the Performing Arts Center in Council Bluffs, Iowa, and one of your many duties is to raise funds to cover operation costs. One of the primary ways you do this is by speaking to businesses, community clubs, and other organizations throughout

If you have a SAM 2010 user profile, an autogradable SAM version of this assignment may be available at http://www.cengage.com/sam2010. Check with your instructor to confirm that this assignment is available in SAM. To use the SAM version of this assignment, log into the SAM 2010 Web site and download the instruction and start files.

the Council Bluffs region. Every year you speak to many organizations, where you give a short presentation detailing what the theater center plans to do for the coming season. You need to continue working on the presentation you started already.

a. Start PowerPoint, open the presentation PPT B-3.pptx from the drive and folder where you store your Data Files, and save it as **PPT B-Arts Center**.

b. Use the Outline tab to enter the following as bulleted text on the Commitment to Excellence slide:
Study
Diligence
Testing
Excellence

c. Apply the Technic design theme to the presentation.

d. Change the font color of each play name on Slide 3 to Gold, Accent 2, Lighter 40%.

e. Change the bulleted text on Slide 5 to the Vertical Accent List SmartArt graphic layout, then apply the Moderate Effect SmartArt Style.

Independent Challenge 1 (continued)

Advanced Challenge Exercise

- Open the Notes Page view.
- To at least two slides, add notes that relate to the slide content that you think would be important when giving this presentation.
- Save the presentation as **Arts Center ACE** to the drive and folder where you store your Data Files. When submitting the presentation to your instructor, submit the Notes Pages.

f. Check the spelling in the presentation (there is at least one spelling error), then view the presentation in Slide Show view.

g. Add your name as a footer on the notes and handouts, then save your changes.

h. Submit your presentation to your instructor, close your presentation, then exit PowerPoint.

Independent Challenge 2

You are a manager for Jess Hauser Investments Inc., a financial services company. You have been asked by your boss to develop a presentation outlining important details and aspects of the mortgage process to be used at a financial seminar.

a. Start PowerPoint, open the presentation PPT B-4.pptx from the drive and folder where you store your Data Files, and save it as **PPT B-Hauser**.

b. Apply the Hardcover design theme to the presentation.

c. On Slide 4 select the three shapes, Banks, Mortgage Bankers, and Private Investors, then using the Align command distribute them vertically and align them to their left edges.

d. On Slide 4 select the three shapes, Borrower, Mortgage Broker, and Mortgage Bankers, then using the Align command distribute them horizontally and align them to their bottom edges.

e. Select all of the shapes, then apply Intense Effect – Black, Dark 1 from the Shape Styles group, then move the shapes down as shown in Figure B-21.

f. Using the Arrow shape from the Shapes gallery, draw a 2 ¼-pt arrow between all of the shapes. (*Hint*: Draw one arrow shape, change the line weight to 2 ¼-pt using the Shape Outline button, then duplicate the shape.)

g. Create a sixth slide to end the presentation, then type the following information in the Outline tab:

Program Summary
> **We will find the right loan for you**
> **You will be able to afford your loan**
> **You will save money with our loan**
> **No government interference**

h. Check the spelling in the presentation, view the presentation in Slide Show view, then view the slides in Slide Sorter view.

FIGURE B-21

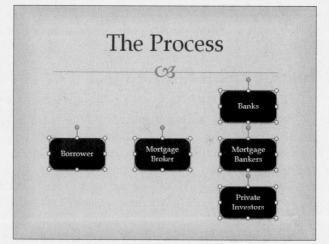

i. Add the page number and your name as a footer on the notes and handouts, then save your changes.

j. Submit your presentation to your instructor, close your presentation, then exit PowerPoint.

Independent Challenge 3

You are an independent distributor of natural foods in Spokane, Washington. Your business, Pacific Coast Natural Foods, has grown progressively since its inception 10 years ago, but sales have leveled off over the last 12 months. In an effort to stimulate growth, you decide to purchase Idaho Foods Inc., a natural food dealer in Idaho, which would allow your company to begin expanding into surrounding states. Use PowerPoint to develop a presentation that you can use to gain a financial backer for the acquisition. Create your own information for the presentation.

a. Start PowerPoint, create a new presentation, then apply the Thatch design theme to the presentation.

b. Type **A Plan for Growth** as the main title on the title slide, and **Pacific Coast Natural Foods** as the subtitle.

c. Save the presentation as **PPT B-Pacific Coast** to the drive and folder where you store your Data Files.

d. Add five more slides with the following titles: Slide 2-**Background**; Slide 3-**Current Situation**; Slide 4-**Acquisition Goals**; Slide 5-**Funding Required**; Slide 6-**Our Management Team**.

e. Enter appropriate text into the text placeholders of the slides. Use both the Slide pane and the Outline tab to enter text.

f. Convert text on one slide to a SmartArt graphic, then apply the SmartArt graphic style Inset Effect.

Advanced Challenge Exercise

■ Click the Replace list arrow in the Editing group on the Home tab, then click Replace Fonts.

■ Replace the Tw Cen MT font with the Eras Medium ITC font.

■ Save the presentation as **PPT B-Pacific Coast ACE** to the drive and folder where you store your Data Files.

g. Check the spelling in the presentation, view the presentation as a slide show, then view the slides in Slide Sorter view.

h. Add the slide number and your name as a footer on the slides, then save your changes.

i. Submit your presentation to your instructor, close your presentation, then exit PowerPoint.

Real Life Independent Challenge

Your computer instructor at City Junior College has been asked by the department head to convert his Computer Basics 101 course into an accelerated course that both students and professional working people can take. Your instructor has asked you to help him create a presentation for the class that he can post on the Internet and use as a promotional tool at local businesses. Most of the raw information is already on the slides, you primarily need to jazz it up by adding a theme and some text formatting.

a. Start PowerPoint, open the presentation PPT B-5.pptx from drive and folder where you store your data files, and save it as **PPT B-Course 101**.

b. Add a new slide after the Course Facts slide with the same layout, type **Course Details** in the title text placeholder, then enter the following as bulleted text in the Outline tab:
Unix/Information Systems
Networking
Applied Methods
Technology Solutions
Software Design
Applications

c. Apply the Paper design theme to the presentation.

d. Select the title text object on Slide 1 (*Hint*: Press [Shift] to select the whole object), then change the text color to Yellow.

e. Change the font of the title text object to Century Gothic.

f. Click the subtitle text object, click the AutoFit Options button, then click Stop Fitting Text to This Placeholder.

g. Change the text on Slide 4 to a SmartArt graphic. Use an appropriate diagram type for a list.

h. Change the style of the SmartArt diagram using one of the SmartArt Styles, then view the presentation in Slide Show view.

i. Add the slide number and your name as a footer on the notes and handouts, then save your changes.

j   Submit your presentation to your instructor, close your presentation, then exit PowerPoint.

Visual Workshop

Create the presentation shown in Figures B-22 and B-23. Add today's date as the date on the title slide. Save the presentation as **PPT B-Ag Trade** to the drive and folder where you store your Data Files. (*Hint*: The SmartArt style used for the SmartArt is a 3-D style.) Review your slides in Slide Show view, then add your name as a footer to the notes and handouts. Submit your presentation to your instructor, save your changes, close the presentation, then exit PowerPoint.

FIGURE B-22

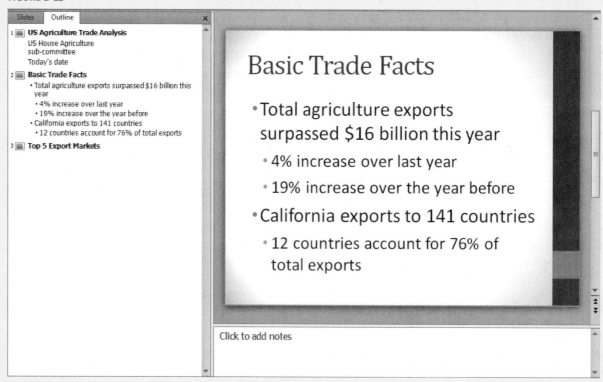

FIGURE B-23

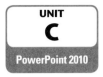

UNIT C
PowerPoint 2010

Inserting Objects into a Presentation

Files You Will Need:

PPT C-1.pptx
PPT C-2.docx
PPT C-3.jpg
PPT C-4.pptx
PPT C-5.docx
PPT C-6.jpg
PPT C-7.pptx
PPT C-8.pptx
PPT C-9.docx
PPT C-10.pptx
PPT C-11.docx
PPT C-12.jpg
PPT C-13.jpg
PPT C-14.jpg
PPT C-15.jpg

A good presenter will make use of visual elements, such as charts, graphics, and photographs, in conjunction with text to help communicate the presentation message. Visual elements keep the presentation interesting, illustrate concepts, and help the audience focus on what the presenter is saying. In this unit, you continue working on the presentation by inserting visual elements, including clip art, a photograph, and a chart, into the presentation. You format these objects using PowerPoint's powerful object-editing features.

OBJECTIVES

Insert text from Microsoft Word

Insert clip art

Insert and style a picture

Insert a text box

Insert a chart

Enter and edit chart data

Insert a table

Insert and format WordArt

Inserting Text from Microsoft Word

It is easy to insert documents saved in Microsoft Word format (.docx), Rich Text Format (.rtf), plain text format (.txt), and HTML format (.htm) into a PowerPoint presentation. If you have an outline saved in a document file, you can import it into PowerPoint to create a new presentation or create additional slides in an existing presentation. When you import a document into a presentation, PowerPoint creates an outline structure based on the styles in the document. For example, a Heading 1 style in the Word document becomes a slide title and a Heading 2 style becomes the first level of text in a bulleted list. If you insert a plain text format document into a presentation, PowerPoint creates an outline based on the tabs at the beginning of the document's paragraphs. Paragraphs without tabs become slide titles and paragraphs with one tab indent become first-level text in bulleted lists. ▓▓▓▓▓ You have a Microsoft Word document with information about the different Canadian train routes that you want to insert into your presentation to create several new slides.

STEPS

1. **Start PowerPoint, open the presentation** PPT C-1.pptx **from the drive and folder where you store your Data Files, save it as** PPT C-QST, **click the** Outline tab, **then click the** Slide 3 icon ▤ **in the Outline tab**

   Slide 3 appears in the Slide pane. Clicking a slide icon in the Outline tab highlights the slide text indicating the slide is selected. Before you insert an outline into a presentation, you need to determine where you want the new slides to be placed. You want the text from the Word document inserted as new slides after Slide 3.

2. **Click the** New Slide list arrow **in the Slides group, then click** Slides from Outline

   The Insert Outline dialog box opens.

3. **Navigate to the drive and folder where you store your Data Files, click the Word document file** PPT C-2.docx, **then click** Insert

   Four new slides (4, 5, 6, and 7) are added to the presentation. See Figure C-1.

QUICK TIP
If your presentation has numerous slides, you can organize them into sections in the Slides tab. To create a section, click the slide in the Slides tab where you want the section to begin, click the Section button in the Slides group on the Home tab, then click Add Section.

4. **Read the text for the new Slide 4 in the Slide pane, then review the text on slides 5, 6, and 7 in the Outline tab**

   Information on Slide 7 refers to an obsolete train route and is not needed for this presentation.

5. **Click the** Slides tab, **then right-click the** Slide 7 thumbnail **in the Slides tab**

   A shortcut menu opens displaying related, or contextual, commands that are currently available.

6. **Click** Delete Slide **on the shortcut menu**

   Slide 7 is deleted, and the next slide down becomes the new Slide 7 and appears in the Slide pane.

7. **Click the** Slide 6 thumbnail **in the Slides tab, then drag it above Slide 5**

   Slide 6 and Slide 5 change places. You want the text of the inserted outline to adopt the presentation theme.

8. **Click the** Slide 4 thumbnail, **then click the** Reset button **in the Slides group**

   Notice that the font type and formatting attributes of the slide text changes to reflect the current theme fonts for the presentation. The Reset button resets the slide placeholders to their default position, size, and text formatting based on the Angles presentation design theme.

9. **Click the** Slide 5 thumbnail, **press and hold** [Shift], **click the** Slide 6 thumbnail, **release** [Shift], **click the** Reset button, **then click the** Save button 🖫 **on the Quick Access toolbar**

   Now all of the newly inserted slides have the same design theme as the rest of the presentation. Compare your screen to Figure C-2.

FIGURE C-1: **Outline tab showing imported text**

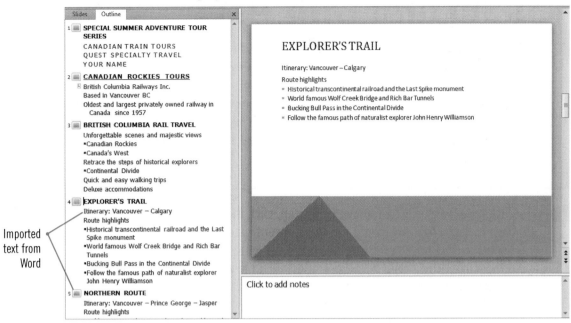

Imported text from Word

FIGURE C-2: **Slide showing correct theme fonts**

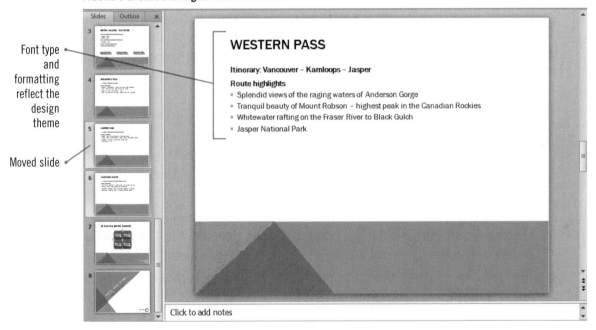

Font type and formatting reflect the design theme

Moved slide

Inserting slides from other presentations

To insert slides from another presentation into the current presentation, click the New Slide list arrow in the Slides group, then click Reuse Slides. The Reuse Slides task pane opens on the right side of the window. Click the Browse button, click Browse File in the drop down list, locate the presentation you want to use, then click Open. Click each slide you want to place in the current presentation. The new slides automatically take on the theme of the current presentation, unless you check the Keep source formatting check box. You can also copy slides from one presentation to another. Open both presentations, change the view of each presentation to Slide Sorter view or use the Arrange All command to see both presentations, select the desired slides, then copy and paste them (or use drag and drop) into the desired presentation.

Inserting Clip Art

In PowerPoint you have access to a collection of assorted types of media clips. The types of clips include illustrations, called **clip art**, photographs, animations, videos, and sounds. Clips are stored in the Microsoft **Clip Organizer**, a separate file index program, and are identified by descriptive keywords. The Clip Organizer is organized into folders called **collections** that you can customize by adding, moving, or deleting clips. Clip art and other media clips are available from many sources, including the Microsoft Office Web site and commercially available collections that you can purchase. ▨▨▨▨ To enhance the QST presentation, you add a clip from the Clip Organizer to one of the slides, and then adjust its size and placement.

STEPS

1. **Click the up scroll arrow in the Slides tab, click the Slide 2 thumbnail in the Slides tab, then click the Clip Art icon ▦ in the Content placeholder**

   The Clip Art task pane opens. At the top of the task pane in the Search for text box, you enter a descriptive keyword to search for clips. If you want to limit or define the types of media clips PowerPoint searches for, click the Results should be list arrow, and then select or deselect specific media types.

2. **Verify that there is a check mark in the Include Office.com content check box, select any text in the Search for text box, type locomotive, then click the Results should be list arrow**

   You are only interested in finding clip art images that are located in the Illustrations category. Searching in only the categories you are interested in significantly reduces the number of media clips PowerPoint needs to search through to produce your results.

3. **Click the check boxes to remove all check marks, click the Illustrations check box, click the Go button, click the down scroll arrow, then click the clip art thumbnail shown in Figure C-3**

   The train clip appears in the content placeholder, and the Picture Tools Format tab is active on the Ribbon. Although you can change a clip's size by dragging a corner sizing handle, you can also **scale** it to change its size proportionally by a specific percentage or size.

4. **Select 2 in the Shape Width text box in the Size group, type 4, then press [Enter]**

   The train clip proportionally doubles in size. Notice the number in the Shape Height text box changes from 1.47 to 2.94.

5. **Click the Picture Border list arrow in the Picture Styles group, then click the Black, Text 1 color box in the top row**

   A black border appears around the train clip.

6. **Click the Picture Border list arrow, point to Weight, then click the 2 ¼ pt solid line style**

   The train clip now has a 2 ¼-point solid border, which creates a frame around the clip.

7. **Drag the train clip object to the middle of the blank area, click the Color button in the Adjust group, then click Orange, Accent color 2 Dark**

   You prefer the original placement and color of the train clip.

8. **Click the Undo button list arrow ↺ ▾ on the Quick Access toolbar, click Move Object, click a blank area of the slide, then save your changes**

   Notice that by using the Undo button list arrow, you can undo multiple actions in one step, in this case the Recolor Picture and the Move Object commands.

9. **Click the Results should be list arrow in the Clip Art task pane, click the All media types check box, click Go, then click the task pane Close button ✕**

   Now the next time you search for a clip, PowerPoint will search through all media types. Compare the slide on your screen to the slide shown in Figure C-4.

FIGURE C-3: Screen showing Clip Art task pane

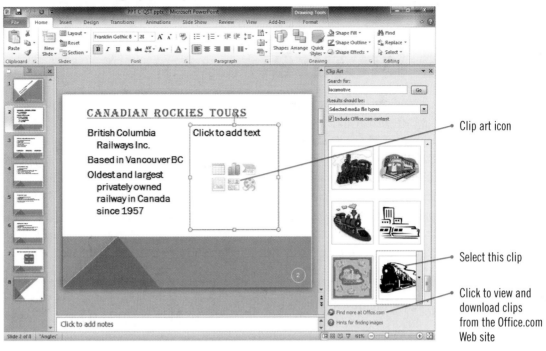

Clip art icon

Select this clip

Click to view and download clips from the Office.com Web site

FIGURE C-4: Slide with formatted train clip

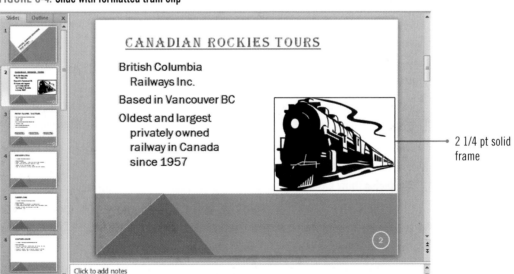

2 1/4 pt solid frame

Finding more clips online

If you can't find exactly what you want using the Clip Art task pane, you can easily find and download clips from the Office.com Web site. To get clips online, click the Find more at Office.com hyperlink at the bottom of the Clip Art task pane. If your computer is connected to the Internet, this will start your Web browser and automatically connect you to the Office.com Web site. You can search the site by keyword or browse by category type. Each clip you download is automatically inserted into the Clip Organizer and appears in the Clip Art task pane.

Inserting and Styling a Picture

In PowerPoint, a **picture** is defined as a digital photograph, a piece of line art or clip art, or other artwork that is created in another program. PowerPoint gives you the ability to insert 14 different types of pictures including JPEG File Interchange Format and BMP Windows Bitmap files into a PowerPoint presentation. As with all objects in PowerPoint, you can format and style inserted pictures to help them fit the theme of your presentation. You can also hide a portion of the picture you don't want to be seen by **cropping** it. The cropped portion of a picture remains a part of the picture file unless you delete the cropped portion by applying picture compression settings in the Compression Settings dialog box. Using your digital camera, you took photographs during your train tours. In this lesson you insert a picture that you saved as a JPG file on your computer, and then you crop and style it to best fit the slide.

STEPS

1. **Click the down scroll arrow in the Slides tab, click the Slide 8 thumbnail, then click the Insert Picture from File icon** in the content placeholder on the slide

   The Insert Picture dialog box opens displaying the pictures available in the default Pictures library.

2. **Navigate to the drive and folder where you store your Data Files, select the picture file PPT C-3.jpg, then click Insert**

   The picture appears in the content placeholder on the slide, and the Picture Tools Format tab opens on the Ribbon. The picture would look better if you cropped some of the window reflection images off the right edge.

3. **Click the Crop button in the Size group, then place the pointer over the lower-right corner cropping handle of the picture**

   The pointer changes to ⌐. When the Crop button is active, cropping handles appear next to the sizing handles.

4. **Drag the corner of the picture up and to the left as shown in Figure C-5, then press [Esc]**

   PowerPoint has a number of picture formatting options, and you decide to experiment with some of them.

5. **On the Picture Tools Format tab, click the More button ⊽ in the Picture Styles group, then click Compound Frame, Black (2nd row)**

   The picture now has a black frame.

6. **Click the Corrections button in the Adjust group, move your pointer over the thumbnails to see how the picture changes, then click Sharpen: 50% in the Sharpen and Soften section**

   The picture clarity is better.

7. **Click the Artistic Effects button in the Adjust group, move your pointer over the thumbnails to see how the picture changes, then click a blank area of the slide**

   The artistic effects are all interesting but none of them will work well for this picture. You decide to compress the picture to delete the cropped areas and make the file smaller.

8. **Click the Compress Pictures button in the Adjust group, make sure the Use document resolution option button is checked, then click OK**

   The cropped portions of the picture are deleted and the picture is compressed.

9. **Drag the lower-right sizing handle down so the right side of the picture increases in size and aligns with the right side of the slide number, click a blank area on the slide, then save your changes**

   Compare your screen to Figure C-6.

Inserting Objects into a Presentation

FIGURE C-5: Using the cropping pointer to crop a picture

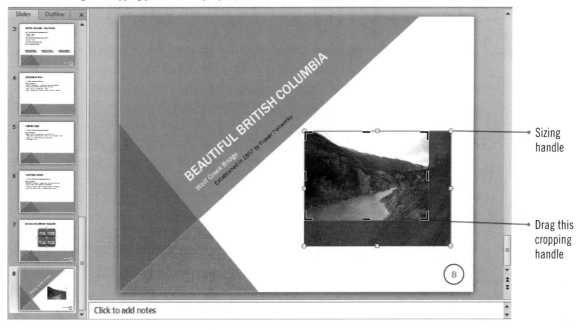

Sizing handle

Drag this cropping handle

FIGURE C-6: Cropped and styled picture

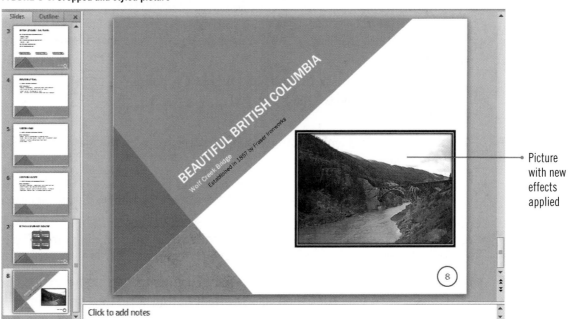

Picture with new effects applied

Things to know about picture compression

It's important to know that when you compress a picture you change the amount of detail in the picture, so it might look different than it did before the compression. Compressing a picture changes the amount of color used in the picture with no loss of quality. By default, all inserted pictures in PowerPoint are automatically compressed using the settings in the PowerPoint Options dialog box. To locate the compression settings, click the File tab, click Options, then click Advanced in the left pane. In the Image Size and Quality section, you can change picture compression settings or stop the automatic compression of pictures.

Inserting a Text Box

As you've already learned, you enter text on a slide using a title or content placeholder that is arranged on the slide based on a slide layout. Every so often you need additional text on a slide where the traditional placeholder does not place text effectively for your message. You can create an individual text box by clicking the Text Box button in the Text group on the Insert tab on the Ribbon. There are two types of text boxes that you can create: a text label, used for a small phrase where text doesn't automatically wrap to the next line inside the box; and a word-processing box, used for a sentence or paragraph where the text wraps inside the boundaries of the box. Either type of text box can be formatted and edited just like any other text object. You decide to add a text box to the picture on Slide 8. You create a word-processing box on the slide, enter text, edit text, and then format the text.

STEPS

1. **Click the Insert tab on the Ribbon, click the Text Box button in the Text group, then move the pointer to the blank area of the slide above and to the left of the title text**

   The pointer changes to ⌄.

2. **Drag down and toward the right about three inches to create a text box**

   When you begin dragging, an outline of the text box appears, indicating how large a text box you are drawing. After you release the mouse button, an insertion point appears inside the text box, in this case a word-processing box, indicating that you can enter text. The font and font style appear in the Font group on the Ribbon.

3. **Type On day 2 of the tour east of Kamloops 20 kilometers**

   Notice that the text box increases in size as your text wraps to a second line inside the text box. Your screen should look similar to Figure C-7. After entering the text you realize the sentence could be clearer if written differently.

4. **Drag I over the phrase 20 kilometers to select it, position ⌖ on top of the selected phrase, then press and hold the mouse button**

   The pointer changes to ⌖.

5. **Drag the selected words to the left of the word "east" in the text box, then release the mouse button**

   A light blue insertion line appears as you drag, indicating where PowerPoint places the text when you release the mouse button. The phrase "20 kilometers" moves before the word "east" and is still selected. Now fix the word spacing.

6. **Click between the words "kilometers" and "east" in the text, then press [Spacebar]**

   The words in the text box now have proper spacing.

7. **Move I to the edge of the text box, which changes to ⌖, click the text box border (changes to a solid line), then click the Italic button _I_ in the Font group**

   All of the text in the text box is italicized.

8. **Drag the right-middle sizing handle of the text box to the right until all the text fits on two lines, position ⌖ over the text box edge, then drag it above the picture**

   Your screen should look similar to Figure C-8.

9. **Click the Reading View button ⊞ on the status bar, review the slide, press [Esc], then save your changes**

FIGURE C-7: **New text object**

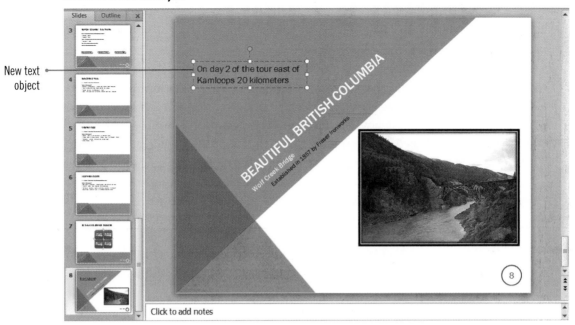

New text
object

FIGURE C-8: **Formatted text object**

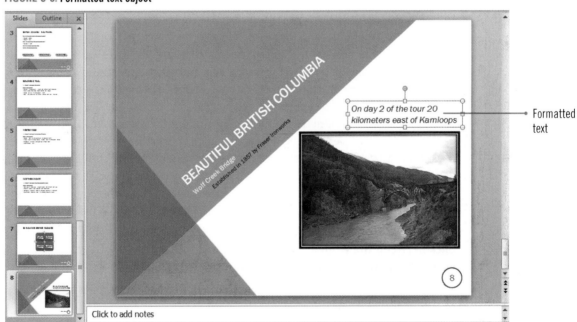

Formatted
text

Sending a presentation using e-mail

You can send a copy of a presentation over the Internet to a reviewer to edit and add comments. You can use Microsoft Outlook to send your presentation. Although your e-mail program allows you to attach files, you can send a presentation using Outlook from within PowerPoint. Click the File tab, click Save & Send, click Send Using E-mail in the center pane, then click Send as Attachment. Outlook opens and automatically creates an e-mail with a copy of the presentation attached to it. You can also attach and send a PDF copy or an XPS copy of the presentation using your e-mail program. Both of these file formats preserve document formatting, enable file sharing, and can be viewed online and printed.

Inserting a Chart

Frequently, the best way to communicate numerical information is with a visual aid such as a chart. If you have Microsoft Excel installed on your computer, PowerPoint uses Excel to create charts. If you don't have Excel installed, a charting program called **Microsoft Graph** opens that you can use to create charts for your slides. A **chart** is the graphical representation of numerical data. Every chart has a corresponding **worksheet** that contains the numerical data displayed by the chart. When you insert a chart object into PowerPoint, you are actually embedding it. An **embedded object** is one that is a part of your presentation (just like any other object you insert into PowerPoint) except that an embedded object's data source can be opened, in this case Excel, for editing purposes. Changes you make to an embedded object in PowerPoint using PowerPoint's features do not affect the data source for the data. You insert a chart on a new slide.

QUICK TIP

You can also add a chart to a slide by clicking the Insert Chart button in the Illustrations group on the Insert tab.

1. **Click Slide 7 in the Slides tab, then press [Enter]**

   Pressing [Enter] adds a new blank slide to your presentation with the slide layout of the selected slide, in this case the Title and Content slide layout.

2. **Click the Title placeholder, then type Vacation Comparison Survey**

3. **Click the Insert Chart icon ▥ in the Content placeholder**

   The Insert Chart dialog box opens as shown in Figure C-9. Each chart type includes a number of 2-D and 3-D styles. The Column chart type, for example, includes 19 different 2-D and 3-D styles. The 2-D Clustered Column chart is the default chart style. For a brief explanation of chart types, refer to Table C-1.

4. **Click OK**

TROUBLE

If Excel is not installed on your computer, Microsoft Graph opens and your screen will look different.

   Excel opens in a split window sharing the screen with the PowerPoint window as shown in Figure C-10. The PowerPoint window displays the clustered column chart, and the Excel window displays sample data in a worksheet. The Chart Tools Design tab on the Ribbon contains commands you use in PowerPoint to work with the chart. The worksheet consists of rows and columns. The intersection of a row and a column is called a **cell**. Cells are referred to by their row and column location; for example, the cell at the intersection of column A and row 1 is called cell A1. Cells in the first or left column contain **axis labels** that identify the data in a row for example, "Category 1" is an axis label. Cells in the first or top row appear in the **legend** and describe the data in the series. Cells below and to the right of the axis labels and legend names contain the data values that are represented in the chart. Each column and row of data in the worksheet is called a **data series**. Each data series has corresponding **data series markers** in the chart, which are graphical representations such as bars, columns, or pie wedges. The gray boxes with the numbers along the left side of the worksheet are **row headings**, and the gray boxes with the letters along the top of the worksheet are **column headings**.

5. **Move the pointer over the worksheet in the Excel window**

   The pointer changes to ✚. Cell A6 is the **active cell**, which means that it is selected. The active cell has a thick black border around it.

6. **Click cell C4**

   Cell C4 is now the active cell.

7. **Click the Excel Window Close button ▭✕▭ on the title bar**

   The Excel window closes, and the PowerPoint window fills the screen. The new chart on the slide displays the data from the Excel worksheet.

8. **Click in a blank area of the slide to deselect the chart, then save your changes**

   The Chart Tools Design tab is no longer active.

FIGURE C-9: Insert Chart dialog box

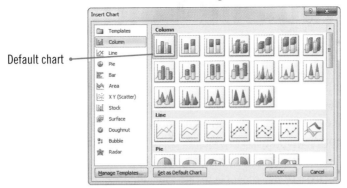

FIGURE C-10: The PowerPoint and Excel split windows

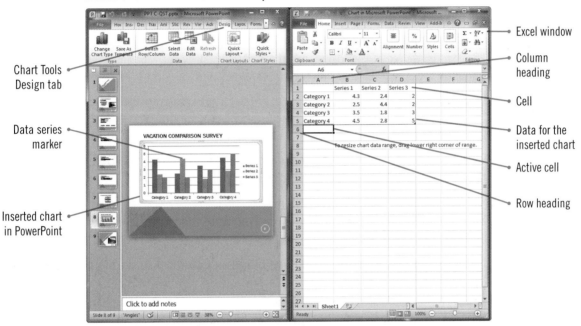

TABLE C-1: Chart types

chart type	icon looks like	use to
Column		Track values over time or across categories
Line		Track values over time
Pie		Compare individual values to the whole
Bar		Compare values in categories or over time
Area		Show contribution of each data series to the total over time
XY (Scatter)		Compare pairs of values
Stock		Show stock market information or scientific data
Surface		Show value trends across two dimensions
Doughnut		Compare individual values to the whole with multiple series
Bubble		Indicate relative size of data points
Radar		Show changes in values in relation to a center point

Entering and Editing Chart Data

After you insert a chart into your presentation, you need to replace the sample data with the correct information. If you have data in an Excel worksheet or another source, you can import it from Excel; otherwise, you can type your own data into the worksheet. As you enter data and make other changes in the Excel worksheet, the chart in PowerPoint automatically reflects the new changes. You enter and format survey data you collected that asked people to rate four categories of vacations with respect to three factors: price, safety, and culture.

STEPS

1. **Click the chart on Slide 8, click the Chart Tools Design tab on the Ribbon, then click the Edit Data button in the Data group**

   The chart is selected in PowerPoint, and the worksheet opens in a separate Excel window. The data in the worksheet needs to be replaced with the correct information.

   > **QUICK TIP**
   > Click the chart in the PowerPoint window, then move your pointer over each bar in the chart to see the data source values.

2. **Click the Series 1 cell, type Price, press [Tab], type Safety, press [Tab], then type Culture**

   The Legend labels are entered. Pressing [Tab] in Excel moves the active cell from left to right one cell at a time in a row. Pressing [Enter] in the worksheet moves the active cell down one cell at a time in a column.

3. **Click the Category 1 cell, type Standard Rail, press [Enter], type Deluxe Rail, press [Enter], type Cruise, press [Enter], type Traditional, then press [Enter]**

   The axis labels are entered, and the chart in the PowerPoint window reflects all the changes.

4. **Enter the data shown in Figure C-11 to complete the worksheet, then press [Enter]**

   Column A needs to be wider to see all of the information in cell A2.

   > **QUICK TIP**
   > You can also drag a column divider line to resize the column width to accommodate the widest entry.

5. **Move ✛ over the column divider line between Column A and Column B, which changes to ↔, then double-click**

   Column A widens so you can see all of the data.

6. **Click the Switch Row/Column button in the Data group in the PowerPoint window**

   The data charted on the x-axis switches and moves to the y-axis. The y-axis is also referred to as the vertical axis or **value axis**, and the x-axis is also referred to as the horizontal axis or **category axis**. Notice the legend now displays the row axis labels instead of the column axis labels. You have finished entering the data in the Excel worksheet.

7. **Click the Excel window Close button** ⬛ x

   Notice that the height of each column in the chart, as well as the values along the y-axis, adjust to reflect the numbers you typed. The column axis labels are now on the x-axis of the chart, and the row axis labels are listed in the legend.

8. **Click the More button ▾ in the Chart Styles group, then click Style 26 (4th row)**

   The new chart style gives the column data markers a three-dimensional look.

9. **Click a blank area on the slide, then save the presentation**

   Compare your chart to Figure C-12.

FIGURE C-11: Worksheet showing chart data

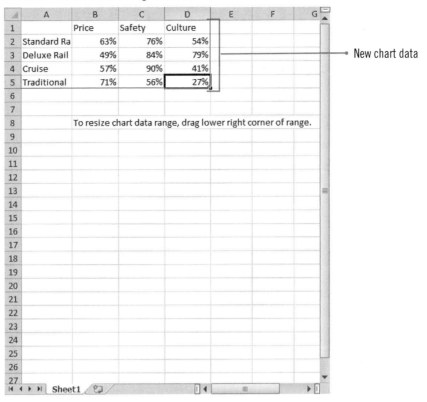

New chart data

FIGURE C-12: Formatted chart

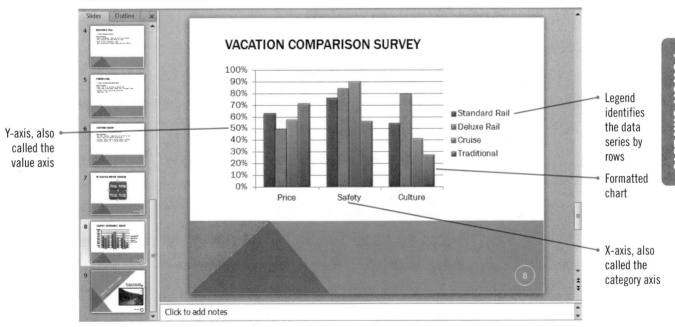

Y-axis, also called the value axis

Legend identifies the data series by rows

Formatted chart

X-axis, also called the category axis

Switching rows and columns

If you have difficulty visualizing what the Switch Row/Column command does, think about what is represented in the chart. **Series in Rows** means that the data in the datasheet rows is plotted on the y-axis, and the row axis labels are shown on the x-axis. The column axis labels are shown in the legend. **Series in Columns** means that the data in the datasheet columns is plotted on the y-axis, and the row axis labels are shown in the legend. The column axis labels are plotted on the x-axis.

Inserting a Table

As you create your presentation, you may have some information that would look best organized in rows and columns. For example, if you wanted to compare the basic details of three different cruise tours side by side, a table is ideal for this type of information. Once you have created a table, two new tabs, the Table Tools Design tab and the Table Tools Layout tab, appear on the Ribbon. You can use the Design tab to apply color styles, change cell borders, and add cell effects. Using the Layout tab, you can add rows and columns to your table, adjust the size of cells, and align text in the cells. ▰▰▰▰ You decide that a table best illustrates the different services offered by the train tour company.

STEPS

QUICK TIP
You can also create a table by clicking the Table button in the Tables group on the Insert tab, then dragging ⬚ over the table grid to create the size table you want.

1. **Right-click** Slide 7 **in the Slides tab, click** New Slide **on the shortcut menu, click the** title placeholder, **then type** Service Levels and Prices

   A new slide with the Title and Content layout appears.

2. **Click the** Insert Table icon ▦, **type** 4 **in the Number of columns text box, click the Number of rows text box, click the up arrow until** 5 **appears, then click** OK

   A formatted table with four columns and five rows appears on the slide, and the Table Tools Design tab opens on the Ribbon. The table has 20 cells. The insertion point is in the first cell of the table and is ready to accept text.

QUICK TIP
Press [Tab] when the insertion point is in the last cell of a table to create a new row.

3. **Type** Classic, **press** [Tab], **type** Deluxe, **press** [Tab], **type** Exclusive, **press** [Tab], **type** Royal, **then press** [Tab]

   The text you typed appears in the top four cells of the table. Pressing [Tab] moves the insertion point to the next cell; pressing [Enter] moves the insertion point to the next line in the same cell.

4. **Enter the rest of the table information shown in Figure C-13**

   The table would look better if it were formatted differently.

5. **Click the** More button ▾ **in the Table Styles group, scroll to the bottom of the gallery, then click** Medium Style 3 – Accent 2

   The background and text color change to reflect the table style you applied.

QUICK TIP
Change the height or width of any table cell by dragging its borders.

6. **Click the** upper-left cell, **click the** Table Tools Layout tab, **click the** Select button **in the Table group, click** Select Row, **then click the** Center button ▤ **in the Alignment group**

   The text in the top row is centered horizontally in each cell.

7. **Click the** Select button **in the Table group, click** Select Table, **then click the** Center Vertically button ▤ **in the Alignment group**

   The text in the whole table is centered vertically within each cell. The table would look better if all the rows were the same height.

8. **Click the** Distribute Rows button ▥ **in the Cell Size group, click the** Table Tools Design tab, **then click the** Effects button ◔▾ **in the Table Styles group**

   The Table Effects gallery opens.

9. **Point to** Cell Bevel, **click** Hard Edge **(3rd row), press** [Down arrow] **three times, click a blank area of the slide, then save the presentation**

   The 3-D effect makes the cells of the table stand out. The table looks better nudged away from the slide title. Compare your screen with Figure C-14.

FIGURE C-13: Inserted table with data

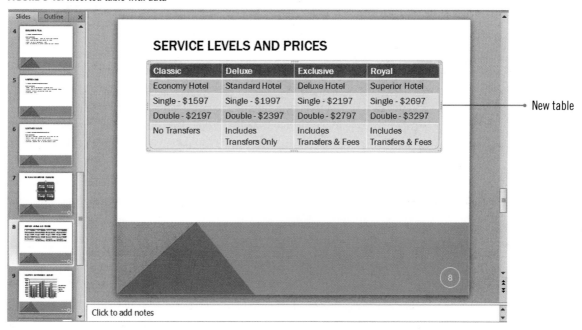

New table

FIGURE C-14: Formatted table

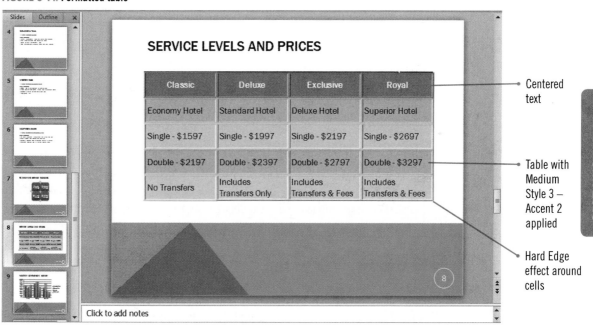

Centered text

Table with Medium Style 3 – Accent 2 applied

Hard Edge effect around cells

Drawing tables

Choose the slide where you want the table, click the Table button in the Tables group on the Insert tab, then click Draw Table. The pointer changes to ✏. Drag to define the boundaries of the table in the area of the slide where you want the table. A dotted outline appears as you draw. Next, you draw to create the rows and columns of your table. Click the Table Tools Design tab on the Ribbon, click the Draw Table button in the Draw Borders group, then draw lines for columns and rows. Be sure to draw within the boundary line of the table.

Inserting and Formatting WordArt

As you work to create an interesting presentation, your goal should include making your slides visually appealing. Sometimes plain text can come across as dull and unexciting in a presentation. **WordArt** is a set of decorative text styles, or text effects, that you can apply to any text object to help direct the attention of your audience to a certain piece of information. You can use WordArt in two different ways: you can apply a WordArt text style to an existing text object that converts the text into WordArt, or you can create a new WordArt object. The WordArt text styles and effects include text shadows, reflections, glows, bevels, 3-D rotations, and transformations. ▓▓▓▓ Use WordArt to create a new WordArt text object on Slide 3.

STEPS

QUICK TIP
You can format any text with a WordArt style. Select the text, click the Drawing Tools Format tab on the Ribbon, then click a WordArt style option in the WordArt Styles group.

1. **Click the** Slide 3 thumbnail **in the Slides tab, click the** Insert tab **on the Ribbon, then click the** WordArt button **in the Text group**
   The WordArt gallery appears displaying 30 WordArt text styles.

2. **Click** Fill – Ice Blue, Text 2, Outline – Background 2, **(first style in the first row)**
   A text object appears in the middle of the slide displaying sample text with the WordArt style you just selected.

3. **Click the edge of the WordArt text object, then when the pointer changes to** ⁺↖, **drag the text object to the blank area of the slide**

4. **Click the** More button ⊽ **in the WordArt Styles group, move your mouse over all of the WordArt styles in the gallery, then click** Fill – Orange, Accent 2, Warm Matte Bevel
   The WordArt Styles change the sample text in the WordArt text object. The new WordArt style is applied to the text object.

5. **Drag to select the text** Your text here **in the WordArt text object, click the** Decrease Font Size button A˅ **in the Mini toolbar until** 40 **appears in the Font Size text box, type** Guaranteed best, **press [Enter], then type** vacation in Canada
   The text is smaller and appears on two lines.

6 **Click the** Text Effects button **in the WordArt Styles group, point to** Transform, **click** Triangle Down **in the Warp section (first row), then click a blank area of the slide**
   The transform effect is applied to the text object. Compare your screen to Figure C-15.

7. **Click the** Reading View button 📖 **on the status bar, click the** Next button ➡ **until you reach Slide 10, click the** Menu button 🗐 **, then click** End Show

8. **Click the** Slide Sorter button 🔡 **on the status bar**
   Compare your screen with Figure C-16.

9. **Click the** Normal button 🗔 **on the status bar, add your name as a footer to the notes and handouts, save your changes, submit your presentation to your instructor, then exit PowerPoint**

FIGURE C-15: WordArt inserted on slide

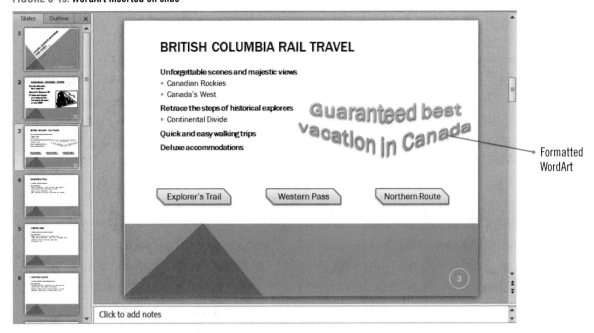

Formatted WordArt

FIGURE C-16: Completed presentation in Slide Sorter view

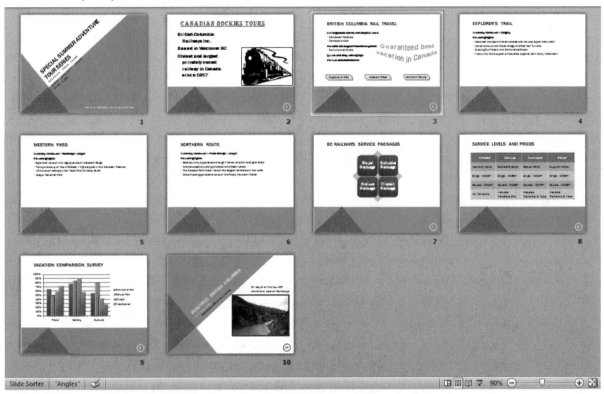

Saving a presentation as a video

You can save your PowerPoint presentation as a full-fidelity video, which incorporates all slide timings, transitions, animations, and narrations. The video can be distributed using a disc, the Web, or e-mail. Depending on how you want to display your video, you have three resolution settings from which to choose: Computer & HD Displays, Internet & DVD, and Portable Devices. The Large setting, Computer & HD Displays (960 × 720), is used for viewing on a computer monitor, projector, or other high definition displays. The Medium setting, Internet & DVD (640 × 480), is used for uploading to the Web or copying to a standard DVD. The Small setting, Portable Devices (320 × 240), is used on portable devices including portable media players such as Microsoft Zune. To save your presentation as a video, click the File tab, click Save & Send, click Create a Video, choose your settings, then click the Create Video button.

Practice

Concepts Review

For current SAM information, including versions and content details, visit SAM Central (http://www.cengage.com/samcentral). If you have a SAM user profile, you may have access to hands-on instruction, practice, and assessment of the skills covered in this unit. Since various versions of SAM are supported throughout the life of this text, check with your instructor for the correct instructions and URL/Web site for accessing assignments.

Label each element of the PowerPoint window shown in Figure C-17.

FIGURE C-17

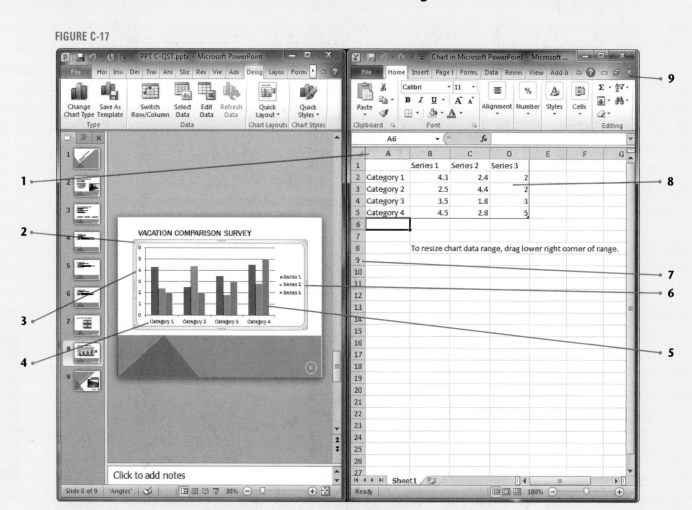

Match each term with the statement that best describes it.

10. Collection   **a.** Contains the numerical data displayed in a chart

11. Crop   **b.** The folder in the Clip Organizer that stores clip art

12. Worksheet   **c.** A presentation that is designed and formatted and usually comes with sample text

13. Table   **d.** PowerPoint object that compares data in columns and rows

14. Template   **e.** Hides a portion of a picture

Select the best answer from the list of choices.

15. **What is the file index system that stores clip art, photographs, and movies called?**
    - **a.** Clip Art Index
    - **b.** WordArt Gallery
    - **c.** Microsoft Clip Organizer
    - **d.** Office Media Collections

16. **According to this unit, which media type is defined as line art or art work created in another program?**
    - **a.** Picture
    - **b.** Clip art
    - **c.** Video
    - **d.** Animation

17. **In PowerPoint, what is the graphical representation of data on a slide called?**
    - **a.** Table
    - **b.** Worksheet
    - **c.** Legend
    - **d.** Chart

18. **According to this unit, to compare data side by side, which of the following objects should you select?**
    - **a.** Table
    - **b.** Chart
    - **c.** Outline
    - **d.** Grid

19. **An object that has its own data source and becomes a part of your presentation after you insert it best describes which of the following?**
    - **a.** A Word outline
    - **b.** An embedded object
    - **c.** A WordArt object
    - **d.** A table

20. **A presentation designed and formatted with background elements, colors, and other graphic elements that you can use to create a new presentation is a _____.**
    - **a.** template
    - **b.** theme
    - **c.** video
    - **d.** gallery

21. **Use _____ to apply a set of decorative text styles or text effects to text.**
    - **a.** a template
    - **b.** rich text format
    - **c.** a collection
    - **d.** WordArt

Skills Review

1. **Insert text from Microsoft Word.**
    - **a.** Open the file PPT C-4.pptx from the drive and folder where you store your Data Files, then save it as **PPT C-Vista**. You will work to create the completed presentation as shown in Figure C-18.
    - **b.** Click Slide 3 in the Slides tab, then use the Slides from Outline command to insert the file PPT C-5.docx from the drive and folder where you store your Data Files.
    - **c.** In the Slides tab, drag Slide 5 above Slide 4.

FIGURE C-18

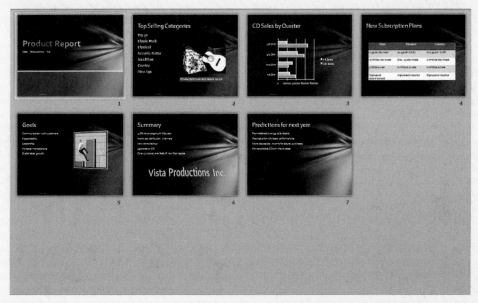

Skills Review (continued)

   d. In the Slides tab, delete Slide 7, Expansion Potential.

   e. Select Slides 4, 5, and 6 in the Slides tab, reset the slides to the default theme settings, then save your work.

2. Insert clip art.

   a. Select Slide 4, then change the slide layout to the Two Content slide layout.

   b. Press [Shift], click the text object, then change the font size to 18.

   c. Click the clip art icon in the right content placeholder, search for clip art using the keywords **business goals**, insert the clip art shown in Figure C-18, then close the Clip Art task pane.

   d. Click the Picture Border list arrow, change the color of the clip art border to White, Text 1.

   e. Click the Picture Border list arrow, change the weight of the clip art border to 3 pt.

   f. Click the Picture Effects button, point to 3-D Rotation, then click Perspective Left.

   g. Drag the clip art so the top lines up with the top of the text object, then save your changes.

3. Insert and style a picture.

   a. Select Slide 2, then insert the picture PPT C-6.jpg.

   b. Completely crop the light blue section off the top of the picture, then crop the right side of the picture about $\frac{1}{4}$ inch.

   c. Drag the picture up so it is in the center of the blank area of the slide.

   d. Click the Color button, then change the picture color to Black and White: 25%.

   e. Save your changes.

4. Insert a text box.

   a. On Slide 2, insert a text box below the picture.

   b. Type **Private client submissions for music up 9%**.

   c. Delete the word **for**, then drag the word **music** after the word **client**.

   d. Select the text object, then click the More button in the Shape Styles group on the Drawing Tools Format tab.

   e. Click Intense Effect – Green, Accent 6.

   f. Center the text object under the picture.

5. Insert a chart.

   a. Go to Slide 3, CD Sales by Quarter, click the Insert tab on the ribbon, click the Chart button in the Illustrations group, then insert a Clustered Bar chart.

   b. Close Excel.

6. Enter and edit chart data.

   a. Show the chart data.

   b. Enter the data shown in Table C-2 into the worksheet.

   c. Delete the data in each cell in Column D, then close Excel.

   d. Change the chart style to Style 12 in the Chart Styles group.

   e. Move the chart to the center of the blank area of the slide, then save your changes.

TABLE C-2

	U.S. Sales	Int. Sales
1st Qtr	390,957	263,902
2nd Qtr	229,840	325,854
3rd Qtr	585,063	435,927
4th Qtr	665,113	203,750

7. Insert a table.

   a. Add a new slide after Slide 3 with the Title and Content layout.

   b. Add the slide title **New Subscription Plans**.

   c. Insert a table with three columns and five rows.

   d. Enter the information shown in Table C-3, then change the table style to Medium Style 3 – Accent 3. (*Hint*: Use the Copy and Paste commands to enter duplicate information in the table.)

   e. Center the text in the top row.

   f. In the Table Tools Layout tab, distribute the table rows.

   g. Move the table to the center of the blank area of the slide, then save your changes.

TABLE C-3

Basic	Standard	Premium
$.99 per download	$4.99 per month	$12.95 per month
Unlimited downloads	Max. 25 downloads	Unlimited downloads
Limited access	Unlimited access	Unlimited access
High-speed recommended	High-speed required	High-speed required

Skills Review (continued)

8. Insert and format WordArt.

  a. Go to Slide 6, then, insert a WordArt text object using the Fill – Brown, Accent 3, Outline – Text 2 style.

  b. Type **Vista Productions Inc.**, then apply the WordArt style Fill – Gold, Accent 2, Warm Matte Bevel.

  c. Apply the Inflate Top Transform effect (seventh row) to the text object, then move the text object to the middle of the blank area of the slide.

  d. View the presentation in Slide Show view, then check the spelling of the presentation.

  e. Add your name as a footer to all the slides, then save your changes.

  f. Submit your presentation to your instructor, close your presentation, and exit PowerPoint.

Independent Challenge 1

You are a financial management consultant for Goodrich & Young Investments LLP, located in Syracuse, New York. One of your responsibilities is to create standardized presentations on different financial investments for use on the company Web site. As part of the presentation for this meeting, you insert some clip art, add a text box, and insert a chart.

If you have a SAM 2010 user profile, an autogradable SAM version of this assignment may be available at http://www.cengage.com/sam2010. Check with your instructor to confirm that this assignment is available in SAM. To use the SAM version of this assignment, log into the SAM 2010 Web site and download the instruction and start files.

  a. Open the file PPT C-7.pptx from the drive and folder where you store your Data Files, then save it as **PPT C-Goodrich**.

  b. Add your name as the footer on all of the slides, then apply the Horizon Design Theme.

  c. Insert a clustered column chart on Slide 6, then enter the data in Table C-4 into the worksheet. Delete the unwanted placeholder data in the chart.

  d. Format the chart using Style 35, then move the chart down slightly away from the title text object.

TABLE C-4

	1 year	3 year	5 year	7 year
Bonds	2.2%	3.2%	3.9%	4.5%
Stocks	1.9%	2.2%	4.2%	3.6%
Mutual Funds	2.6%	4.0%	8.4%	6.4%

Advanced Challenge Exercise

  ■ Click the Chart Tools Layout tab, click the Legend button, then click Show Legend at Top.

  ■ Click the Chart Tools Format tab, then click the Chart Elements list arrow in the Current Selection group, then click Series "3 year."

  ■ Click the Shape Fill list arrow in the Shape Styles group, then click Gold, Text 2, under Theme Colors.

  e. Insert clip art of a set of balance scales on Slide 2, then position and format as necessary. (*Hint*: Use the keyword **balance scales** to search for clips.)

  f. On Slide 3, use the Align command and Distribute command on the Drawing Tools Format tab in the Arrange group to align and distribute the objects so that the shapes are aligned on top and distributed horizontally.

  g. Check the spelling of the presentation, view the slide show, make any necessary changes, then save your work. See Figure C-19.

  h. Submit the presentation to your instructor, then close the presentation, and exit PowerPoint.

FIGURE C-19

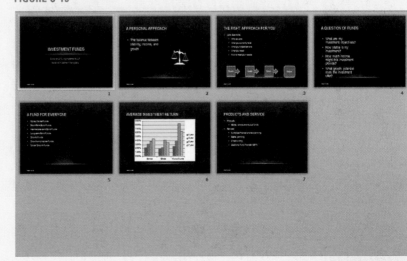

PowerPoint 2010

Independent Challenge 2

You work for Veil Home Systems, a company based in Michigan that provides integrated data, security, and voice command systems for homes. You have been asked to enhance a marketing presentation on a new product that the company is going to promote at a large trade fair in Las Vegas. You work on completing a presentation for the show. You insert some clip art, add a text box, and insert a chart.

a. Start PowerPoint, open the file PPT C-8.pptx from the drive and folder where you store your Data Files, and save it as **PPT C-Veil**.

b. Add your name and today's date to Slide 1 in the Subtitle text box.

c. Organize the objects on Slide 2 using the Align, Distribute, and Group commands. Add and format additional shapes to enhance the presentation.

d. On Slide 3, style the picture, recolor the picture, and use a picture effect.

e. Apply the Hardcover theme to the presentation.

f. Insert the Word document file PPT C-9.docx to create additional slides from an outline after Slide 2.

g. Select Slides 3 and 4, then reset the slides to their default settings.

h. Create a new slide after Slide 4, title the slide **Growth of Integrated Systems**, then insert a chart.

i. Enter the data in Table C-5, then format the chart using at least two formatting commands. Be able to name which formatting commands you applied to the chart.

TABLE C-5

	Last Yr.	Current Yr.	Next Yr.
Traditional	73	94	103
Integrated	15	36	55

j. Insert a text box on the Veil Home Systems slide (Slide 7). Create your own company contact and address information. Format the text box.

k. Check the spelling, then view the final slide show (refer to Figure C-20). Make any necessary changes.

l. Save the presentation, submit the presentation to your instructor, close the file, and exit PowerPoint.

FIGURE C-20

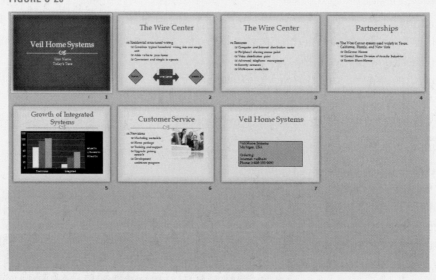

Independent Challenge 3

You work for LearnRight Inc. a company that produces instructional software to help people learn foreign languages. Once a year, LearnRight holds a meeting with their biggest client, the Department of State, to brief the government on new products and to receive feedback on existing products. Your boss has started a presentation and has asked you to look it over and add other elements to make it look better.

a. Start PowerPoint, open the file PPT C-10.pptx from the drive and folder where you store your Data Files, and save it as **PPT C-LearnRight**.

Independent Challenge 3 (continued)

b. Add an appropriate design theme to the presentation.

c. Insert the Word outline PPT C-11.docx after the Product Revisions slide, then reset Slides 5, 6, and 7 to the default settings.

d. Format the text so that the most important information is the most prominent.

e. Insert an appropriate table on a slide of your choice. Use your own information, or use text from a bulleted list on one of the slides.

f. Add at least two appropriate shapes that emphasize slide content. Format the objects using shape styles. If appropriate, use the Align, Distribute, and Group commands to organize your shapes.

Advanced Challenge Exercise (*Internet connection required*)

- Select a slide on which you want to add a clip art image. Open the Clip Art task pane, then click the Find more at Office.com link to go to the Office.com Web site.
- Download and insert an appropriate media clip from the Academic category. (*Hint*: Make sure you know the media clip's keywords; it will make searching for it in the Clip art task pane much easier.)
- Format the clip using Picture Tools Format tab.
- Be ready to explain how you formatted the clip.

g. Check the spelling and view the final slide show. Make any necessary changes.

h. Add your name as footer text on the notes and handouts, then save the presentation.

i. Submit your presentation to your instructor, close the file, then exit PowerPoint.

Real Life Independent Challenge

You are on the Foreign Exchange Commission at your college, and one of your responsibilities is to present information on past foreign student exchanges to different organizations on and off campus. You need to create a pictorial presentation that highlights a trip to a different country. Create a presentation using your own pictures or pictures given to you with permission by a friend.

Note: Three photographs (PPT C-12.jpg, PPT C-13.jpg, and PPT C-14.jpg) from Dijon, France, are provided to help you complete this Independent Challenge. You can use the provided photos if you have none of your own to use.

a. Start PowerPoint, create a new blank presentation, and save it as **PPT C-Exchange** to the drive and folder where you store your Data Files.

b. Locate and insert the pictures you want to use. Place one picture on each slide using the Content with Caption slide layout.

c. Add information about each picture in the text placeholder, and enter a slide title. If you use the pictures provided, research Dijon, France, using the Internet for relevant information to place on the slides (*Internet connection required*).

d. Apply an appropriate design theme, then apply an appropriate title and your name to the title slide.

e. Check the spelling, then view the final slide show (refer to Figure C-21).

f. Add a slide number and your class name as footer text to all of the slides, save your work, then submit your presentation to your instructor.

g. Close the file, and exit PowerPoint.

FIGURE C-21

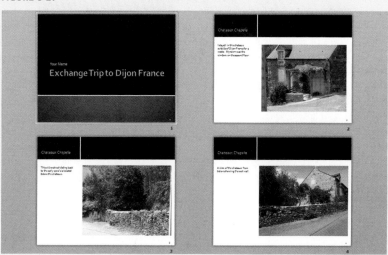

Visual Workshop

Create a one-slide presentation that looks like Figure C-22. The slide layout shown in Figure C-22 is a specific layout designed for pictures. Insert the picture file PPT C-15.jpg to complete this presentation. Add your name as footer text to the slide, save the presentation as **PPT C-Guide** to the drive and folder where you store your Data Files, check the spelling of the presentation, then submit your presentation to your instructor.

FIGURE C-22

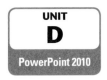

Finishing a Presentation

Though not required, having a consistent professional-looking theme throughout your presentation is best if you want to gain and retain your audience's interest in the subject you are presenting. PowerPoint helps you achieve a consistent look by providing ways to customize your slides' layout and background. Once you are finished working with the text and other objects of your presentation, you are ready to apply slide show effects, which determine the way the slides and objects on the slides appear in Slide Show view. You have reviewed the presentation and are pleased with the slides you created for the Quest Specialty Travel presentation. Now you are ready to finalize the look of the slides and add effects to make the presentation interesting to watch.

OBJECTIVES

Modify masters

Customize the background and theme

Use slide show commands

Set slide transitions and timings

Animate objects

Inspect a presentation

Evaluate a presentation

Create a template

Modifying Masters

Each presentation in PowerPoint has a set of **masters** that store information about the theme and slide layouts, including the position and size of text and content placeholders, fonts, slide background, color, and effects. There are three Master views: Slide Master view, Notes Master view, and Handout Master view. Changes made in Slide Master view are reflected on the slides in Normal view; changes made in Notes Master view are reflected in Notes Page view, and changes made in Handout Master view appear when you print your presentation using a handout printing option. The primary benefit to modifying a master is that you can make universal changes to your whole presentation instead of making individual repetitive changes to each of your slides. You want to add the QST company logo to every slide in your presentation, so you open your presentation and insert the logo to the slide master.

STEPS

1. **Start PowerPoint, open the presentation PPT D-1.pptx from the drive and folder where you store your Data Files, save the presentation as PPT D-QST, then click the View tab on the Ribbon**

   The title slide of the presentation appears.

   QUICK TIP
   You can press and hold [Shift] and click the Normal button on the status bar to display the slide master.

2. **Click the Slide Master button in the Master Views group, scroll to the top of the slide thumbnail pane, then click the Angles Slide Master thumbnail (first thumbnail)**

   A new tab, the Slide Master tab, appears next to the Home tab on the Ribbon. The Slide Master view appears with the slide master displayed in the Slide pane as shown in Figure D-1. The slide master is the theme slide master (the Angles theme in this case). Each theme comes with its own associated slide masters. Each master text placeholder on the slide master identifies the font size, style, color, and position of text placeholders on the slides in Normal view. For example, the Master title placeholder positioned at the top of the slide uses a black, 28 pt, uppercase, Franklin Gothic Medium font. Slide titles use this font style and formatting. Design elements that you place on the slide master appear on every slide in the presentation. The slide layouts located below the slide master in the slide thumbnail pane follow the information on the slide master. All changes you make to the slide master, including font changes, are reflected in all of the slide layouts.

   QUICK TIP
   When working with slide layouts, you can right-click the thumbnail to open a shortcut list of commands.

3. **Point to the slide layouts in the slide thumbnail pane, then click the Two Content Layout thumbnail**

   As you point to each slide layout, a ScreenTip appears identifying each slide layout by name and lists if any slides in the presentation are using the layout. Slides 2, 5, 7, and 9 are using the Two Content Layout.

4. **Click the Angles Slide Master thumbnail (first thumbnail), click the Insert tab on the Ribbon, then click the Picture button in the Images group**

   The Insert Picture dialog box opens.

5. **Select the picture file PPT D-2.jpg from the drive and folder where you store your Data Files, then click Insert**

   The QST graphic logo appears on the slide master and will appear on all slides in the presentation. The graphic is too large and needs to be repositioned on the slide.

6. **Click 1.61" in the Shape Width text box in the Size group, type 1, press [Enter], drag the graphic to the upper-left corner of the slide, then click a blank area of the slide**

   The graphic snaps into the corner of the slide.

7. **Click the Slide Master tab on the Ribbon, then click the Preserve button in the Edit Master group**

   Preserving the selected master assures that the Angles slide master remains with this presentation even if you eventually use another master. Compare your screen to Figure D-2.

8. **Click the Normal button ▣ on the status bar, then save your changes**

Slide Master tab

Angles slide master

Slide thumbnail pane

Slide layouts

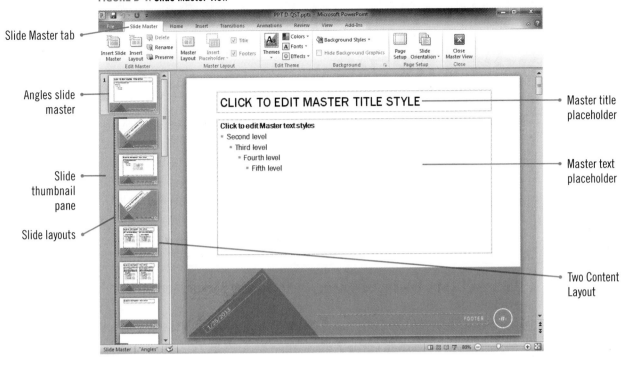

Master title placeholder

Master text placeholder

Two Content Layout

Preserve icon identifies the master as preserved

New graphic

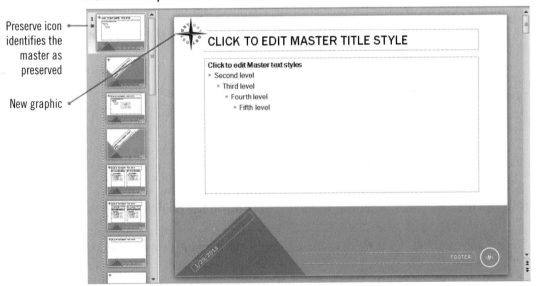

Create custom slide layouts

As you work with PowerPoint, you may find that you need to develop a customized slide layout. For example, you may need to create presentations for a client that has slides that display four pictures with a caption underneath each picture. To make everyone's job easier, you can create a custom slide layout that includes only the placeholders that you need. To create a custom slide layout, open Slide Master view, and then click the Insert Layout button in the Edit Master group. A new slide layout appears in the slide thumbnail pane. You can choose to add several different placeholders including Content, Text, Picture, Chart, Table, SmartArt, Media, and Clip Art. Click the Insert Placeholder list arrow in the Master Layout group, click the placeholder you want to add, drag ✛ to create the placeholder, then position the placeholder on the slide. In Slide Master view, you can add or delete placeholders in any of the slide layouts. You can rename a custom slide layout by clicking the Rename button in the Edit Master group and entering a descriptive name to better identify the layout.

PowerPoint 2010

Customizing the Background and Theme

Every slide in a PowerPoint presentation has a **background**, the area behind the text and graphics. You modify the background to enhance the slides using images and color. A **background graphic** is an object placed on the slide master. You can quickly change the background appearance by applying a background style, which is a set of color variations derived from the theme colors. Theme colors determine the colors for all slide elements in your presentation, including slide background, text and lines, shadows, fills, accents, and hyperlinks. Every PowerPoint theme has its own set of theme colors. See Table D-1 for a description of the theme colors. ██████ The QST presentation needs some design enhancements. You decide to modify the background of the slides by changing the theme colors and fonts.

STEPS

1. **Click the Design tab on the Ribbon, then click the Background Styles button in the Background group**

   A gallery of background styles opens. Review the different backgrounds using Live Preview.

2. **Move ◌ over each style in the gallery, then click Style 2**

   Figure D-3 shows the new background on Slide 1 of the presentation and the other slides in the Slides tab. Even though you are working in Normal view, the new background style is applied to the slide master and slide layouts. The new background style does not appear over the whole slide, which indicates there are background items on the slide master preventing you from seeing the entire slide background.

3. **Click the Slide 2 thumbnail in the Slides tab, then click the Hide Background Graphics check box in the Background group**

   All of the background items (the QST graphic and colored shapes at the bottom of the slide) are hidden from view, and only the text objects, slide number, and train clip remain visible.

4. **Click the Hide Background Graphics check box, click the Background Styles button in the Background group, then click Style 1**

   All of the background items and the white background appear again. The white background color you started with actually looks the best. Theme colors that better match the QST logo would look better than the current theme colors.

5. **Click the Colors button in the Themes group, move the pointer over each of the built-in themes, then click Aspect**

   The new theme colors are applied to the slide master and all of the elements in the presentation including background items, tables, the SmartArt graphic on Slide 4, and the chart on Slide 11. Notice the title text font, color, and formatting did not change; this is known as an **exception**. Exceptions are changes that you make directly to text on the slide, which do not match the theme fonts on the slide master.

6. **Click the Slide 4 thumbnail in the Slides tab, click the Effects button in the Themes group, move the pointer over each of the built-in themes, then click Elemental**

   Notice how the new theme effects change the SmartArt graphic. Like the theme colors, the new theme effects are applied to the slide master and to all of the slides in the presentation.

7. **Click the Slide 5 thumbnail in the Slides tab, click the Fonts button in the Themes group, move the pointer over each of the built-in themes, click Composite, then save your work**

   The new theme fonts are applied to the presentation. Compare your screen to Figure D-4.

FIGURE D-3: Slide with new background style applied

New background style appears on every slide

Background style appears behind all slide objects

FIGURE D-4: Slide showing new theme colors and theme fonts

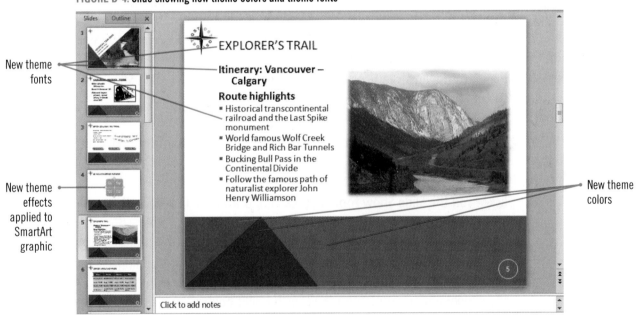

New theme fonts

New theme effects applied to SmartArt graphic

New theme colors

TABLE D-1: Theme colors

color element	description
Text/Background colors	Contrasting colors for typed characters and the slide background
Accent colors	There are six accent colors used for shapes, drawn lines, and text; the shadow color for text and objects and the fill and outline color for shapes are all accent colors; all of these colors contrast appropriately with background and text colors
Hyperlink color	Colors used for hyperlinks you insert
Followed Hyperlink color	Color used for hyperlinks after they have been clicked

Using Slide Show Commands

With PowerPoint, you can show a presentation on a computer using Slide Show view. Slide Show view is used primarily to deliver a presentation to an audience, either over the Internet using your computer or through a projector connected to your computer. As you've seen, Slide Show view fills your computer screen with the slides of the presentation, showing them one at a time. Once the presentation is in Slide Show view, you can use a number of slide show options to tailor the show to meet your needs. For example, you can draw, or **annotate**, on slides or jump to different slides in other parts of the presentation. ▨▨▨ You want to learn how to run a slide show and use the slide show options so you will be prepared when you give your presentation. You run the slide show of the presentation and practice using some of the custom slide show options.

STEPS

1. **Click the Slide 1 thumbnail in the Slides tab, then click the Slide Show button 🖵 on the status bar**

   The first slide of the presentation fills the screen.

2. **Press [Spacebar]**

   Slide 2 appears on the screen. Pressing [Spacebar] or clicking the left mouse button is the easiest way to move through a slide show. See Table D-2 for other Slide Show view keyboard commands. You can also use the Slide Show shortcut menu for on-screen navigation during a slide show.

3. **Right-click anywhere on the screen, point to Go to Slide on the shortcut menu, then click 7 Western Pass**

   The slide show jumps to Slide 7. You can highlight or emphasize major points in your presentation by annotating the slide during a slide show using one of PowerPoint's annotation tools.

4. **Move ⌖ to the lower-left corner of the screen to display the Slide Show toolbar, click the Pen Options menu button 🖉, then click Highlighter**

   The pointer changes to the highlighter pointer ▮.

5. **Drag ▮ to highlight the text in the first and fourth bullet points on the slide**

   While the annotation tool is visible, mouse clicks do not advance the slide show; however, you can still move to the next slide by pressing [Spacebar] or [Enter].

6. **Click 🖉 on the Slide Show toolbar, click Pen, draw a circle around the train tunnel in the picture, then press [Esc]**

   Pressing [Esc] or [Ctrl][A] while using an annotation pointer (pen pointer or highlighter pointer) switches the pointer back to ⌖. Compare your screen to Figure D-5.

7. **Click 🖉 on the Slide Show toolbar, click Eraser, the pointer changes to ✎◺, then click the yellow highlight annotation on the fourth bullet point**

   The annotation is erased.

8. **Press [Esc], click 🖉, then click Erase All Ink on Slide**

   The annotations on Slide 7 are erased. You also have the option of saving annotations you don't delete in Slide Show view when you quit the slide show. Saved annotations appear as drawn objects in Normal view.

9. **Click the Slide Show menu button ▤ on the Slide Show toolbar, point to Go to Slide, then click 1 Adventure Tour Series on the menu**

   Slide 1 appears.

10. **Press [Enter] to advance through the slide show, then when you see a black slide, press [Spacebar]**

    The black slide indicates the end of the slide show, and you are returned to Slide 1 in Normal view.

FIGURE D-5: Slide 7 in Slide Show view showing annotations

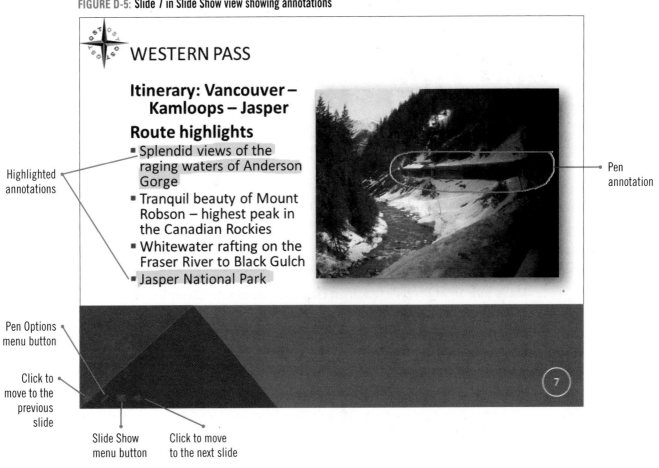

TABLE D-2: Basic slide show keyboard commands

keyboard commands	description
[Enter], [Spacebar], [PgDn], [N], [down arrow], or [right arrow]	Advances to the next slide
[E]	Erases the annotation drawing
[Home], [End]	Moves to the first or last slide in the slide show
[H]	Displays a hidden slide
[up arrow] or [PgUp]	Returns to the previous slide
[W]	Changes the screen to white; press again to return
[S]	Pauses the slide show; press again to continue
[B]	Changes the screen to black; press again to return
[Ctrl][M]	Shows or hides annotations on the slide
[Ctrl][A]	Changes pointer to
[Esc]	Stops the slide show

Setting Slide Transitions and Timings

In a slide show, you can specify how each slide advances in and out of view, and for how long each slide appears on the screen. **Slide transitions** are the special visual and audio effects you apply to a slide that determine how it moves on and off the screen during the slide show. **Slide timing** refers to the amount of time a slide is visible on the screen. Typically, you only set slide timings if you want the presentation to automatically progress through the slides during a slide show. Setting the correct slide timing, in this case, is important because it determines how much time your audience has to view each slide. Each slide can have a different slide timing. You decide to set slide transitions and seven-second slide timings for all the slides.

STEPS

1. **Make sure Slide 1 is selected, then click the Transitions tab on the Ribbon**

   Transitions are organized by type into three groups.

2. **Click the More button ⦇ in the Transition to This Slide group, then click Glitter in the Exciting section**

   The new slide transition plays on the slide, and a transition icon ⭐ appears next to the slide thumbnail in the Slides tab as shown in Figure D-6. You can customize the slide transition by changing its direction and speed.

   QUICK TIP
   You can add a sound that plays with the transition from the Sound list arrow in the Timing group.

3. **Click the Effect Options button in the Transition to This Slide group, click Diamonds from Top, click the Duration down arrow in the Timing group until 2.00 appears, then click the Preview button in the Preview group**

   The Glitter slide transition now plays from the top of the slide for 2.00 seconds. You can apply this transition with the custom settings to all of the slides in the presentation.

4. **Click the Apply To All button in the Timing group, then click the Slide Sorter button 🔲 on the status bar**

   All of the slides now have the customized Glitter transition applied to them as identified by the transition icons located below each slide. You also have the ability to determine how slides progress during a slide show—either manually by mouse click or automatically by slide timing.

5. **Click the On Mouse Click check box under Advance Slide in the Timing group to clear the check mark**

   This clears the option that manually advances slides during a slide show. You can set both manual and automatic slide timings within the same presentation, which is why you need to clear the manual option. Now you can set an automatic slide timing.

   QUICK TIP
   Click the transition icon under any slide in Slide Sorter view to see its transition play.

6. **Click the After up arrow until 00:07.00 appears in the text box, then click the Apply To All button**

   The timing between slides is 7 seconds as indicated by the time under each slide in Slide Sorter view. See Figure D-7. When you run the slide show, each slide will remain on the screen for 7 seconds. You can override a slide's timing and speed up the slide show by pressing [Spacebar], [Enter], or clicking the left mouse button.

7. **Click the Slide Show button 🖵 on the status bar, then watch the slide show advance automatically**

8. **When you see the black slide at the end of the slide show, press [Spacebar], then save your changes**

   The slide show ends and returns to Slide Sorter view with Slide 1 selected.

FIGURE D-6: Applied slide transition

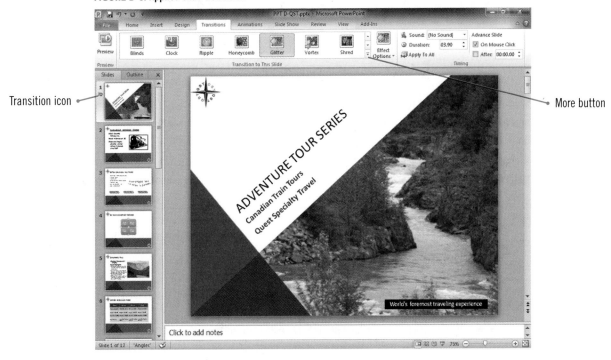

Transition icon

More button

FIGURE D-7: Slide Sorter view showing applied transition and timing

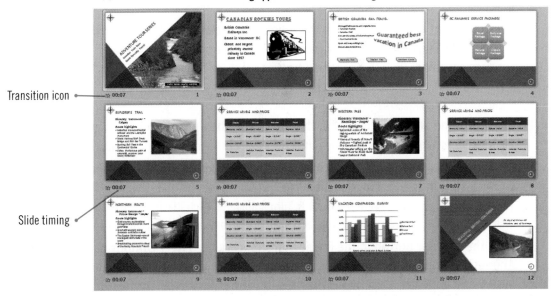

Transition icon

Slide timing

Rehearsing slide show timings

You can set different slide timings for each slide. For example, you can have the title slide appear for 20 seconds, the second slide for 1 minute, and so on. You can set timings by clicking the Rehearse Timings button in the Set Up group on the Slide Show tab. Slide Show view opens and the Recording toolbar shown in Figure D-8 opens. It contains buttons to pause between slides and to advance to the next slide. After opening the Recording toolbar, practice giving your presentation. PowerPoint keeps track of how long each slide appears and sets the timing accordingly. When you are finished rehearsing, PowerPoint displays the total recorded time for the presentation. The next time you run the slide show, you can use the timings you rehearsed.

FIGURE D-8: Recording toolbar

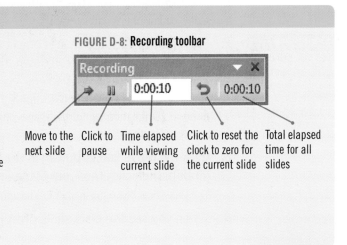

Move to the next slide

Click to pause

Time elapsed while viewing current slide

Click to reset the clock to zero for the current slide

Total elapsed time for all slides

Animating Objects

Animations let you control how objects and text appear on the screen during a slide show and allow you to manage the flow of information and emphasize specific facts. You can animate text, pictures, sounds, hyperlinks, SmartArt diagrams, charts, and individual chart elements. For example, you can apply a Fade animation to bulleted text so that each paragraph enters the slide separately from the others. Animations are organized into four categories, Entrance, Emphasis, Exit, and Motion Paths. The Entrance and Exit animations cause an object to enter or exit the slide with an effect. An Emphasis animation causes an object visible on the slide to have an effect and a Motion Path animation causes an object to move on a specified path on the slide. **████** You animate the text and graphics of several slides in the presentation.

STEPS

1. **Double-click the Slide 1 thumbnail to return to Normal view, click the Animations tab on the Ribbon, then click the river picture**

   Text as well as other objects, like a picture, can be animated during a slide show.

QUICK TIP
There are additional animation options for each animation category located at the bottom of the animations gallery.

2. **Click the More button ▾ in the Animation group, point to each of the animation options in the gallery, then click Shape in the Entrance section**

   As you point to each animation option a Live Preview of the effect plays. Animations can be serious and business-like or humorous, so be sure to choose appropriate effects for your presentation. A small numeral 1, called an animation tag **1**, appears at the top corner of the picture. **Animation tags** identify the order in which objects are animated during slide show.

3. **Click the Effect Options button in the Animation group, click Diamond, then click the Duration up arrow in the Timing group until 04.00 appears**

   Effect options change for each animation. Changing the shape of the animation to diamond complements the shape of the picture, and increasing the duration of the animation gives it a more dramatic effect. Compare your screen to Figure D-9.

4. **Click the Slide Show button ▣ on the status bar, then press [Esc] when you see Slide 3**

   The Shape animation, with the Diamond effect, which begins after the slide transition, is active on Slide 1.

5. **On Slide 3, click the bulleted list text object, click ▾ in the Animation group, then click Grow & Turn in the Entrance section**

   The text object is animated with the Grow & Turn animation. Each line of text has an animation tag with each paragraph displaying a different number. Accordingly, each paragraph is animated separately.

6. **Click the Preview button in the Preview group, click the Effect Options button in the Animation group, click All at Once, then click the Duration up arrow in the Timing group until 02.50 appears**

   Notice that the animation tags for each line of text in the text object now have the same numeral (1), indicating that each line of text animates at the same time.

QUICK TIP
If you want to individually animate the parts of a grouped object, then you must ungroup the objects before you animate them.

7. **Press [Shift], click the shapes object at the bottom of the slide, release [Shift], click ▾ in the Animation group, scroll down, then click Loops in the Motion Paths section**

   A motion path object appears over the shapes object and identifies the direction and shape, or path, of the animation. When needed, you can move, resize, and change the direction of the motion path. Notice the numeral 2 animation tag for the shapes object indicating it is animated *after* the text object. Compare your screen to Figure D-10.

8. **Click the Move Earlier button in the Timing group, click the Slide Show tab on the Ribbon, then click the From Beginning button in the Start Slide Show group**

   The slide show begins from Slide 1. The animations make the presentation more interesting to view.

9. **When you see the black slide, press [Spacebar], then save your changes**

FIGURE D-9: Slide showing animation applied to picture

Animation tag

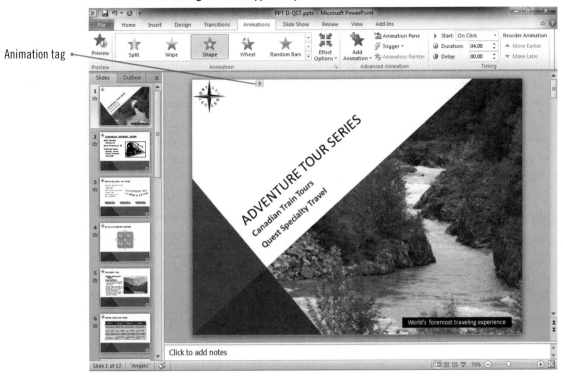

FIGURE D-10: Screen showing animated shapes object

Animation tags

Animation tag

Motion path object

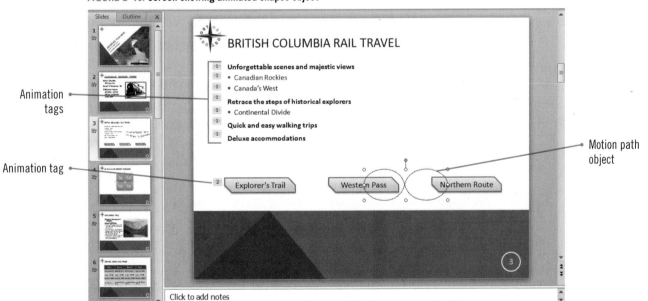

Presentation checklist

You should always rehearse your slide show. If possible, rehearse your presentation in the room and with the computer that you will use. Use the following checklist to prepare for the slide show:

- Is PowerPoint or PowerPoint Viewer installed on the computer?
- Is your presentation file on the hard drive of the computer you will be using? Try putting a shortcut for the file on the desktop. Do you have a backup copy of your presentation file on a removable storage device, like a flash drive?
- Is the projection device working correctly? Can the slides be seen from the back of the room?

- Do you know how to control **room lighting** so the audience can see both your slides and their handouts and notes? You may want to designate someone to control the lights if the controls are not close to you.
- Will the **computer** be situated so you can advance and annotate the slides yourself? If not, designate someone to advance them for you.
- Do you have enough copies of your **handouts**? Bring extras. Decide when to hand them out, or whether you prefer to have them waiting at the audience members' seats when they enter.

Finishing a Presentation

Inspecting a Presentation

Reviewing your presentation can be an important step, not only to find and fix errors, but also to locate and delete private company or personal information and document properties you do not want to share with others. If you share presentations with others, especially over the Internet, it is a good idea to inspect the presentation file using the Document Inspector. The **Document Inspector** looks for hidden data and personal information that is stored in the file itself or in the document properties. Document properties, also known as **metadata**, includes specific data about the presentation, such as the author's name, subject matter, title, who saved the file last, and when the file was created. Other types of information the Document Inspector can locate and remove include presentation notes, comments, ink annotations, invisible on-slide content, off-slide content, and custom XML data. You decide to view and add some document properties, inspect your presentation file, and learn about the Mark as Final command.

STEPS

QUICK TIP

Click the Properties button, then click Advanced Properties to open the Properties dialog box to see or change more document properties.

1. **Click the File tab on the Ribbon, with Info selected, click the Properties button in the right pane, then click Show Document Panel**

   The Document Properties pane opens showing the file location and the title of the presentation. Now enter some descriptive data for this presentation file.

2. **Enter the data shown in Figure D-11, then click the Document Properties pane Close button ☒**

   This data provides detailed information about the presentation file that you can use to identify and organize your file. You can also use this information as search criteria to locate the file at a later time. You now use the Document Inspector to search for information you might want to delete in the presentation.

3. **Click the File tab on the Ribbon, with Info selected, click the Check for Issues button in the center pane, click Inspect Document, then click Yes to save the changes to the document**

   The Document Inspector dialog box opens. The Document Inspector searches the presentation file for six different types of information that you might want removed from the presentation before sharing it.

QUICK TIP

If you need to save a presentation to run in an earlier version of PowerPoint, check for unsupported features using the Check Compatibility feature.

4. **Make sure all of the check boxes are selected, then click Inspect**

   The presentation file is reviewed, and the results are shown in Figure D-12. The Document Inspector found items having to do with document properties, which you just entered, and presentation notes, which are on Slides 11 and 12. You decide to leave the document properties alone but delete the notes for all of the slides.

5. **Click the Remove All button in the Presentation Notes section, then click Close**

   All notes are removed from the Notes pane for the slides in the presentation.

6. **Click the Protect Presentation button, click Mark as Final, then click OK in the alert box**

   A message box opens. Be sure to read the message to understand what happens to the file and how to recognize a marked-as-final presentation. You decide to complete this procedure.

QUICK TIP

Presentations marked as final in PowerPoint 2010 are not read-only if they are opened in earlier versions of PowerPoint.

7. **Click OK, click the Home tab on the Ribbon, click the Slide 1 thumbnail in the Slides tab, then click anywhere in the title text object**

   Notice in Figure D-13 that the Ribbon is no longer displayed and an information alert box notes that the presentation is marked as final, making it a read-only file. A **read-only** file is one that can't be edited or modified in any way. Anyone who has received a read-only presentation can only edit the presentation by changing its marked-as-final status. You still want to work on the presentation, so you remove the marked-as-final status.

8. **Click the Edit Anyway button in the information alert box, then save your changes**

   The Ribbon and all commands are active again, and the file can now be modified.

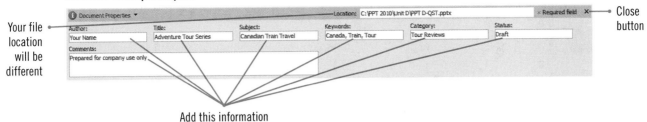

Your file location will be different

Location: C:\PPT 2010\Unit D\PPT D-QST.pptx   * Required field X

Close button

Add this information

FIGURE D-12: **Document Inspector dialog box**

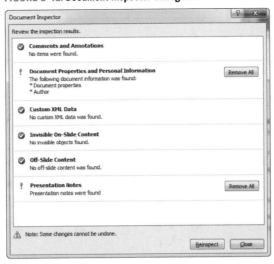

FIGURE D-13: **Marked as final presentation**

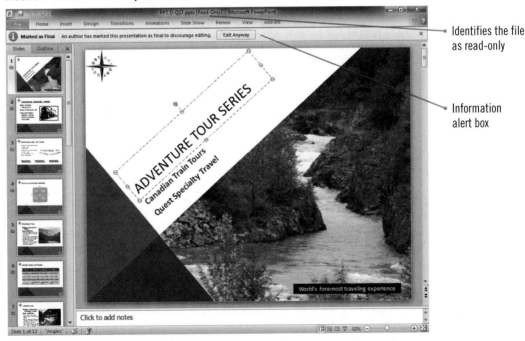

Identifies the file as read-only

Information alert box

Digitally sign a presentation

What is a digital signature, and why would you want to use one in PowerPoint? A **digital signature** is similar to a hand-written signature in that it authenticates your document; however, a digital signature, unlike a hand-written signature, is created using computer cryptography and is not visible within the presentation itself. There are three primary reasons you would add a digital signature to a presentation: one, to authenticate the signer of the document; two, to assure that the content of the presentation has not been changed since it was signed; and three, to assure the origin of the signed document. To add a digital signature, click the File tab on the Ribbon, click the Protect Presentation button, click Add a Digital Signature, then follow the dialog boxes.

PowerPoint 2010

Evaluating a Presentation

A well-designed and organized presentation requires thought and preparation. An effective presentation is focused and visually appealing—easy for the speaker to present and simple for the audience to understand. Visual elements can strongly influence the audience's attention and can influence the success of your presentation. See Table D-3 for general information on the impact a visual presentation has on an audience. ▓▓▓▓ You know your boss and other colleagues will critique your presentation, so you take the time to evaluate your presentation's organization and effectiveness.

STEPS

1. **Click the Reading View button 📖 on the status bar, then press [Spacebar] when the slide show finishes**

QUICK TIP
You can also move, delete, collapse, and expand a section in the Slides tab or in Slide Sorter view.

2. **Click the Slide 5 thumbnail in the Slides tab, click the Section button in the Slides group, then click Add Section**

   Two new sections appear in the Slides tab, the section you created, called the Untitled Section and a section for all the slides before the new section, called the Default Section. Sections help you organize your slides into logical groups.

3. **Right-click Untitled Section in the Slides tab, click Rename Section, type Tour Packages, then click Rename**

4. **Click the Slide Sorter view button 🔡 on the status bar, save your work, then compare your screen to Figure D-14**

5. **Double-click Slide 1, add your name to the notes and handouts footer, evaluate your presentation according to the guidelines below, submit your presentation to your instructor, then close the presentation**

   Figure D-15 shows a poorly designed slide. Contrast this slide with guidelines below and your presentation.

DETAILS

When evaluating a presentation, it is important to:

- **Keep your message focused and your text concise**

  Don't put every point you plan to say on your slides. Keep the audience anticipating explanations to the key points in the presentation. Limit each slide to six words per line and six lines per slide. Use bulleted lists to help prioritize your points visually. Your presentation text should only provide highlights of your message. Supplement the information on your slides with further explanation and details during your presentation.

- **Keep the design simple, easy to read, and appropriate for the content**

  A design theme makes the presentation consistent. If you design your own layout, keep it simple and use design elements sparingly. Use similar design elements consistently throughout the presentation; otherwise, your audience may get confused.

- **Choose attractive colors that make the slide easy to read**

  Use contrasting colors for slide background and text to make the text readable. If you are giving an on-screen presentation, you can use almost any combination of colors that look good together.

- **Choose fonts and styles that are easy to read and emphasize important text**

  As a general rule, use no more than two fonts in a presentation and vary the font size, using nothing smaller than 24 points. Use bold and italic attributes selectively.

- **Use visuals to help communicate the message of your presentation**

  Commonly used visuals include clip art, photographs, charts, worksheets, tables, and videos. Whenever possible, replace text with a visual, but be careful not to overcrowd your slides. White space on your slides is okay!

FIGURE D-14: The final presentation in Slide Sorter view

New default section

New renamed section

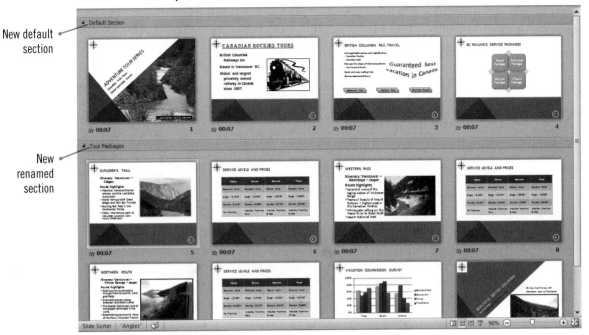

FIGURE D-15: A poorly designed slide

Too many fonts and font styles used

Too many words used

Shape serves no purpose and does not fit theme

Theme does not fit content

Duplicate clip art not necessary

Too many font colors

Too much text on the slide

Font is hard to read and is lost on the slide

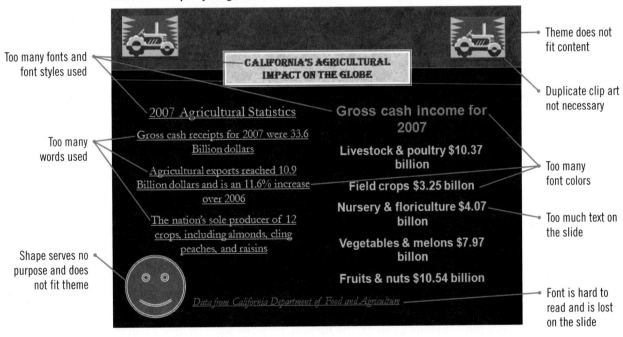

TABLE D-3: Audience impact from a visual presentation

impact	description
Visual reception	75% of all environmental stimuli is received through visual reception
Learning	55% of what an audience learns comes directly from visual messages
Retention	Combining visual messages with verbal messages can increase memory retention by as much as 50%
Presentation goals	You are twice as likely (67%) to achieve your communication objectives using a visual presentation
Meeting length	You are likely to decrease the average meeting length by 26.8% when you use a visual presentation

Source: Presenters Online, www.presentersonline.com

PowerPoint 2010

Creating a Template

When planning the design of your presentation, keep in mind that you are not limited to using the standard themes PowerPoint provides or the ones you find on the Web. You can also create a presentation using a template. A **template** is a type of presentation file that contains custom design elements on the slide master, background, slide layouts, and a theme, and can include graphics and content. You can create a new template from a blank presentation, or you can modify an existing PowerPoint presentation and save it as a template. If you modify an existing presentation, you can modify or delete any color, graphic, or font as necessary. When you save a presentation as a template file the .potx extension is added to the filename. You can then use your template presentation as the basis for new presentations. You are finished working on your presentation for now. You want to create a template using the design theme of this presentation so others can use it.

STEPS

1. **Click the File tab on the Ribbon, click New, make sure Blank presentation is selected in the Available Templates and Themes section, then click Create**

   A new presentation appears. Now save this presentation as a template.

2. **Click the File tab on the Ribbon, click Save As, click the Save as type list arrow, then click PowerPoint Template (*.potx)**

   Because this is a template, PowerPoint automatically opens the Templates folder on your hard drive.

   QUICK TIP

   Presentations saved to the Templates folder appear in the Recent templates folder. To locate this folder, click the File tab on the Ribbon, click New, then click Recent templates.

3. **Locate the drive and folder where you store your Data Files, click to select the default filename Presentation 1 in the File name text box, type PPT D-QST Template as shown in Figure D-16, then click Save**

   The presentation is saved as a PowerPoint template to the drive and folder where you store your Data Files, and the new template presentation appears in the PowerPoint window.

4. **Click the Design tab on the Ribbon, click the More button ⊡ in the Themes group, then click Browse for Themes**

   The Choose Theme or Themed Document dialog box opens.

5. **Locate the drive and folder where you store your Data Files, click PPT D-QST, then click Apply**

   The design theme, including slide transitions and slide timings, from the presentation PPT D-QST is applied to the PPT D-QST Template presentation. All slide master elements, including slide layouts, colors, shapes, fonts, and background elements from the PPT D-QST presentation are applied over the existing design theme of the PPT D-QST Template presentation.

   QUICK TIP

   To quickly replace a word you have typed with a common synonym, right-click the word, then point to Synonyms on the shortcut menu.

6. **Click the title text placeholder, type QST Template, click the subtitle placeholder, type Standard Company Use Template – Your Name, then save your changes**

   You don't need to keep the slide transitions and slide timings that were applied from the PPT D-QST presentation.

7. **Click the Transitions tab on the Ribbon, click the More button ⊡ in the Transition to This Slide group, click None, click the After check box in the Timing group, then click the Apply to All button in the Timing group**

   The slide transitions and slide timing are removed from the presentation.

8. **Click the View tab, click the Slide Sorter button in the Presentation Views group, then drag the Zoom Slider all the way to the right**

   Figure D-17 shows the final template presentation in Slide Sorter view.

9. **Double-click Slide 1, save your work, submit your presentation to your instructor, close the presentation, then exit PowerPoint**

FIGURE D-16: Save As dialog box

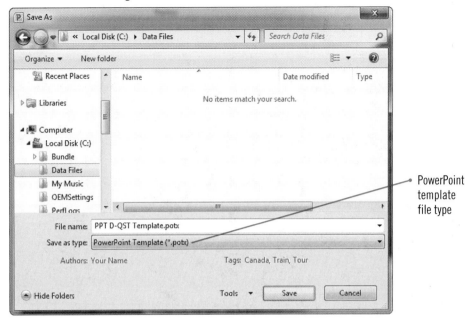

PowerPoint template file type

FIGURE D-17: Completed template presentation in Slide Sorter view

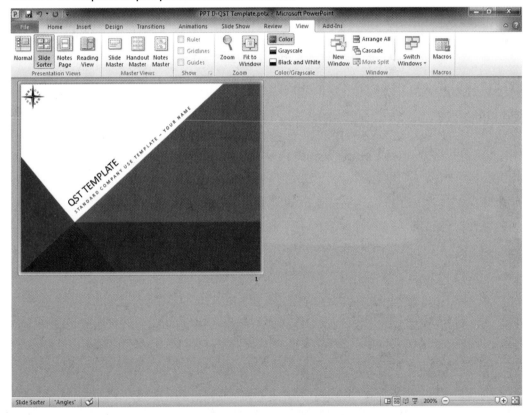

Using Paste Special

Paste Special is used to paste text or objects into PowerPoint using a specific file format. For example, you may want to paste some text as a picture or as plain text without formatting. Copy the text, then in PowerPoint click the Paste list arrow, click Paste Special, then select the appropriate file format option. You can also link an object or selected information from another program to PowerPoint using the Paste Special command. This technique is useful when you want to link part of an Excel worksheet or a chart from a workbook that contains both a worksheet and a chart. To link just the chart, open the Microsoft Excel worksheet, then copy the chart. Leaving Excel and the source file open, click the Paste list arrow, click Paste Special, click the Paste link option button, then click OK.

Practice

Concepts Review

Label each element of the PowerPoint window shown in Figure D-18.

FIGURE D-18

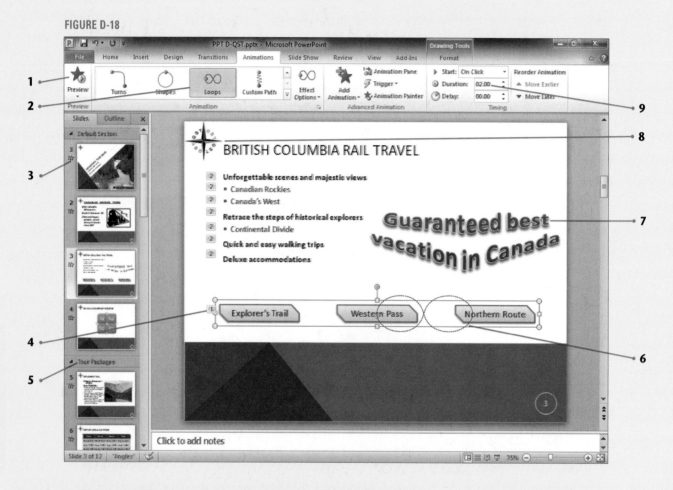

Match each term with the statement that best describes it.

10. **Masters**
11. **Annotate**
12. **Metadata**
13. **Animation tag**
14. **Transitions**
15. **Background**

a. Identifies the order in which objects are animated
b. The area behind text and graphics
c. Includes document properties such as the author's name
d. To draw on a slide during a slide show
e. Slides that store theme and placeholder information
f. Visual effects that determine how a slide moves in and out of view during a slide show

Select the best answer from the list of choices.

16. **The effect that determines how a slide moves in and out of view during a slide show is called a(n):**
    - **a.** Transition.
    - **b.** Timing.
    - **c.** Theme.
    - **d.** Animation.

17. **An object placed on the slide master defines which of the following items?**
    - **a.** Background graphic
    - **b.** Logo
    - **c.** Shape
    - **d.** Master placeholder

18. **Which of the following statements about masters is *not* true?**
    - **a.** Each slide layout in the presentation has a corresponding slide layout in Slide Master view.
    - **b.** The design theme is placed on the slide master.
    - **c.** Masters store information.
    - **d.** Changes made to the slide master are reflected in the handout and notes masters as well.

19. **Which PowerPoint file *can't* be edited or modified?**
    - **a.** Inspected file
    - **b.** File saved in another file format
    - **c.** Read-only file
    - **d.** Template file

20. **The effect that controls how an object appears on the screen during a slide show is called a(n):**
    - **a.** Transition.
    - **b.** Animation.
    - **c.** Path.
    - **d.** Template.

21. **The Document Inspector looks for _____ and personal information that is stored in the presentation file.**
    - **a.** themes
    - **b.** hidden data
    - **c.** animation tags
    - **d.** video settings

22. **According to the book, which standard should you follow to evaluate a presentation?**
    - **a.** Replace visuals with text as often as possible.
    - **b.** Slides should include most of the information you wish to present.
    - **c.** Use many different design elements to keep your audience from getting bored.
    - **d.** The message should be outlined in a concise way.

Skills Review

1. **Modify masters.**
   a. Open the presentation PPT D-3.pptx from the drive and folder where you store your Data Files, then save the presentation as **PPT D-New Product**.
   b. Open Slide Master view using the View tab, then click the Origin Slide Master thumbnail.
   c. Insert the picture PPT D-4.jpg, then resize the picture so it is 0.8" wide.
   d. Drag the picture to the upper-right corner of the slide within the design frame of the slide, then deselect the picture.
   e. Preserve the Origin master, switch to Normal view, then save your changes.

2. **Customize the background and theme.**
   a. Switch to Slide 3, click the Design tab, then open the background styles gallery.
   b. Change the background style to Style 5.
   c. Open the Format Background dialog box.
   d. Set the Transparency to 25%, apply the background to all of the slides, then close the dialog box.
   e. Click the Colors button, then click Office. Click the Fonts button, then click Office Classic 2.
   f. Save your changes.

3. **Use slide show commands.**
   a. Begin the slide show on Slide 1, then proceed to Slide 4.
   b. Use the Pen to circle the words **Early Adopters**, **Mass Adopters**, and **Late Adopters**.
   c. Move to Slide 5, then use the Highlighter to highlight the words **Pricing**, **Look**, and **Fulfillment issues**.

Skills Review (continued)

d. Right-click the slide and go to Slide 1, move to Slide 4, then erase all ink on the slide.

e. Move to Slide 5, erase the ink on the slide, then change the pointer back to ⌖.

f. Press [Home], advance through the slide show, don't save any ink annotations, then save your work.

4. Set slide transitions and timings.

a. Go to Slide Sorter view, click the Slide 1 thumbnail, then apply the Vortex transition to the slide.

b. Change the effect option to From Bottom, change the duration speed to 3.00, then apply to all the slides.

c. Change the slide timing to 5 seconds, then apply to all of the slides.

d. Switch to Normal view, view the slide show, then save your work.

5. Animate objects.

a. Go to Slide 3, click the Animations tab, then select the E shape on the slide.

b. Apply the Swivel effect to the object, click the Price arrow, apply the Float In effect, then preview the animations.

c. On Slide 4 apply the Spin effect (Emphasis section) to the title text object.

d. Select the six objects in the graphic, click the More button in the Animation group, click More Entrance Effects, then apply an animation of your choice from the Exciting group to the six selected objects in the graphic.

e. Apply animation effects to objects on at least two more slides in the presentation.

f. Edit the animations effects as needed, then save your changes.

6. Inspect a presentation.

a. Open the Document Properties pane, type **Internet Product** in the Subject text box, then type **Review** in the Status text box.

b. Close the Document Properties pane, then open the Document Inspector dialog box.

c. Make sure the Off-Slide Content check box is selected, then inspect the presentation.

d. Delete the off-slide content and the presentation notes, then close the dialog box. Save your changes.

7. Evaluate a presentation.

a. Go to Slide 1, then run a slide show.

b. Evaluate the presentation using the points described in the lesson as criteria, then submit a written evaluation to your instructor.

c. Move Slide 6 below Slide 8.

d. Check the spelling of the presentation, add the slide number and your name to the slide footer on all the slides, then save your changes.

e. Switch to Slide Sorter view, then compare your presentation to Figure D-19.

f. Submit your presentation to your instructor, then close the presentation.

FIGURE D-19

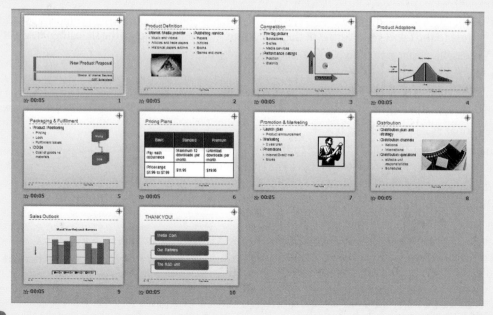

Skills Review (continued)

8. Create a template.

    a. Create a new presentation, then save it as a PowerPoint template with the name **PPT D-Template** to the drive and folder where your Data Files are stored.

    b. Click the More button in the Themes group, browse for themes, locate the drive and folder where you store your Data files, click PPT D-New Product, then click Apply.

    c. Type **QST Template** in the title placeholder, then type your name in the subtitle placeholder.

    d. Delete the slide transitions and animations, remove the slide timing, then select the On Mouse Click option in the Timing group.

    e. Save your work, then submit your presentation to your instructor.

    f. Close the presentation, then exit PowerPoint.

Independent Challenge 1

You are a travel consultant for Island Travel Services, located in Tampa, Florida. You have been working on a sales presentation that is going to be accessed by customers on the company Web site. You need to finish up what you have been working on by adding transitions, timings, and animation effects to the sales presentation.

If you have a SAM 2010 user profile, an autogradable SAM version of this assignment may be available at http://www.cengage.com/sam2010. Check with your instructor to confirm that this assignment is available in SAM. To use the SAM version of this assignment, log into the SAM 2010 Web site and download the instruction and start files.

    a. Open the file PPT D-5.pptx from the drive and folder where you store your Data Files, and save the presentation as **PPT D-Island**.

    b. Add the slide number and your name as the footer on all slides, except the title slide.

    c. Apply the Float In animation to the title text on each slide.

    d. Apply the Wipe animation to the bulleted text objects on each slide.

    e. Apply the Shape animation to the table on Slide 8, then change the effect option to Box.

    f. Apply the Shred slide transition, apply a 7-second slide timing, then apply to all of the slides.

    g. Check the spelling of the presentation, then save your changes.

    h. View the slide show, and evaluate your presentation. Make changes if necessary.

    i. Submit your presentation to your instructor, close the presentation, then exit PowerPoint.

Independent Challenge 2

You are a development engineer at Extreme Sports, Inc., an international sports product design company located in Fargo, North Dakota. Extreme Sports designs and manufactures items such as bike helmets, bike racks, and kayak paddles, and markets these items primarily to countries in North America and Western Europe. You need to finish the work on a quarterly presentation that outlines the progress of the company's newest technologies by adding animations, customizing the background, and using the Document Inspector.

    a. Open the file PPT D-6.pptx from the drive and folder where you store your Data Files, and save the presentation as **PPT D-Extreme**.

    b. Apply an appropriate design theme, then apply a new slide background style. Make sure the new background style is appropriate for the design theme you have chosen.

    c. Apply the Ripple slide transition to all slides, then animate the following objects: the text on Slide 2, the clip art object on Slide 3, the table on Slide 4, and the clip art on Slide 6. View the slide show to evaluate the effects you added and make adjustments as necessary.

    d. Run the Document Inspector with all options selected, identify what items the Document Inspector finds, close the Document Inspector dialog box, then review the slides to find the items.

Independent Challenge 2 (continued)

e. Add a slide at the end of the presentation that identifies the items the Document Inspector found.

f. Run the Document Inspector again, and remove all items except the document properties.

Advanced Challenge Exercise

- Click the Rehearse Timings button on the Slide Sorter toolbar.
- Set slide timings for each slide in the presentation.
- Save new slide timings.

g. Add your name as a footer to all slides, run the spell checker, save your work, then run a slide show to evaluate your presentation.

h. Submit your presentation to your instructor, then close the presentation and exit PowerPoint.

Independent Challenge 3

You work for Young & Associates, a full-service investment and pension firm. Your boss wants you to create a presentation on small business pension plan options to be published on the company Web site. You have completed adding the information to the presentation, now you need to add a design theme, format some information, add some animation effects, and add slide timings.

a. Open the file PPT D-7.pptx from the drive and folder where you store your Data Files, and save the presentation as **PPT D-IRAPlans**.

b. Apply an appropriate design theme.

c. Apply animation effects to the following objects: the shapes on Slide 3 and the text and clip art on Slide 5. View the slide show to evaluate the effects you added, and make adjustments as necessary.

d. Convert the text on Slide 4 to a Basic Radial SmartArt graphic (Found in the Cycle category).

e. Apply the Intense Effect style to the SmartArt graphic, then change the colors of the graphic to Colorful Range – Accent Colors 2 to 3.

f. Switch to Slide 3, align the Sector and Quality arrow shapes to one another, then align the Allocation and Maturity arrow shapes to one another.

g. Adjust the aligned arrow shapes so they are centered on the Buy/Sell oval shape, then apply a 15-second timing to Slides 3–7 and a 5-second timing to Slides 1 and 2.

h. Add a section between Slide 5 and Slide 6, then rename the section **Plans**.

i. Rename the Default section in the Slides tab to **Intro**.

Advanced Challenge Exercise

- Open Slide Master view, select the last slide layout, then click the Insert Layout button.
- Click the Insert Placeholder list arrow, click Table, then drag a placeholder in the blank area of the Slide Master layout. (*Hint*: Draw the table placeholder so it takes up most of the blank space in the layout.)
- Return to Normal view, apply the new Custom Layout to Slides 6 and 7. Adjust the placeholder in Slide Master view if necessary.

j. Add your name as a footer to the slides, run the spell checker, save your work, then run a slide show to evaluate your presentation.

k. Submit your presentation to your instructor, then close the presentation and exit PowerPoint.

Real Life Independent Challenge

You work for the operations supervisor at the Tennessee State University student union. Create a presentation that you can eventually publish to the college Web site that describes all of the services offered at the student union.

a. Plan and create the slide presentation that describes the services and events offered at the student union. To help create content, use the student union at your school or use the Internet to locate information on college student unions. The presentation should contain at least six slides.

b. Use an appropriate design theme.

c. Add clip art and photographs available in the Clip Organizer, then style and customize at least one photo.

d. Save the presentation as **PPT D-TSU** to the drive and folder where you store your Data Files. View the slide show, and evaluate the contents of your presentation. Make any necessary adjustments.

e. Add slide transitions, animation effects, and timings to the presentation. View the slide show again to evaluate the effects you added.

f. Add your name as a footer to the slides. Spell check the presentation, save, inspect, then submit your presentation to your instructor. An example of a finished presentation is shown in Figure D-20.

g. Create a template from this presentation using a new presentation, then save the presentation as **PPT D-TSU Template** to the drive and folder where you store your Data Files.

h. Type **TSU Template** in the title placeholder, type your name in the subtitle placeholder, delete transitions and animations, submit your presentation to your instructor, close the template presentation, then exit PowerPoint.

FIGURE D-20

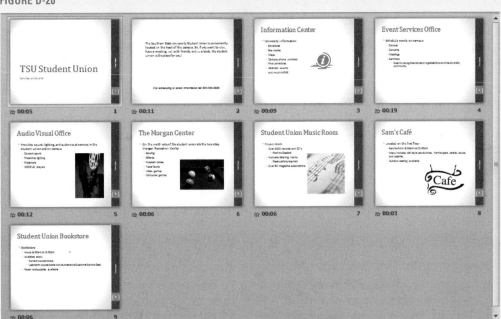

Visual Workshop

Create a new PowerPoint template (.potx) with the filename **PPT D-School Template** and save it to the drive and folder where you store your Data Files. Change the presentation to look like Figures D-21 and D-22. Figure D-22 shows a slide with a custom slide layout that you need to create. Submit your presentation to your instructor.

FIGURE D-21

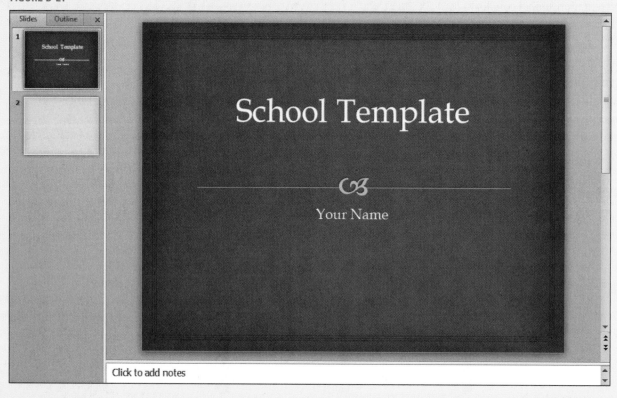

FIGURE D-22

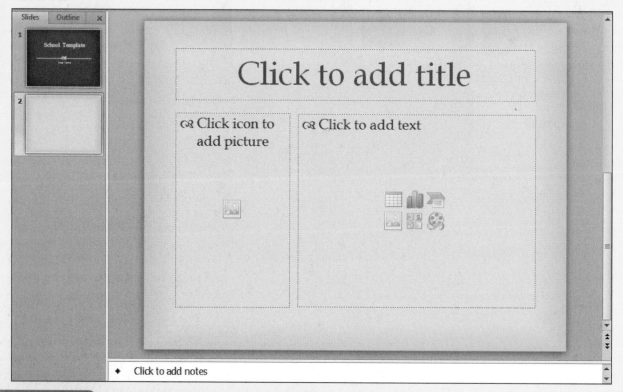

Working with Advanced Tools and Masters

Once you have learned the basics of creating a presentation and running a slide show, you are ready to learn more advanced features of PowerPoint. Advanced features such as connector shapes, the Animation and Format Painters, and customized slide layouts can help you create impressive presentations. Knowing how to modify masters allows you the freedom to customize the slides, handouts, and notes of your presentation. As sales associate for Quest Specialty Travel, you have been working on a train tour presentation that details the specifics of Canadian train tours. After receiving some initial feedback, you revise the presentation by enhancing shapes, customizing animations, and customizing the master views.

OBJECTIVES

Draw and format connectors

Use advanced formatting tools

Customize animation effects

Create custom slide layouts

Format master text

Change master text indents

Adjust text objects

Customize handout and notes masters

Drawing and Formatting Connectors

PowerPoint has a number of connector tools that enable you to create three different types of connector lines or arrows—straight, elbow (bent), or curved. For example, use the connector tools to connect shapes with a line or arrow. Use the Curve tool to create a freeform curved line. Once you have drawn a line or connector, you can format it using Quick Styles, outline color, and effects. ▓▓▓▓▓ Drawing and formatting connecting lines between the shapes on Slide 3 will enhance the look of the shapes.

STEPS

1. **Start PowerPoint, open the presentation PPT E-1.pptx from the drive and folder where you store your Data Files, save the presentation as PPT E-QST, then click the Slide 3 thumbnail in the Slides tab**

   Slide 3 of the presentation appears.

2. **Click the Shapes button in the Drawing group, right-click the Elbow Connector button ⌐ in the Lines section, click Lock Drawing Mode on the shortcut menu, then position + on the top connection site ⊙ on the Explorer's Trail shape**

   Notice the shape has four possible connection sites to anchor a line or arrow. Locking the drawing mode allows you to draw the same shape multiple times without having to reselect it in the Shapes Gallery. See Figure E-1.

TROUBLE
If you accidentally release the mouse before you reach a ⊙, an endpoint is created at the end of the connector. Drag the connector endpoint to the correct connection site.

3. **Press and hold the left mouse button on the ⊙, the pointer changes to +, then drag to the right to connect to the left ⊙ on the Western Pass shape**

   Red handles (circles) appear at either end of the connector line, indicating that it is attached to the two shapes. The line has two adjustment handles (yellow diamonds) which allow you to alter the path of the line.

4. **Position + over the bottom ⊙ on the Western Pass shape, then drag + to the bottom ⊙ on the Northern Route shape**

   A second connector line now flows from the bottom of the Western Pass shape to the bottom of the Northern Route shape.

QUICK TIP
If you rearrange shapes that are joined with connector lines, the connector lines remain attached and move with the shapes.

5. **Press [Esc], click the left connector line, position ⬉ over the red handle on the Western Pass shape, then drag the red handle to the top ⊙ on the Western Pass shape**

   Pressing [Esc] unlocks the drawing mode. The left connector line now flows from the top of the Explorer's Trail shape to the top of the Western Pass shape as shown in Figure E-2.

6. **Click the Drawing Tools Format tab on the Ribbon, click the More button ▼ in the Shape Styles group, then click Moderate Line – Accent 2 (second row)**

   The style of the line becomes more distinct with a shadow effect.

7. **Click the Shape Outline list arrow in the Shape Styles group to open the gallery, point to Weight, then click 3 pt**

   The line is wider and easier to see.

QUICK TIP
To reroute a connector to the closest points between shapes, right-click the connector, then click Reroute Connectors on the shortcut menu.

8. **Right-click the left connector line, point to Connector Types on the shortcut menu, then click Curved Connector**

   The connector line is now curved. You prefer the previous connector style.

9. **Click the Undo button ↶ on the Quick Access toolbar, click a blank area of the slide, then save your presentation**

   Compare your screen to Figure E-3.

FIGURE E-1: Shape showing connection sites

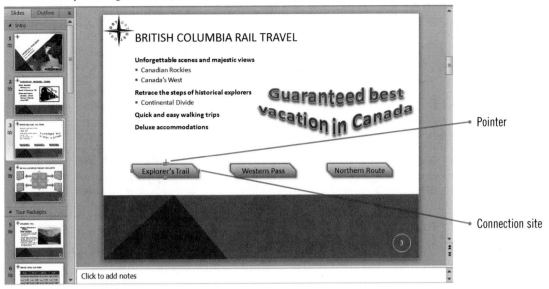

FIGURE E-2: Moved connector line

FIGURE E-3: Slide showing formatted connector line

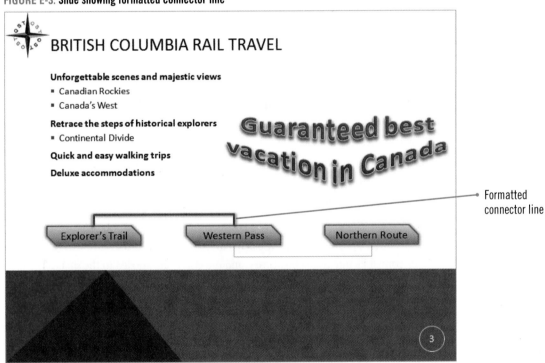

Drawing a freeform shape

A freeform shape can consist of straight lines, freehand (curved) lines, or a combination of the two. To draw a freeform shape, click the Home tab on the Ribbon, click the Shapes button in the Drawing group, then click the Freeform button 🖰 in the Lines section. Drag the pointer to draw the desired shape, then double-click when you are done. To draw a straight line with the Freeform tool, click where you want to begin the line, move the mouse in the direction you want the line, click to insert a stopping point or corner, then double-click to deactivate the Freeform tool when you are finished. To edit a freeform object, right-click the object, then click Edit Points on the shortcut menu.

Using Advanced Formatting Tools

With the advanced formatting tools available in PowerPoint, you can change the attributes of any object. You can format text and shapes using solid and texture fills, 3-D effects, and shadows. If you have multiple objects that you want to format using the same effects to create a cohesive look on the slide, you can use the Format Painter to copy the attributes from one object and apply them to other objects. In this lesson, you finish formatting the connector lines on Slide 3 and then use the advanced formatting tools to enhance the diagram on Slide 4.

STEPS

QUICK TIP

You can also apply effects and shape styles to text objects using commands on the Drawing Tools Format tab.

1. **Right-click the left connector line, click the Format Painter button** 🖌 **on the Mini toolbar, then position** ⬐🖌 **over the right connector line**
   The Format Painter tool "picks up" or copies the attributes of an object and pastes them to the next object you select.

2. **Click the right connector line, then click a blank area of the slide**
   Both connector lines are formatted using the same line width, color, and effects, as shown in Figure E-4.

3. **Click Slide 4 in the Slides tab, right-click the flowchart shape that begins with "Best tour price", click Format Shape on the shortcut menu, then click the Picture or texture fill option button**
   The Format Picture dialog box opens.

QUICK TIP

To fill a shape with a picture, right-click the shape, click Format Shape, click the Picture or texture fill option button, then click the File button to locate and insert a picture.

4. **Drag the dialog box so you can see the selected flowchart shape, click the Texture list arrow, click the Green marble square, then click 3-D Format in the left pane of the dialog box**
   The green marble texture fills the shape. The 3-D Format options appear in the dialog box.

5. **In the Bevel section click the Top list arrow, click the Cool Slant icon, in the Surface section click the Lighting list arrow, then in the Cool section click the Freezing icon**
   The lighting effect will define the bevel effect better.

6. **Click 3-D Rotation in the left pane, click the Presets list arrow, then in the Perspective section click the Perspective Right icon in the top row**
   The shape changes perspective, and you can see the effect and the depth of the effect.

7. **In the Text section click the Keep text flat check box, click Line Style in the left pane, click the Width up arrow until 4pt appears, then click Close**
   The Format Picture dialog box closes, and the effects are applied to the shape. The text in the shape remains flat and does not take on the right perspective of the shape. The line around the shape increases to 4 point and is easier to see.

QUICK TIP

You can also press [Esc] to turn off the Format Painter.

8. **Click the Home tab on the Ribbon, double-click** 🖌 **in the Clipboard group, click each of the three remaining flowchart shapes, then click** 🖌 **again to turn off the Format Painter**
   Double-clicking the Format Painter button allows you to apply the same formatting to multiple objects on the slide without having to reselect the tool. Now the four flowchart shapes on the slide have the same fill, font, and 3-D effects.

9. **Click a blank area of the slide, then save your changes**
   Compare your screen with Figure E-5.

FIGURE E-4: Slide showing formatted connector lines

Left connector line

Both connector lines are formatted with the same attributes

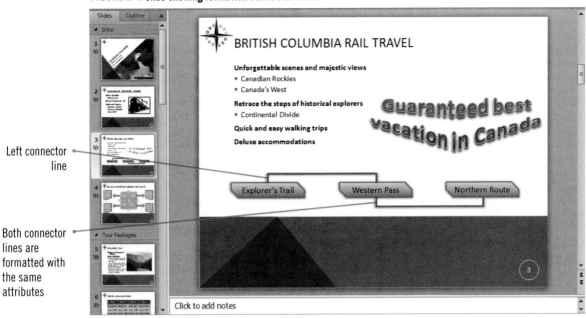

FIGURE E-5: Slide showing formatted shapes

Each flowchart shape is formatted with the same attributes

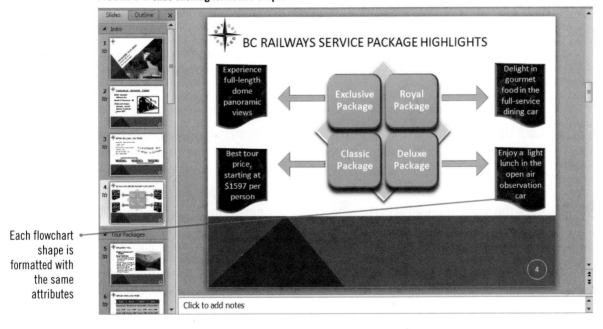

Creating columns in a text box

When the information you are working with fits better in a column format, you have the ability to create columns within text objects. Select the text object, click the Columns button in the Paragraph group on the Home tab, then click either Two Columns, Three Columns, or More Columns. The More Columns option allows you to set up to 16 columns and customize the spacing between columns. You can display the ruler to set specific widths for the columns and further customize the columns.

PowerPoint 2010

Customizing Animation Effects

Animating objects allows you to control how information flows on the slide during a slide show. The simplest way to animate an object is to apply a standard animation effect from the Animation group on the Animations tab. There are additional entrance, emphasis, exit, and motion path animation effects available through the menu at the bottom of the Animation group that you can apply to objects. You can customize effect options including starting time, direction, and speed. And when you want to apply animation settings from one object to another, you can use the Animation Painter. You have been working on animating shapes on Slide 4, and you need to finish your work.

STEPS

1. **Click the Animations tab on the Ribbon, then click the Preview button in the Preview group**
   Watch the animations already applied to the objects on the slide.

QUICK TIP

To delete all animation effects from an object, select the object on the slide, click the More button in the Animation group, then click None.

2. **Click the upper-left arrow shape, click the More button ⊡ in the Animation group, click More Entrance Effects at the bottom of the gallery to open the Change Entrance Effect dialog box, click Wipe in the Basic section, then click OK**
   Notice a preview of the animation plays and an animation tag appears next to the arrow shape.

3. **Click the Effect Options button in the Animation group, click From Right, click the Start list arrow in the Timing group, click After Previous, then click the Preview button**
   Notice the animation tag number on the arrow shape changes from a 1 to a 0 indicating that the animation effect is now associated with the last object animated, which in this case is the lower-right flowchart shape.

4. **Click the upper-left flowchart shape, click Fade in the Animation group, click the Start list arrow in the Timing group, click After Previous, then click the Duration up arrow until 00.75 appears**
   The flowchart shape is animated after the arrow shape. Compare your screen to Figure E-6.

5. **Click the lower-right arrow shape, click the Animation Painter button in the Advanced Animation group, then click the upper-right arrow shape**
   Notice that when you use the Animation Painter all the animation settings from the lower-right arrow shape are applied to the upper-right arrow shape, including the Start setting (After Previous).

QUICK TIP

To set an animation to run after you click another object, click the Trigger button in the Advanced Animation group, point to On Click of, then select an object.

6. **Click the lower-right flowchart shape, click the Animation Painter button, click the upper-right flowchart shape, then click the Preview button**
   All of the animations play on the slide. Some of the animations would look better if they were delayed.

7. **Click the SmartArt graphic, click the Delay up arrow in the Timing group until 01.00 appears, click the lower-left arrow shape, click the Delay up arrow until 01.00 appears, then click the Preview button**
   There is more time to view the flowchart shapes.

8. **Apply a 01.00 delay to the other three arrow shapes, click the SmartArt graphic, click the Add Animation button in the Advanced Animation group, then click Swivel**
   The Add Animation feature allows you to apply multiple animations to the same object. The SmartArt graphic now has two animations.

9. **Click the Preview button, click the SmartArt graphic, then save your changes**
   Compare your screen to Figure E-7.

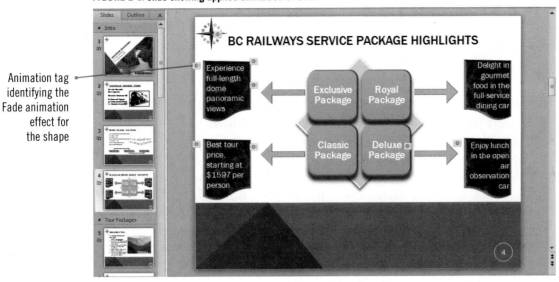

Animation tag identifying the Fade animation effect for the shape

FIGURE E-7: Slide showing completed animation effects

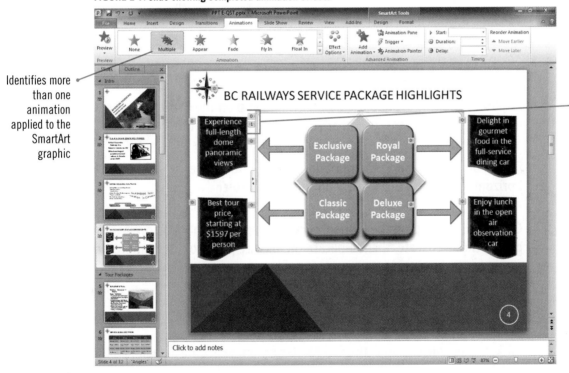

Identifies more than one animation applied to the SmartArt graphic

Identifies the two animations applied to the SmartArt graphic

Understanding animation timings

Each animated object on a slide has a starting time in relation to the other animated objects. There are three different starting time options: Start On Click, Start With Previous, and Start After Previous. The Start On Click timing option starts the animation effect when you click the mouse. The Start With Previous timing option begins the animation effect at the same time as the previous effect in the animation list, so two or more animation effects play at once. The Start After Previous timing option begins the animation immediately after the previous animation without clicking the mouse.

PowerPoint 2010

Creating Custom Slide Layouts

The standard slide layouts supplied in PowerPoint are adequate to create most of the slides for your presentation. However, if you are consistently modifying a standard slide layout for presentations, having a custom slide layout that you can reuse would be helpful. To create a custom slide layout, you choose from eight different placeholders to draw on the slide, including text, chart, and media placeholders. You create and save custom slide layouts in Slide Master view; these then become a part of the presentation. ▄▄▄ You decide to create a custom slide layout that displays picture thumbnails on the slide that you can use as navigation buttons during a slide show.

STEPS

1. **Click the View tab on the Ribbon, click the Ruler check box in the Show group, then click the Slide Master button in the Master Views group**

   Slide Master view opens, and the ruler is displayed.

2. **Click the last slide layout in the slide thumbnail pane, then click the Insert Layout button in the Edit Master group**

   A new slide layout is added to the presentation and appears in the slide thumbnail pane with a title text placeholder and footer placeholders as shown in Figure E-8. The new slide layout contains all of the slide background elements associated with the current theme.

3. **Click the Insert Placeholder list arrow in the Master Layout group, then click Picture**

   The pointer changes to ╋.

4. **Position ╋ on the slide so the pointer is lined up on the 4" mark on the left side of the horizontal ruler and the 2 ½" mark on the top of the vertical ruler**

   As you move the pointer on the slide its position is identified on the rulers by dotted lines.

5. **Drag a box down and to the right until the pointer is lined up with the 2 ½" mark on the horizontal ruler and the 1" mark on the vertical ruler**

   A 1 ½" square picture placeholder appears on the slide. You can duplicate the placeholder.

6. **Click the Home tab on the Ribbon, click the Copy button list arrow ▤ ▾ in the Clipboard group, click Duplicate, then duplicate the picture placeholder six more times**

   There are eight picture placeholders on the slide.

7. **Drag each picture placeholder to a position on the slide as shown in Figure E-9, then click the Slide Master tab on the Ribbon**

   The placeholders are arranged on the slide layout.

8. **Click the Rename button in the Edit Master group, select the default name, type Picture, click Rename, then position the pointer over the last slide layout in the slide thumbnail pane**

   The new name of the custom slide layout appears in the ScreenTip. The new Picture layout now appears when you click the Layout button or the New Slide list button in the Slides group on the Home tab.

9. **Right-click a blank area of the slide, click Ruler, click the Close Master View button in the Close group, then save your changes**

FIGURE E-8: New custom slide layout

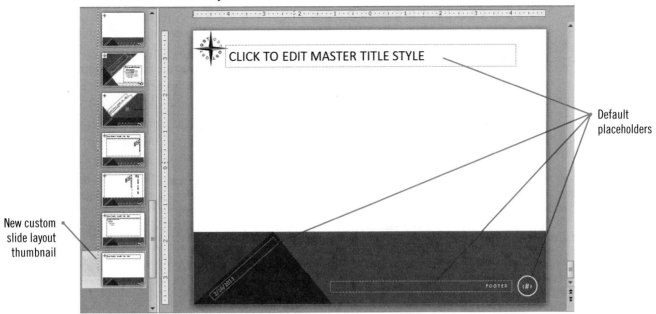

New custom slide layout thumbnail

Default placeholders

FIGURE E-9: Custom slide layout with new placeholders

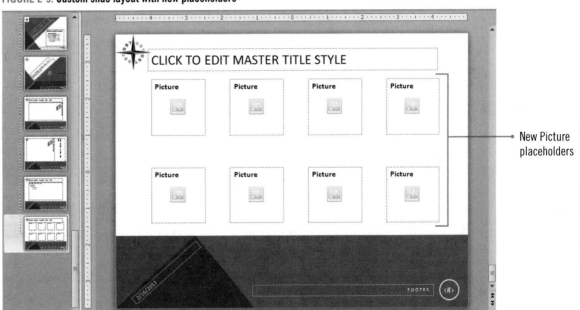

New Picture placeholders

Restoring the slide master layout

If the slide master is missing a placeholder, you can click the Master Layout button in the Master Layout group to reapply the placeholder. Clicking the Master Layout button opens the Master Layout dialog box, as shown in Figure E-10. Click the placeholder check box to reapply the placeholder. To restore a slide layout in Slide Master view, click the Insert Placeholder list arrow in the Master Layout group, click the desired type of placeholder, then draw the placeholder on the slide layout.

FIGURE E-10: Master Layout dialog box

Formatting Master Text

To ensure that you use a consistent blend of fonts and font styles throughout the presentation, you should format slide text using standard theme fonts or make changes to the text placeholders in Slide Master view. A font theme defines two fonts—a major font (for headings) and a minor font (for body text). The fonts used in a theme can be the same font or two contrasting fonts. You can also make specific changes to master text, by opening the Slide Master view and changing the text color, style, size, and bullet type. When you change a bullet type, you can use a character symbol from a font, a picture from the Clip Gallery (or other source), or an image that you scan into your computer. ▰▰▰▰ You decide to make a few formatting changes to the master text placeholder of your presentation.

STEPS

1. **Press [Shift], click the Normal button ⊞ on the status bar, release [Shift], then click the Angles Slide Master thumbnail in the slide thumbnail pane**
    Slide Master view appears with the slide master displayed in the Slide pane.

QUICK TIP
To insert a picture bullet, click Picture in the Bullets and Numbering dialog box, then click the desired image.

2. **Right-click Second level in the master text placeholder, point to Bullets on the shortcut menu, then click Bullets and Numbering**
    The Bullets and Numbering dialog box opens. The Bulleted tab is selected; the Numbered tab in this dialog box is used to create sequentially numbered or lettered bullets.

3. **Click Customize, click the Font list arrow, scroll down the list, then click Webdings**
    The Symbol dialog box displays the available bullet choices for the Webdings font.

4. **Scroll to the bottom of the symbol list, click the symbol shown in Figure E-11, then click OK**
    The new symbol appears in the Bullets and Numbering dialog box.

5. **Click the Color list arrow, then click Dark Green, Accent 4 in the Theme Colors section**

QUICK TIP
To reset the bullet to the default symbol, click Reset in the Bullets and Numbering dialog box. Clicking Reset does not change the color or size back to their original default settings.

6. **Click the Size down arrow until 80 appears, then click OK**
    The symbol and color of the new bullet in the second level of the master text placeholder changes. The size of the bullet is decreased to 80% of the size of the second-level text.

7. **Click the Fonts button in the Edit Theme group, scroll to the bottom of the font list, then click Trek**
    All of the fonts change for the presentation including all of the slide layouts in the slide thumbnail pane.

8. **Click the Close Master View button in the Close group, click the Slide 5 thumbnail in the Slides tab, then save your changes**
    You see how the changes affect the body text bullets in Normal view. Compare your screen to Figure E-12.

FIGURE E-11: **Symbol dialog box**

Webdings font

Click this bullet symbol

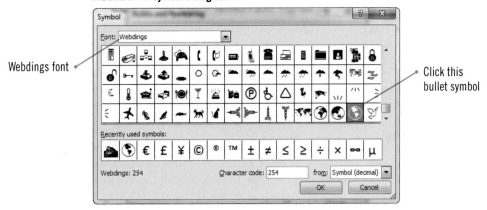

FIGURE E-12: **Slide showing new bullets and font theme**

New font theme

New bullet symbol

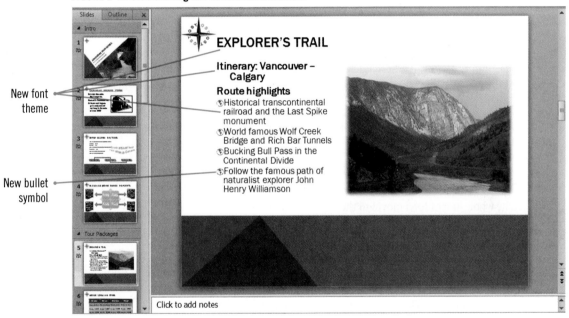

EXPLORER'S TRAIL

Itinerary: Vancouver – Calgary

Route highlights
- Historical transcontinental railroad and the Last Spike monument
- World famous Wolf Creek Bridge and Rich Bar Tunnels
- Bucking Bull Pass in the Continental Divide
- Follow the famous path of naturalist explorer John Henry Williamson

Click to add notes

Understanding exceptions to the slide master

If you change the format of text on a slide and then apply a different theme to the presentation, the slide that you formatted retains the text-formatting changes you made rather than taking the new theme formats. These format changes that differ from the slide master are known as exceptions. Exceptions can only be changed on the individual slides where they occur. For example, you might change the font and size of a particular text object on a slide to make it stand out and then decide later to add a different theme to your presentation. The text you formatted before you applied the theme is an exception, and it is unaffected by the new theme. Another way to override the slide master is to remove the background graphics on one or more slides. You might want to do this to get a clearer view of your slide text. Click the Design tab, then click the Hide Background Graphics check box in the Background group to select it.

Changing Master Text Indents

Master text and content placeholders have five levels of text, called **indent levels**. You can modify indent levels using PowerPoint's ruler. For example, you can change the space between a bullet and text of an indent level or change the position of the whole indent level. The position of each indent level on the ruler is represented by two small triangles and a square called **indent markers**. You can modify an indent level by moving these indent markers on the ruler. You can also set tabs on the horizontal ruler, which identifies where a text indent or a column of text begins. By clicking the **tab selector** located at the far left of the horizontal ruler, you are able to choose which of the four tab options you want to use. Table E-1 describes PowerPoint's indent and tab markers. ░░░░░ To better emphasize the text in the master text placeholder, you change the first two indent levels.

STEPS

1. **Press [Shift], click the** Normal button 🔲 **on the status bar, release [Shift], then click the** Angles Slide Master thumbnail **slide thumbnail pane**

   Slide Master view opens.

2. **Click** Second level **in the master text placeholder, click the** View tab **on the Ribbon, then click the** Ruler check box **in the Show group**

   The horizontal and vertical rulers for the master text placeholder appear. The indent markers, on the horizontal ruler, are set so that the first line of text—in this case, the bullet—begins to the left of subsequent lines of text. This is called a **hanging indent**.

   TROUBLE
   If you accidentally drag an indent marker past the ³⁄₈" mark, click the Undo button on the Quick Access toolbar and try again.

3. **Position** ⌖ **over the** Hanging Indent marker △, **then drag to the** ³⁄₈" **mark on the ruler**

   The space between the first indent-level bullet and text increases. Compare your screen to Figure E-13.

4. **Click** Third level **in the master text placeholder, then drag the** Left indent marker 🔲 **to the** ⁵⁄₈" **mark shown in Figure E-14**

   The whole indent level moves to the right.

5. **Click anywhere in the first line of text in the master text placeholder, then drag** △ **all the way to the left**

   This eliminates the hanging indent for this text level. Since there is no bullet for this level of text, there is no reason to have a hanging indent.

6. **Click** 🔲 **on the status bar, then click to the left of the word** Route **in the text object**

   Slide Master view closes, and Slide 5 appears in Normal view, showing the Master text indent changes in the text object. A left tab stop on the ruler allows you to move a word and align it with text below it.

7. **Click under the** ³⁄₈" **mark on the ruler, then press [Tab]**

   A left-aligned tab appears on the ruler. When you press [Tab] the word "Route" moves to the right and is aligned with the bullet text below it, as shown in Figure E-15.

8. **Add and apply left tabs at the** ³⁄₈" **mark on the ruler to the text objects on Slide 7 and Slide 9**

   Now Slides 5, 7, and 9 each have left tabs in the text objects.

9. **Click a blank area of Slide 9, click the** Ruler check box **in the Show group, click the** Home tab **on the Ribbon, then save your changes**

   The rulers close.

FIGURE E-13: Second-level text with moved hanging indent marker

Move the hanging indent marker to here

Space between the bullet and text increases

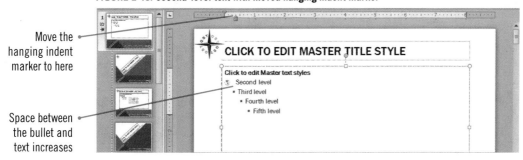

FIGURE E-14: Slide showing moved third-level indent level

Left indent marker

Indent level moves to the right

FIGURE E-15: Slide showing left tab stop

Left tab stop

Tabbed word

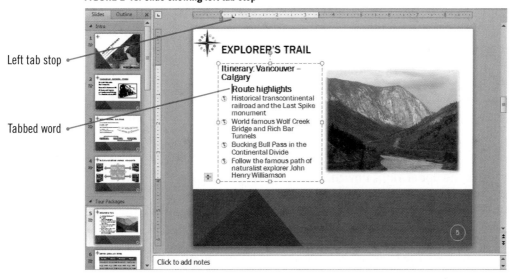

TABLE E-1: Indent and tab markers

symbol	name	function
▽	First line indent marker	Controls the position of the first line of text in an indent level
△	Hanging indent marker	Controls the position of the hanging indent
▭	Left indent marker	Controls the position of subsequent lines of text in an indent level
└	Left-aligned tab	Aligns tab text on the left
┴	Center-aligned tab	Aligns tab text in the center
┘	Right-aligned tab	Aligns tab text on the right
┴	Decimal-aligned tab	Aligns tab text on a decimal point

Adjusting Text Objects

You have complete control over the placement of text on slides in PowerPoint, whether the text is in a shape or in a text object. All text in PowerPoint is created within a text box, which has **margins** that determine the distance between the edge of the text and all four edges of the text box. The space between lines of text or bullets can also be modified. There are two types of text spacing in PowerPoint: paragraph spacing and leading (rhymes with "wedding"). **Paragraph spacing** is the space before and after paragraphs (bullet levels). **Leading** refers to the amount of space between lines of text within the same paragraph (bullet level). Using the text-alignment feature, you can move text within text boxes or shapes. ▰▰▰ You decide to move the text margin in the shapes on Slide 4, and then change paragraph spacing of the text object on Slide 2.

STEPS

1. **Click the** Slide 4 thumbnail **in the Slides tab, right-click a blank area of the slide, then click** Ruler **on the shortcut menu**
   Slide 4 appears in the slide pane with the rulers showing.

2. **Right-click the text in the upper-left flowchart shape, click** Format Picture **on the shortcut menu, then drag the Format Picture dialog box so you can see the shape on the slide**
   The Format Picture dialog box opens.

3. **Click** Text Box **in the left pane, in the Internal margin section click the** Top up arrow **until** 0.2" **appears, then click** Close
   This adjusts the top text margin down in the shape and centers the text within the shape.

4. **Adjust the text margins for the other three flowchart shapes so the text is centered in the shapes, then click a blank area of the slide**
   Not every flowchart shape requires the same amount of text margin adjustment. Compare your screen to Figure E-16.

5. **Click the** upper-left flowchart shape, **press [Shift], click the** lower-left flowchart shape, **release [Shift], click the** Home tab **on the Ribbon, then click** Align Text Left **button** ▤ **in the Paragraph group**
   The text in the left flowchart shape is aligned left and fits the shape better.

6. **Click the** upper-right flowchart shape, **press [Shift], click the** lower-right flowchart shape, **release [Shift], then click the** Align Text Right button ▤ **in the Paragraph group**
   The text in the right flowchart shapes is aligned right and fits the shape.

7. **Click the** Slide 2 thumbnail **in the Slides tab, press [Shift], click the** text object, **release [Shift], click the** Line Spacing button ▤ **in the Paragraph group, then click** Line Spacing Options
   The Paragraph dialog box opens.

8. **In the Spacing section type** 12 **in the Before text box, type** 8 **in the After text box, then click** OK
   The spacing before and after each bullet on Slide 2 increases. Compare your screen to Figure E-17.

9. **Right-click a blank area of the slide, click** Ruler **to close the ruler, then save your changes**

FIGURE E-16: Slide showing changed text margin

Changed text margin

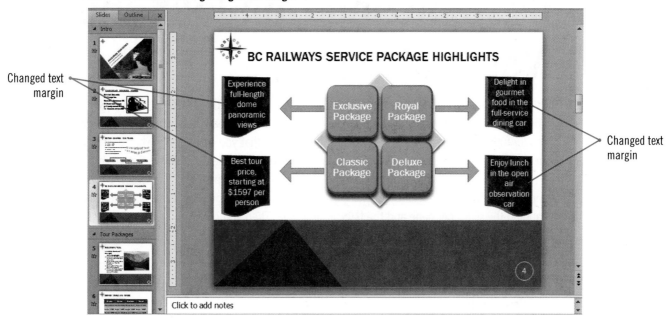

Changed text margin

FIGURE E-17: Slide showing changed line spacing

Changed line spacing between bullets

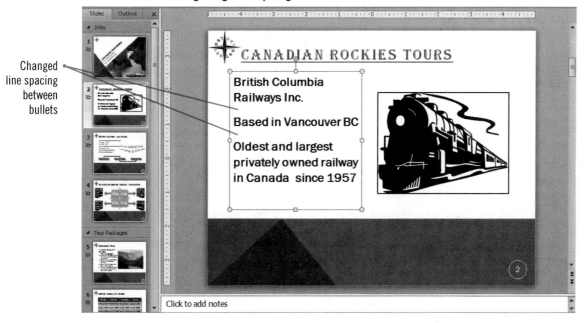

Changing text direction

Using the Text Direction button in the Paragraph group on the Home tab, you can change the direction of text in a text object or shape. There are four text direction options available: Horizontal, Rotate all text 90°, Rotate all text 270°, and Stacked. The Horizontal option is the standard default text direction for all text in PowerPoint. The Rotate all text 90° text direction rotates text so it faces the right margin of a text object or shape. The Rotate all text 270° text direction rotates text so it faces the left margin of a text object or shape. The Stacked text direction stacks letters vertically on top of one another.

Customizing Handout and Notes Masters

It is often helpful to provide your audience with supplemental materials to use during a presentation. Creating handouts for your audience provides them a way to follow along and take notes during your presentation and keep for future use. As the presenter, creating notes pages that you can refer to while giving the presentation can be extremely useful, especially when your presentation is complex or detailed. Before you create handouts or notes pages you might want to customize them to fit your specific needs. ░░░░░ You plan to create supplemental materials to hand out when you give the presentation. You customize the handout master by changing the slides per page and the background style. Then you change the notes master by changing the page setup and the notes page orientation. Finally, you print both handouts and notes pages.

STEPS

1. **Click the** View tab **on the Ribbon, then click the** Handout Master button **in the Master Views group**

   The presentation's Handout Master view appears, showing a page with six large empty placeholders that represent where the slides will appear when you print handouts. There are four smaller placeholders, one in each corner of the page, which are the header, footer, date, and number placeholders. Notice that the date placeholder displays today's date.

2. **Click the** Background Styles button **in the Background group, then click** Style 10

   When you print handouts on a color printer, they will have a gradient fill background.

3. **Click the** Slides Per Page button **in the Page Setup group, then click** 3 Slides

   Three slide placeholders appear on the left side of the handout as shown in Figure E-18.

4. **Click the** Header placeholder, **drag the** Zoom Slider **on the status bar to 100%, type** Canadian Train Tours, **press [Pg Dn], click the** Footer placeholder, **then type your name**

   Now your handouts are ready to print.

5. **Click the** Fit slide to current window button ▦ **on the status bar, click the** Close Master View **button in the Close group, then submit the presentation to your instructor**

   If you print the presentation for your instructor in this step, print using the Handouts 3 Slides print setting. Using this print setting, the presentation prints using the master options you've set.

6. **Click the** View tab **on the Ribbon, then click the** Notes Master button **in the Master Views group**

   Notes Master view opens showing four corner placeholders—one each for the header, footer, date, and page number—a large notes text box placeholder, and a large slide master image placeholder.

7. **Click the** Notes Page Orientation button **in the Page Setup group, then click** Landscape

   The page orientation changes to landscape. Notice that all of the text placeholders are now stretched out to fill the width of the page. Compare your screen to Figure E-19.

8. **Click the** Close Master View button **in the Close group, then submit the presentation to your instructor**

   If you print the presentation for your instructor in this step, print using the Notes Pages print setting. Using this print setting, notes pages of the presentation print in landscape orientation.

9. **Save your work, then exit PowerPoint**

FIGURE E-18: Handout Master view

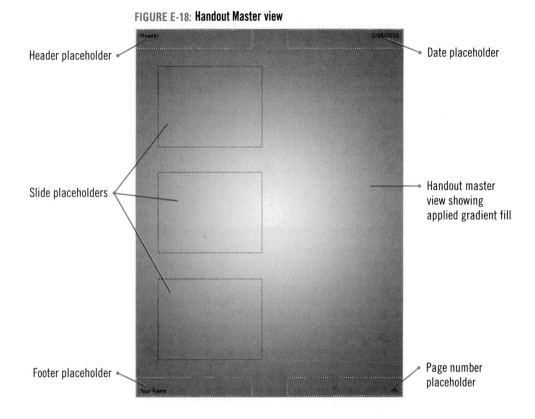

Header placeholder

Date placeholder

Slide placeholders

Handout master
view showing
applied gradient fill

Footer placeholder

Page number
placeholder

FIGURE E-19: Notes Master view with landscape orientation

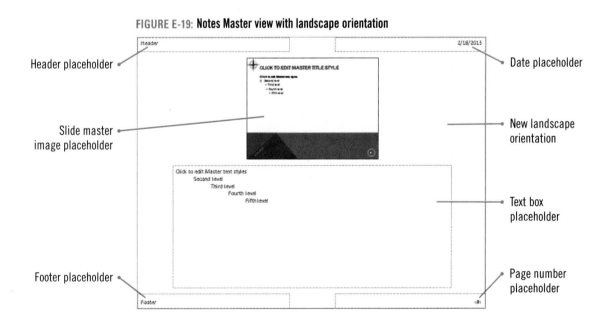

Header placeholder

Date placeholder

Slide master
image placeholder

New landscape
orientation

Text box
placeholder

Footer placeholder

Page number
placeholder

Creating handouts in Microsoft Word

Sometimes it's helpful to use a word-processing program like Microsoft Word to create detailed handouts or notes pages. You might also want to create a Word document based on the outline of your presentation. To send your presentation to Word, click the File tab on the Ribbon, click Save & Send, click Create Handouts, then click the Create Handouts button. The Send to Microsoft Word dialog box opens and provides you with five document layout options from which to choose. There are two layouts that include notes entered in the Notes pane. Select a layout, then click OK. Word opens and a new document opens with your inserted presentation, using the layout you selected. To send just the text of your presentation to Word, click the Outline only document layout.

Practice

For current SAM information, including versions and content details, visit SAM Central (http://www.cengage.com/samcentral). If you have a SAM user profile, you may have access to hands-on instruction, practice, and assessment of the skills covered in this unit. Since various versions of SAM are supported throughout the life of this text, check with your instructor for the correct instructions and URL/Web site for accessing assignments.

Concepts Review

Label each element of the PowerPoint window shown in Figure E-20.

FIGURE E-20

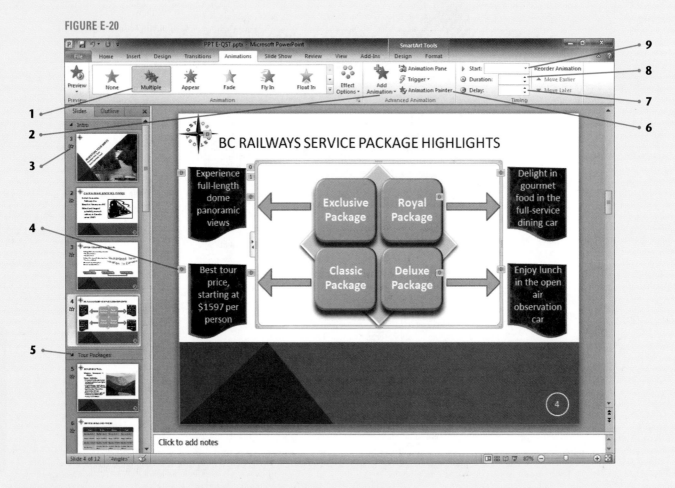

Match each term with the statement that best describes it.

10. **Indent marker**
11. **Indent level**
12. **Tab**
13. **Paragraph spacing**
14. **Hanging indent**
15. **Leading**

a. The space after a hard return
b. The space between lines of text
c. Represents the position of a text on the ruler
d. A text level in a text object, usually started with a bullet
e. Identifies where the text indent or column of text begins
f. The first line of text begins to the left of subsequent lines of text

Select the best answer from the list of choices.

16. Locking the _____ allows you to draw the same shape multiple times.

    a. connector shape

    b. shapes button

    c. drawing mode

    d. drawing pointer

17. Adjustment handles on a connector line:

    a. Alter the path of the line.

    b. Adjust the most prominent aspect of the line.

    c. Change the size of the line.

    d. Allow you to move a line off a connection site.

18. Which of the following statements about connectors is *not* true?

    a. The line connector has an adjustment handle in the middle of it to adjust the line's path.

    b. You can attach a connector to different points on a shape.

    c. A connector has red handles that attach to connection sites on shapes.

    d. Rearranging shapes connected with connectors moves the connectors to better connection sites.

19. The small triangles and square that represent the position of each level in a text placeholder are:

    a. Indent markers.

    b. Tabs.

    c. Ruler marks.

    d. Indent levels.

20. In PowerPoint, tabs:

    a. Determine the location of margins.

    b. Determine spacing between lines of text.

    c. Identify where a text indent begins.

    d. Can be only left- or center-aligned.

21. The Start _____ animation timing option allows you to play more than one animation at the same time.

    a. Before Previous

    b. With Previous

    c. On Click

    d. After Previous

Skills Review

1. Draw and format connectors.

    a. Start PowerPoint and open the presentation PPT E-2.pptx, then save it as **PPT E-General Report** to the drive and folder where you store your Data Files.

    b. Go to Slide 4, click the Shapes button in the Drawing group, right-click the Elbow Arrow Connector shape icon, then click Lock Drawing Mode.

    c. Position the pointer over the left connection site on the Plant shape, then drag to the top connection site on the Regional Warehouse shape.

    d. Position the pointer over the right connection site on the Plant shape, drag to the top connection site on the Individual Stores shape, then press [Esc].

    e. Click the Shapes button, click Line (top row), position the pointer over the right connection site on the Regional Warehouse shape, then drag to the left connection site on the Individual Stores shape.

    f. Click the Select button in the Editing group, click Selection Pane, press [Ctrl], click Elbow Connector 4, click Elbow Connector 2, release [Ctrl], then click the Selection and Visibility task pane Close button.

    g. Right-click one of the connectors, click Format Shape, make the line style for the connectors 2 point wide and change the line color to a black solid line, click Close, then deselect the objects.

    h. Right-click the connector between Regional Warehouse shape and the Individual Stores shape, click Format Shape, click the Dash type list arrow, click Dash Dot, then click Close.

    i. Save the presentation.

2. Use advanced formatting tools.

    a. Go to Slide 1, right-click the shape in the middle of the slide, then click Format Shape.

    b. Click the Gradient fill option button, click the Preset colors list arrow, then click Gold.

    c. Click Line Style in the left pane, then click the Width up arrow until **3 pt** appears.

    d. Click Shadow in the left pane, click the Presets list arrow, click Offset Bottom in the Outer section, click the Distance up arrow until **8 pt** appears, then click Close.

Skills Review (continued)

e. Click the Font Color button list arrow in the Font group, then click Black, Text 1.

f. Double-click the Format Painter button in the Clipboard group, go to Slide 4, apply the picked up styles to each of the diamond objects, press [Esc], then save your changes.

3. **Customize animation effects.**

a. Click the Animations tab, click the Plant shape, click the More button in the Animation group, then click Shape in the Entrance section.

b. Click the Effect Options button in the Animation group, then click Diamond.

c. Select the left elbow arrow connector, click the More button in the Animation group, click More Entrance Effects, apply the Strips animation, then click the Duration up arrow until **1.00** appears.

d. Click the Animation Painter button, then click the right elbow arrow connector.

e. Click Effects Options button, click Right Down, then click the Preview button.

f. Select the Regional Warehouse shape, add the Shape animation, then change the Effect Options to Diamond.

g. Use the Animation Painter to apply the same animation to the Individual Stores shape, then click the Preview button.

h. Click the Animation Pane button in the Advanced Animation group, click 4 Diamond 9 in the list, click the Re-Order up arrow button, then click Play in the Animation task pane.

i. Select the dotted line, click the More button in the Animation group, click More Entrance Effects, click Wipe, click OK, then change the Effect Options to From Right.

j. Click the Add Animation button, click Wipe, change the Effect Options to From Left, then click Play in the Animation Pane.

k. Click 2 Elbow Connector in the Animation Pane, press [Shift], click 6 Straight Connector 6 in the animation list, release [Shift] click the Start list arrow in the Timing group, then click After Previous.

l. Close the Animation task pane, preview the animations, then save your changes.

4. **Create custom slide layouts.**

a. Switch to Slide Master view, then click the last slide layout in the slide thumbnail pane.

b. Display the ruler and the drawing guides, then insert a new custom slide layout.

c. Add a 3" square Media placeholder, move the vertical guide left to 4.13, move the horizontal guide up to 1.02, then move the Media placeholder to the intersection of the guides.

d. Move the vertical guide right to 0.00, add a 4" × 3" Table placeholder, then move the placeholder to the intersection of the guides.

e. Name the custom slide layout **Media Table**, turn off guides, then save your changes.

5. **Format Master text.**

a. Click the Grid Slide Master thumbnail in the slide thumbnail pane, then format the first-level bulleted item in the master text placeholder as bold.

b. Change the bullet symbol of the first-level bullet to the Wingdings open book character bullet (code 38).

c. Use the Bullets and Numbering dialog box to set the size of the bullet to 75% of the text.

d. Change the bullet color to Black (Automatic).

e. Change the bullet symbol color of the second indent level to the Theme Color Tan, Accent 1, then save your changes.

6. **Change Master text indents.**

a. Move the hanging indent marker of the first-level bullet to the ½" mark on the ruler and left indent marker of the second-level bullet as shown in Figure E-21.

b. Hide the rulers, switch to Normal view, go to Slide 2, then save the presentation.

FIGURE E-21

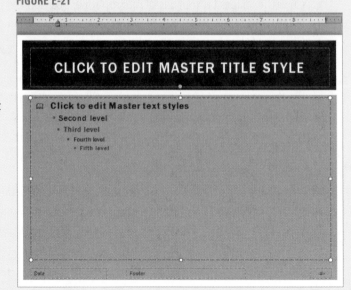

CLICK TO EDIT MASTER TITLE STYLE

Click to edit Master text styles
- Second level
  - Third level
    - Fourth level
      - Fifth level

Date   Footer

Skills Review (continued)

7. Adjust text objects.

a. Press [Shift], right-click anywhere in the text object on Slide 2, release [Shift] then click Format Shape on the shortcut menu.

b. Click Text Box in the left pane, then change the vertical alignment of the text to Top Centered.

c. Adjust the internal margin on the left and right sides to 0.5".

d. Click the Resize shape to fit text option button, then click Close. Figure E-22 shows you the completed presentation.

e. Save your changes.

8. Customize handout and notes masters.

a. Switch to Handout Master view.

b. Change the slides per page to 4 slides, then change the handout orientation to Landscape.

c. In the header text placeholder type **Corner BookStore**, then in the footer text placeholder type **Your Name**.

d. Close Handout Master view, then switch to Notes Master view.

e. Change the background style to Style 9, in the header text placeholder type **Product Report**, then in the footer text placeholder type your name.

f. Close Notes Master view, check the spelling, save your changes, then submit your presentation to your instructor. If you print the presentation, print as handouts, 2 slides per page.

g. Close the presentation and exit PowerPoint.

FIGURE E-22

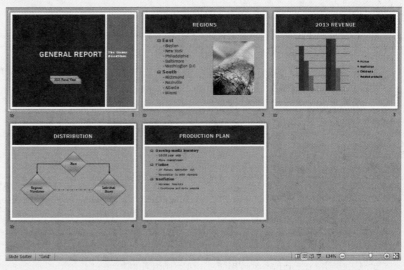

Independent Challenge 1

You work in marketing at gateWAY Records in Los Angeles, California. gateWAY Records is a record label that specializes in alternative music and hip hop. As a growing record company, your business is looking for investment capital to expand its business markets and increase sales. It is your responsibility to develop a presentation that the owners can present to potential investors. You have been working on the content of the presentation, and now you are ready to add custom animations and customize slide master text.

a. Open the presentation PPT E-3.pptx from the drive and folder where you store your Data Files, then save it as **PPT E-gateWAY**.

b. Preview the presentation in Reading View.

c. Open Slide Master view, click the Mylar Slide Master thumbnail, then bold the text in the first-level indent.

d. Add a bullet to the first-level indent. Apply the Webdings font character code 34 at 90% the size of text.

e. Adjust the indent markers for the second indent level as shown in Figure E-23.

FIGURE E-23

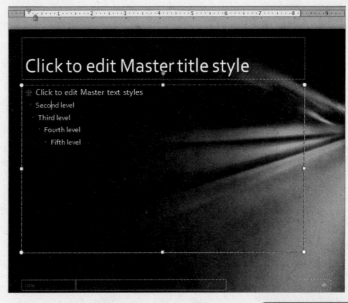

Independent Challenge 1 (continued)

f. Convert the text on Slide 4 to a SmartArt graphic using the Vertical Box List SmartArt graphic layout, then apply the Subtle Effect SmartArt Style to the graphic.

g. Go to Slide 6, create at least two shapes connected by connectors and format all of the objects using advanced formatting techniques you learned in the lesson.

h. Apply animation effects to objects and text on at least three slides, then preview the presentation in Slide Show view.

i. Add your name and the slide number to the slides footer (except the title slide), check spelling, save the presentation, then submit your presentation to your instructor.

j. Close the presentation and exit PowerPoint.

Independent Challenge 2

You are the owner of 2 Guys Gourmet catering company in Vancouver, British Columbia. You have built your business on private parties, wedding receptions, and special events over the last five years. To expand your business, you decide to pursue the business and formal events markets. Use PowerPoint to develop a presentation that you can use to gain corporate catering accounts.

a. Open the presentation PPT E-4.pptx from the drive and folder where you store your Data Files, then save it as **PPT E-Gourmet**.

b. Open Slide Master view, then click the Paper Slide Master thumbnail. Change the Font theme to Waveform, then change the bullet in the first-level indent level to an arrow bullet 90% of text size.

c. Adjust the indent marker for the first indent level so there is $1/8$" of space between the arrow bullet and the text.

d. Search PowerPoint clip art and add an image of a polar bear to the slide master. Format the clip art as necessary.

e. Connect the shapes on Slide 4 using arrow connectors. Draw an Elbow Double-Arrow connector between each shape formatted with a black 3 pt Square Dot dash line.

f. Change the left internal margin of each shape on Slide 4 to 0".

g. Switch to Slide 2 and change the line spacing to 3 pt Before and 6 pt After in the text object.

h. Create a new custom slide layout using at least two different placeholders, then save the new layout as **Custom1**.

i. View the presentation in Reading view, then add your name and slide number to the slides footer (except the title slide).

Advanced Challenge Exercise

- Switch to Slide 5, then select the bulleted list text object.
- Click the Home tab on the Ribbon, then click the Columns button in the Paragraph group.
- Click Two Columns, click the Columns button again, then click More Columns.
- Click the Spacing up arrow until 0.3 appears, then click OK.
- Save the presentation as **PPT E-Gourmet ACE** to the drive and folder where you store your Data Files.

j. Check spelling, save the presentation, then submit your presentation to your instructor.

k. Close the presentation and exit PowerPoint.

Independent Challenge 3

You are a computer game designer for Ultimate Games, an Internet interactive game developer. One of your responsibilities is to develop new interactive game concepts and present the information at a company meeting. Complete the presentation provided, which promotes two new interactive Internet game concepts you've developed. Use the following game ideas in your presentation or create two of your own game ideas.

- *Army Ghosts* is an interactive World War II game where you play a military spy who goes on missions behind enemy lines. You have the option to play with and against others online to achieve one of six different objectives.
- *The Knights Order* is an interactive medieval action/adventure game where you play a mercenary who battles against evil forces to save kingdoms from destruction.

Independent Challenge 3 (continued)

a. Open the presentation PPT E-5.pptx from the drive and folder where you store your Data Files, then save it as **PPT E-Ultimate**. If you develop your own material, open a new presentation, storyboard the ideas for the presentation, then create at least six slides. What do you want your audience to know about the product idea?

b. Apply a theme. Modify the theme as necessary, such as changing background objects, font theme, color theme, or effect theme.

c. Use clip art, photos, shapes, connectors, and other objects as necessary to enhance the presentation.

d. Edit any text and add any additional information to create a professional presentation.

e. Format the Master text and title placeholders on the slide master to fit the subject matter. Change the bullet for the first indent level in the Master text placeholder.

f. Create a custom slide layout, name it **Concept**, then apply it to at least one slide in the presentation.

g. Change the page orientation of the Notes Master view to Landscape, add your name to the notes and handouts footer, then save the presentation.

h. View the presentation in Slide Show view, check spelling, save the presentation, then submit your presentation to your instructor.

Advanced Challenge Exercise

- Click the File button, click Save and Send, click Create Handouts, then click the Create Handouts button.
- Click the Blank lines below slides option button, then click OK.
- Save the document as **PPT E-Ultimate Handouts** to the drive and folder where you store your Data Files.
- Submit the document to your instructor, close the document, then exit Word.

i. Close the presentation and exit PowerPoint.

Real Life Independent Challenge

You work for the operations manager at the Capital University Student Activities Center. You have been working on a presentation that you eventually will publish to the college Web site that describes all of the services offered at the Student Activities Center. Complete work on the presentation by working with masters and animation effects.

a. Open the presentation PPT E-6.pptx from the drive and folder where you store your Data Files, then save it as **PPT E-Capital U**.

b. Apply animation effects to at least four objects in the presentation. Customize the animation settings as necessary.

c. Create a custom slide layout, and apply it to a slide.

d. Format the bullet and text in the Master text and title placeholders on the slide master to fit the subject matter.

e. Modify Master text indents on the slide master.

f. Change the page orientation of Handout Master view to Landscape, add your name to the notes and handouts footer, and save the presentation.

g. Adjust the alignment and line spacing of at least one text object.

h. Check spelling, view the final slide show, then submit your presentation to your instructor.

i. Close the presentation and exit PowerPoint.

Visual Workshop

Create a slide that looks like the example in Figure E-24. Be sure to use connector lines. Use the features on the Drawing Tools Format tab and specifically the Shape Outline button to customize the connector lines. Add your name to the slide footer, then save the presentation as **PPT E-Development**. Submit your presentation to your instructor, then exit PowerPoint.

FIGURE E-24

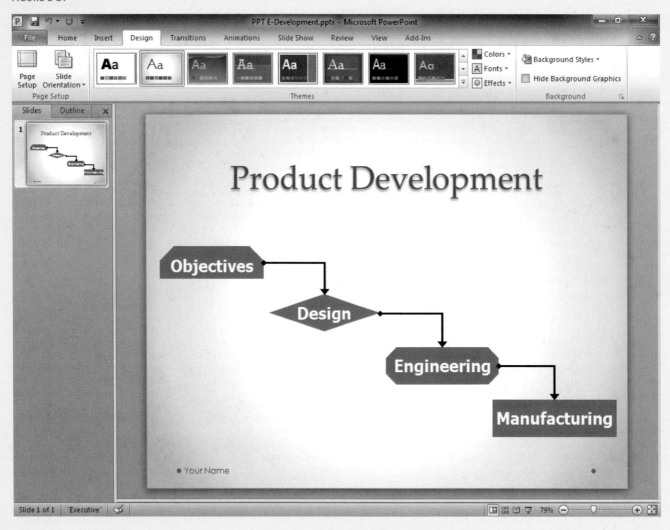

Enhancing Charts

A PowerPoint presentation is first and foremost a visual communication tool. Slides that deliver information with relevant graphics have a more lasting impact on an audience than slides with plain text. The most effective way to display numerical data is to show the data graphically in a chart. You can show numerical data in many different ways including columns, bars, lines, or pie wedges. When choosing a chart type, it is important to consider which type of chart best illustrates your data. For example, a pie chart is designed to display data from one data series in proportion to the sum of all the data series; whereas, a column chart is designed to display data changes over time or for demonstrating comparisons among data points.  In this unit, you continue to work on the Quest Specialty Travel (QST) presentation that includes charts. You customize the chart layout, format chart elements, and animate the chart. Finally, you embed an Excel chart, and then you link an Excel worksheet to the presentation.

OBJECTIVES

Work with charts in PowerPoint

Change chart design and style

Customize a chart layout

Format chart elements

Animate a chart

Embed an Excel chart

Link an Excel worksheet

Update a linked Excel worksheet

Working with Charts in PowerPoint

One of the best ways to enhance a presentation is to insert graphic elements such as a chart. When you have numerical data that you want to compare, a chart helps the audience visualize and understand the information. Because Excel is integrated with PowerPoint, you can easily create fantastic-looking charts on the presentation slides. ▆▆▆▆▆ As you continue to develop the QST presentation, you plan to include charts on several slides. You review the features, benefits, and methods of charting in PowerPoint.

DETAILS

- **Create charts using Excel from within PowerPoint**

  If you have Microsoft Office 2010 installed on your computer, PowerPoint uses Excel, by default, to create charts. When you create a chart using the Chart button in PowerPoint, a sample chart is placed on the slide and a separate Excel window opens beside the PowerPoint window displaying the chart's data in a worksheet. Displaying both program windows at the same time provides you with the ability to work directly on the chart in the Excel window and see the changes on the slide in the PowerPoint window. See Figure F-1. If you don't have Excel, Microsoft Graph opens and displays a chart and a datasheet where you can enter your own data.

- **Embed or link a chart**

  You have some options to choose from when inserting an Excel chart to your presentation. There are two ways to add a chart to a slide: you can embed it or link it. An embedded chart is an object created in another program and inserted in a slide. An embedded chart becomes a part of the presentation like a picture or a piece of clip art. The embedded chart's data is stored in an Excel worksheet that is included with the presentation file. You can embed a chart in PowerPoint using the Chart button on the Insert tab or by copying a chart from Excel and pasting it on a slide. A linked chart is also created in another program, but it is saved in a separate file and not with the presentation. If you want to make changes to a linked Excel chart, you must open the saved Excel file that contains the chart.

- **Modify charts using styles and layouts**

  Because themes and theme effects are alike for all Office programs, you can apply a specific theme or effect to a chart in Excel, and PowerPoint will recognize the theme or effect. Using themes gives your chart a consistent look with other objects in your presentation; however, you can fine-tune individual elements, such as the data series or legend of your chart. In addition, there are a number of chart layouts that you can apply to your chart. A chart layout specifies where chart elements, such as axes titles, data labels, and the legend, are displayed within the chart area. You cannot create your own chart layouts and styles, but you can create a template of a customized chart, which you can use later to apply to another chart.

- **Add advanced formatting to charts**

  If the basic predefined chart styles do not provide you with the formatting options you want, you can choose to modify individual elements. For example, you may want to alter the way data labels look or how axes are displayed. You can specify the axes scales and adjust the interval between the values or categories. You can also add trendlines and error bars to a chart to provide more information about the data. A **trendline** is a graphical representation of an upward or downward trend in a data series, also used to predict future trends. **Error bars** identify potential error amounts relative to each data marker in a data series. Figure F-2 displays some advanced formatting items.

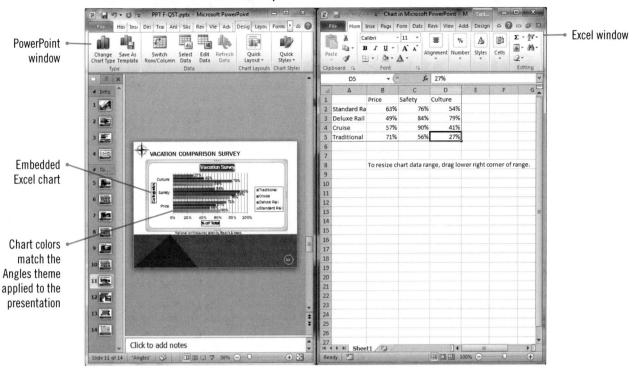

PowerPoint window

Excel window

Embedded Excel chart

Chart colors match the Angles theme applied to the presentation

FIGURE F-2: Formatted chart

Data label

Vertical axis title

Error bar

Horizontal axis title

Changing page setup and slide orientation

When you need to customize the size and orientation of the slides in your presentation, you can do so using the commands in the Page Setup group on the Design tab on the Ribbon. Click the Page Setup button to open the Page Setup dialog box. In the Page Setup dialog box, you can change the width and height of the slides to 12 different settings, including On-screen Show, Letter Paper, 35mm Slides, and Banner. You can also set a custom slide size by determining the height and width of the slides. If the presentation would work better in Portrait rather than Landscape mode, you can set the slide orientation in the Page Setup dialog box by clicking the Slide Orientation option button in the Slides section. The orientation setting for the slides is separate from the orientation setting for the notes, handouts, and outline. To change slide orientation of the presentation from the Ribbon, click the Slide Orientation button in the Page Setup group on the Design tab.

PowerPoint 2010

Changing Chart Design and Style

Being able to use Excel to create charts in PowerPoint offers you many advantages, including the ability to format charts using Excel Chart tools to customize the design, layout, and formatting. After you create a chart, you can immediately alter the way it looks by changing different individual chart elements or by applying a predefined chart layout or style. For example, you can select a chart layout that adds a chart title and moves the legend to the bottom of the chart. You can also easily change the color and effects of chart elements by applying one of the styles found in the Chart Styles gallery. The chart that includes survey results needs some work. You change the chart layout, style, and type of the chart on Slide 11.

STEPS

1. **Start PowerPoint, open the presentation** PPT F-1.pptx **from the drive and folder where you store your Data Files, save the presentation as** PPT F-QST, **then click the** Slide 11 **thumbnail in the Slides tab**
   Slide 11 appears in the Slide pane.

2. **Click the** chart, **then click the** Chart Tools Design tab **on the Ribbon**
   The chart is selected and ready to edit.

3. **Click the** More button ⏷ **in the Chart Layouts group, then click** Layout 9 **in the Layout gallery**
   This particular layout option adds a chart title and value and category axis titles to the chart, as shown in Figure F-3.

4. **Click** Chart Title, **type** Vacation Survey, **click** Vertical (Value) Axis Title, **type** % of Total, **click** Horizontal (Category) Axis Title, **type** Categories, **then click in a blank area of the chart**
   The new chart labels help identify aspects of the chart.

5. **Click the** More button ⏷ **in the Chart Styles group, then click** Style 18
   The Style 18 option removes some shading and dark colors to make the chart easier to read. This new style option also adds a light outline to the data series markers, for better contrast between the markers.

6. **Click the** Change Chart Type button **in the Type group**
   The Change Chart Type dialog box opens.

7. **Click** Bar **in the left pane, make sure that** Clustered Bar **is selected, then click** OK
   The data series markers change from columns to bars and rotate 90 degrees. Notice also that the value and category axis have switched places with this new chart type. Compare your screen to Figure F-4.

8. **Click a blank area of the slide, then save your presentation**

FIGURE F-3: Chart showing new layout

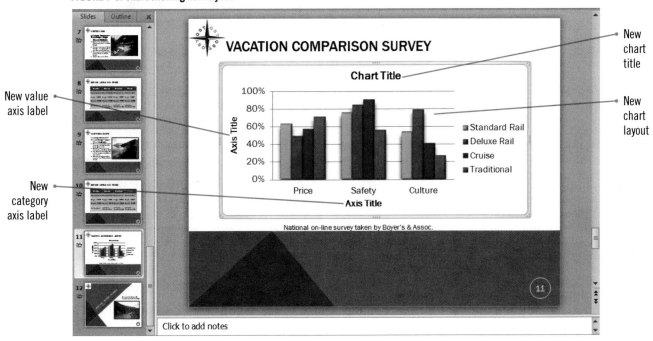

New value axis label

New category axis label

New chart title

New chart layout

FIGURE F-4: Chart showing new style and axis labels

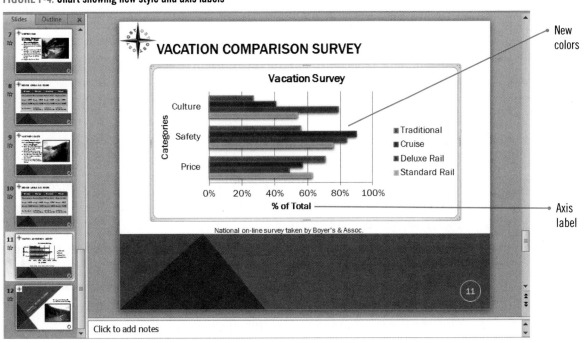

New colors

Axis label

Saving a chart as a template

If you create a customized chart that you want to reuse, you can save it as a template (*.crtx) to the Charts Template folder. A chart template stores the formatting and layout of a chart. Then, instead of re-creating the chart type, you simply apply the chart template to an existing chart or create a new chart based on the template. To

save a chart as a template, select the chart you want to save, then click the Save As Template button in the Type group on the Chart Tools Design tab. To apply a chart template to an existing chart, click the Change Chart Type button in the Type group, click Templates, then click the chart template.

Customizing a Chart Layout

One of the many advantages of using Excel to create charts in PowerPoint is the ability you have to customize chart elements, such as labels, axes, gridlines, and the chart background. For example, you can change the plot area color so the data markers are distinctly set off, or you can add gridlines to a chart. Gridlines help make the data easier to read in the chart and extend from the horizontal axis or the vertical axis across the plot area. There are two types of gridlines: major gridlines and minor gridlines. **Major gridlines** identify major units on the axis and are usually identified by a tick mark. **Tick marks** are small lines of measurement that intersect an axis and identify the categories, values, or series in a chart. **Minor gridlines** identify minor units on the axis and can also be identified by a tick mark. You decide to improve the appearance of the chart by customizing some elements of the chart.

STEPS

QUICK TIP
You can easily add or remove a legend by clicking the Legend button in the Labels group on the Chart Tools Layout tab.

1. **Click the chart, click the Chart Tools Layout tab on the Ribbon, then click the Gridlines button in the Axes group**

   The Gridlines menu opens. The chart already has major gridlines on the vertical axis.

2. **Point to Primary Vertical Gridlines, then click Major & Minor Gridlines**

   This adds minor vertical gridlines to the chart as shown in Figure F-5. Notice that the major gridlines are darker in color than the minor gridlines and are identified by a tick mark on the value axis at each unit of value.

3. **Click the Data Table button in the Labels group, then click Show Data Table with Legend Keys**

   You like seeing the data displayed in the data table because it helps define the data markers. However, using the data table takes up too much room on the slide and significantly decreases the size of the chart making it unreadable.

4. **Click the Data Table button in the Labels group, click None, click the Data Labels button in the Labels group, then click Center**

   The data table closes, and data labels appear in the center of each data marker. The data labels are a little hard to read in the center of the data markers.

5. **Click the Data Labels button in the Labels group, click Outside End**

   The data labels move to the end of the data markers.

QUICK TIP
To format any chart element quickly, right-click the element, then choose a command from the submenu or the Mini toolbar.

6. **Click the Axis Titles button in the Labels group, point to Primary Horizontal Axis Title, then click More Primary Horizontal Axis Title Options**

   The Format Axis Title dialog box opens.

7. **Click Border Color in the left pane, click the Solid line option button, click the Color list arrow, click Red, Accent 2 in the top row, then click Close**

   A dark red border appears around the value axis title. The category axis title would also look good with a border around it.

8. **Click the Vertical (Category) Axis Title, then press [F4]**

   A dark red border appears around the category axis title. Pressing [F4] repeats the last formatting action.

9. **Click a blank area of the slide, then save your presentation**

   Compare your screen to Figure F-6.

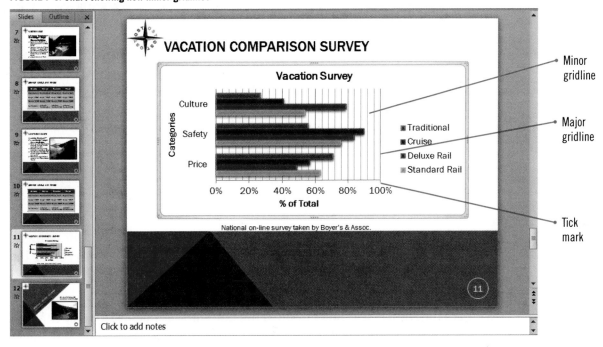

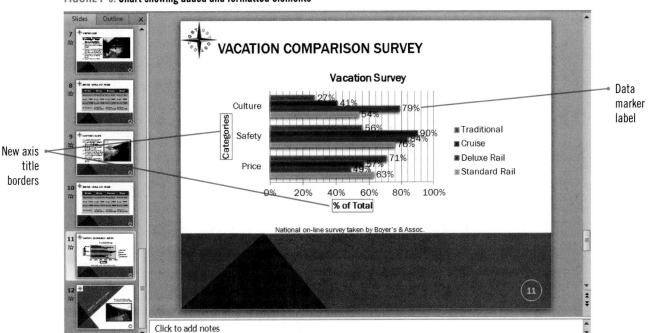

Using the Research task pane

Sometimes when you are developing a presentation, you need help formulating your ideas or researching a subject. PowerPoint has an extensive set of online tools found in the Research task pane that gives you immediate access to many different kinds of information. The Research task pane provides the following research tools: an English dictionary; an English, French, and Spanish thesaurus; a word and phrase translator; three research Web sites; and two business research Web sites. To open the Research task pane, click the Research button in the Proofing group on the Review tab. The Research options link at the bottom of the Research task pane provides additional research books and research sites that you can add to the Research task pane.

Formatting Chart Elements

Quick Styles in PowerPoint provide you with a number of choices to modify all the elements in a chart. Even with all the Quick Style choices, you still may want to format individual elements to make the chart easy to read and understand. Overall, you like what you have done to the vacation survey chart so far, but you decide to format some individual elements of the chart to better fit the QST presentation design. You also consider using the copy and paste commands for inserting other charts on a slide.

1. **Click a blank area in the Chart, click the Chart Tools Layout tab on the Ribbon, click the Chart Area list arrow in the Current Selection group, then click Series "Standard Rail"**
   All of the Standard Rail data markers are selected in the chart.

2. **Click the Chart Tools Format tab on the Ribbon, click the Shape Fill list arrow in the Shape Styles group, point to Gradient, then click Linear Diagonal – Bottom Left to Top Right in the Dark Variations section (bottom row)**
   The Standard Rail data series markers change to gradient fill.

3. **Click the Format Selection button in the Current Selection group to open the Format Data Series dialog box, drag the Series Overlap slider to the left towards Separated until –50% appears in the Series Overlap text box, then click Close**
   A small space is applied between the data markers for each data series in the chart. You can enter a value from –100 percent to 100 percent in the Series Overlap text box. A negative number adds space between each data marker, and a positive number overlaps the data markers. Compare your screen to Figure F-7.

4. **Click the Vacation Survey chart title, then click the More button ▾ in the Shape Styles group**
   The Shapes Style gallery opens.

5. **Click Moderate Effect – Dark Purple, Accent 5 (5th row), then click any one of the numbers on the Horizontal (Value) Axis**
   Applying the new style to the chart title makes it stand out. Clicking any of the numbers on the value axis selects the entire axis.

6. **Click the More button ▾ in the Shape Styles group, click Subtle Line – Accent 1 (1st row), click any one of the words on the Vertical (Category) Axis, then click Subtle Line – Accent 1 in the Shape Styles group**
   The new style applies an orange color to the axis and better defines the plot area.

7. **Right-click the chart legend, then click Format Legend in the shortcut menu**
   The Format Legend dialog box opens.

8 **Click Border Color in the left pane, click the Solid line option button, click the Color list arrow ▨ ▾, click Dark Green, Accent 4 (top row), then click Close**
   A solid dark green border line appears around the legend.

9. **Click a blank area of the slide, then save the presentation**
   Compare your screen to Figure F-8.

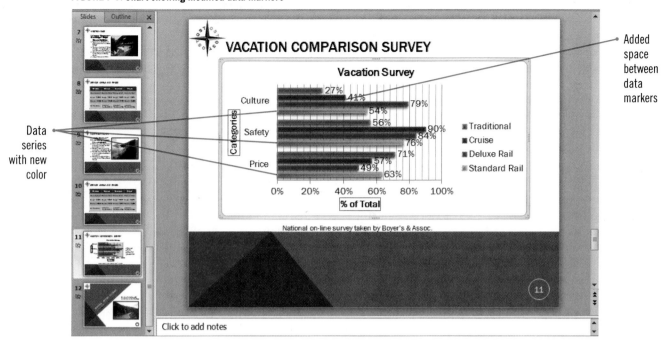

Added space between data markers

Data series with new color

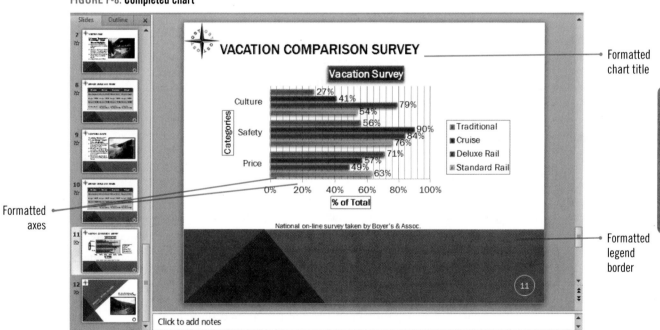

Formatted chart title

Formatted axes

Formatted legend border

Changing PowerPoint options

You can customize your installation of PowerPoint by changing various settings and preferences. To change PowerPoint settings, click the File tab on the Ribbon, then click Options to open the PowerPoint Options dialog box. In the dialog box there are nine sections identified in the left pane, which offer you ways to customize PowerPoint. For example, the General area includes options for viewing the Mini toolbar, enabling Live Preview, and personalizing your copy of Office.

Animating a Chart

You can animate elements of a chart, much in the same way you animate text and graphics. You can animate the entire chart as one object, or you can animate the data markers. There are two options for animating data markers individually: by series or by category. Animating data markers individually by series displays data markers of each data series (or the same-colored data markers). Animating data markers individually by category displays the data markers of each category in the chart. If you choose to animate the chart's data markers as a series, the entire data series is animated as a group; the same is true for animating data markers by category. 💾💾 You decide to animate the data series markers of the chart.

STEPS

1. **Verify that the chart is selected, click the Animations tab on the Ribbon, click the More button ▾ in the Animation group, then click Random Bars**

   The Random Bars entrance animation is applied to the entire chart, and PowerPoint plays the animation.

2. **Click the Animation Pane button in the Advanced Animation group, then click the Content Placeholder 8 list arrow**

   The Animation Pane opens and displays specific information, such as the type of animation (Entrance, Exit, Emphasis, or Motion Path), the sequence and timeline of the animation, and the name of the animated object. Clicking an animation's list arrow provides access to other custom options. Compare your screen to Figure F-9.

3. **Click ▾ in the Animation group, click Fly In, then click the Duration up arrow in the Timing group until 1.00 appears**

   The Fly In entrance animation replaces the Random Bars entrance animation. A longer duration, or animation timing, slows down the animation.

4. **Click the Effect Options button in the Animation group, point to each option in the Direction and Sequence sections of the gallery and watch the Live Preview of the animation, then click By Elements in Series in the Sequence section**

   Each data series marker, by series, flies in from the left of the slide beginning with the Standard Rail data series. There are now 13 animation tags, one for the chart background and one for each data series marker.

5. **Click the Expand contents arrow ⩔ in the Animation Pane, click the first animation tag 1 on the slide, click Fade in the Animation group, then click the Duration up arrow until 1.50 appears**

   The Fade animation is now applied to the chart background. Notice the timeline icon for the chart background animation is wider to account for the longer duration.

6. **Click the Play button in the Animation Pane, then watch all the animations**

   The chart background fades into view, then data series markers fly in from the left one after another. Notice the advancing timeline (vertical blue line) as it moves over each animation in the Animation Pane.

7. **Click the Hide contents arrow ⩓ in the Animation Pane, click the Delay up arrow until .50 appears, then click the Play button in the Animation Pane**

   A half second delay is applied between each animation. Watch closely at how the changed settings affect the progression of the animated data series markers.

8. **Click the Start list arrow in the Timing group, click After Previous, click the Trigger button in the Advanced Animation group, point to On Click of, then click Title 1**

   Now when Slide 11 appears in Slide Show view, you can click the slide title to play the chart animations. The animation tags combine into one lightning bolt tag indicating the animation has a trigger.

9. **Click the Slide Show button ▣ on the status bar, click the slide title, watch the animation, press [Esc], close the Animation Pane, then save the presentation**

   Compare your screen to Figure F-10.

FIGURE F-9: Screen showing added animation effect

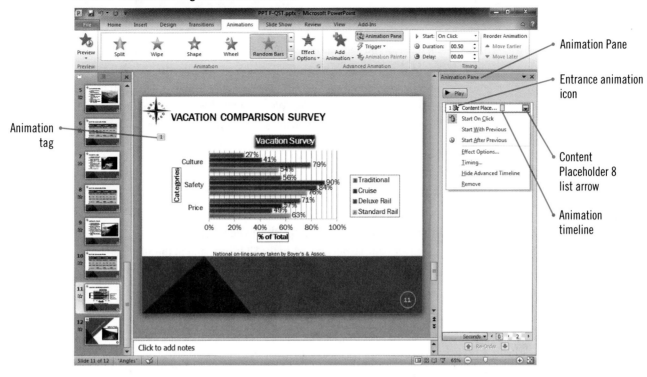

Animation Pane

Entrance animation icon

Animation tag

Content Placeholder 8 list arrow

Animation timeline

FIGURE F-10: Finished chart

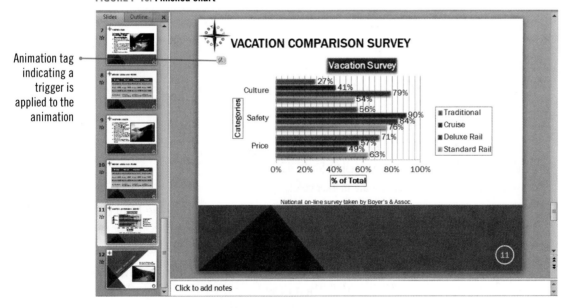

Animation tag indicating a trigger is applied to the animation

Adjusting screen resolution and improving performance

If your presentation runs too slow or shudders during a slide show, one possible solution is to adjust the resolution setting PowerPoint uses during a slide show. By default, the resolution used during a slide show is the resolution of the monitor displaying the show. To change the slide show resolution, click the Slide Show tab on the Ribbon, click the Resolution button in the Monitors group, then click a different resolution option. Lower resolutions provide faster speeds but poor picture quality, while higher resolutions provide slower speeds and better picture quality. Other ways to improve performance include reducing single letter and single word animations, reducing the size of animated pictures, and reducing the number of simultaneous animations. Objects that have gradient or transparent fills also slow performance.

PowerPoint 2010

Embedding an Excel Chart

When a chart is the best way to present information on a slide, you can create one within PowerPoint or you can embed an existing Excel chart directly to the slide. When you use another program to create an object, the program, Excel in this case, is known as the **source program**. The object you create with the source program is saved to a file called the **source file**. When you embed a chart into a presentation, the presentation file in which the chart is embedded becomes the **destination file**. ▰▰▰▰ You want to include other supporting data from last year's sales numbers in your presentation, so you embed an Excel chart on a new slide.

STEPS

QUICK TIP
You can also press [Ctrl][D] to duplicate a slide in the Slides tab.

1. **Click the** Slide 12 thumbnail **in the Slides tab, click the** Home tab **on the Ribbon, click the** New Slide list arrow **in the Slides group, then click** Title Only

   A new slide with the Title Only layout appears in the Slide pane and in the Slides tab.

2. **Click the** slide title placeholder, **type** Quarterly Profit Figures, **click the** Insert tab **on the Ribbon, then click the** Object button **in the Text group**

   The new slide title appears in capital letters because of the presentation theme. The Insert Object dialog box opens. Using this dialog box, you can create a new chart or locate an existing one to insert on a slide.

QUICK TIP
Another way to embed a chart is to open the chart in Excel, copy it, and then paste it into your slide.

3. **Click the** Create from file option button, **click** Browse, **locate the drive and folder where you store your Data Files, click the file** PPT F-2.xlsx, **click OK, then click OK in the Insert Object dialog box**

   The chart containing the quarterly profit figures appears and is embedded on the slide. You can open the chart and use the commands in Excel to make any changes to it.

4. **Double-click the** chart **to open it in Microsoft Office Excel**

   The chart appears inside an Excel worksheet on the slide. Excel commands and tabs appear on the Ribbon under the PowerPoint title bar as shown in Figure F-11.

5. **Click the** Sheet 2 tab **at the bottom of the Excel worksheet, click cell B5, type** 17490.10, **press [Enter], then click the** Sheet 3 tab

   The changed number is reflected for the Quarter 1 UK data series in the chart.

QUICK TIP
If the chart you want to embed is in another presentation, you can open both presentations and then copy and paste the chart from one presentation to the other.

6. **Click the** chart, **click the** Chart Tools Design tab **on the Ribbon, click the** More button ▾ **in the Chart Styles group, then click** Style 42 (bottom row)

   The chart style changes with new data marker colors and a new plot area color.

7. **Right-click the** Vertical (Value) Axis, **click the** Bold button **B** **on the Mini toolbar, click the** Horizontal (Category) Axis, **then press [F4]**

   Both the value and category axes labels are bold and now easier to read.

8. **Click outside the chart to exit Excel, drag the chart's** upper-left sizing handle **until the chart is under the word "Quarterly", then drag the** upper-right sizing handle **up and to the right until the chart is directly under the slide title**

   Compare your screen to Figure F-12.

9. **Click a blank area of the slide, then save the presentation**

FIGURE F-11: **Inserted Excel chart**

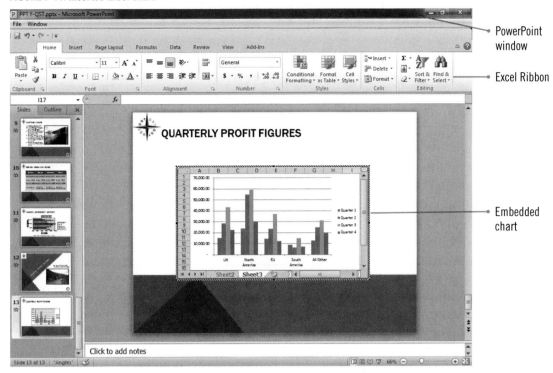

- PowerPoint window
- Excel Ribbon
- Embedded chart

FIGURE F-12: **Formatted Excel chart**

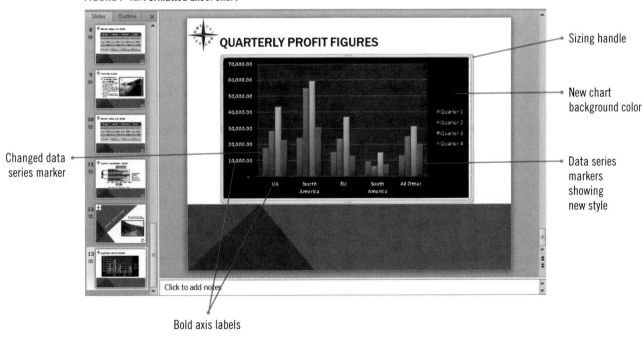

- Sizing handle
- New chart background color
- Data series markers showing new style
- Changed data series marker
- Bold axis labels

Embedding a worksheet

You can embed all or part of an Excel worksheet in a PowerPoint slide. To embed an entire worksheet, go to the slide where you want to place the worksheet. Click the Insert tab on the Ribbon, then click the Object button in the Text group. The Insert Object dialog box opens. Click the Create from file option button, click Browse, locate and double-click the worksheet filename, then click OK. The worksheet is embedded in the slide. Double-click it to edit it using Excel commands as needed to work with the worksheet. To insert only a portion of a worksheet, open the Excel workbook and copy the cells you want to include in your presentation.

PowerPoint 2010

Linking an Excel Worksheet

Another way to connect objects to your presentation is to establish a **link**, or connection, between the source file and the destination file. Unlike embedded objects, a linked object is stored in its source file, not on the slide or in the presentation file. So when you link an object to a PowerPoint slide, a representation (picture) of the object, not the object itself, appears on the slide. Any changes made to the source file using the source program of a linked object are automatically reflected in the linked representation in your PowerPoint presentation. Some of the objects that you can link to PowerPoint include bitmap images, Microsoft Excel worksheets, and PowerPoint slides from other presentations. Use linking when you want to be sure your presentation contains the latest information and when you want to include an object, such as an accounting spreadsheet, that may change over time. See Table F-1 for suggestions on when to embed an object and when to link an object. You need to link and format an Excel worksheet to the presentation. The worksheet was created by the QST Accounting Department earlier in the year.

STEPS

QUICK TIP
If you plan to do the steps in this lesson again, make a copy of the Excel file PPT F-3.xlsx to keep the original data intact.

1. **Click the** Home tab **on the Ribbon, click the** New Slide button, **then type** QST Revenue
    A new slide, Slide 14, is created and appears in the Slide pane and Slides tab.

2. **Click the** Insert tab **on the Ribbon, then click the** Object button **in the Text group**
    The Insert Object dialog box opens.

3. **Click the** Create from file option button, **click** Browse, **locate the file** PPT F-3.xlsx **in the drive and folder where you store your Data Files, click** OK, **click the** Link check box, **then click** OK
    The Excel worksheet appears on the slide. The worksheet would be easier to see if it were larger.

4. **Drag the** upper-left sizing handle **up and to the left, drag the** upper-right sizing handle **up and to the right, then position the worksheet in the middle of the slide as shown in Figure F-13**
    If the worksheet had a background fill color, it would help to emphasize the data and direct the audience's attention.

5. **Right-click the** worksheet, **then click** Format Object **on the shortcut menu**
    The Format Object dialog box opens.

6. **Drag the dialog box out of the way if it is blocking the worksheet, then click the** Solid fill option button
    A dark orange color is applied behind the worksheet. The color is too dark for the presentation.

7. **Click the** Color list arrow 🎨▾, **click** Dark Green, Accent 4 (top row), **type** 40 **in the Transparency text box, then click** Line Color **in the left pane**
    The transparency of the background color is at 40 percent and looks better.

8. **Click the** Solid line option button, **click the** Color list arrow, **click** Orange, Accent 1, **then click** Line Style **in the left pane**
    The worksheet appears with a new border color.

9. **Click the** Width up arrow **until** 2pt **appears, click** Close, **click a blank area of the slide, then save the presentation**
    The border is thicker and easier to see. Compare your screen to Figure F-14.

FIGURE F-13: Slide with linked Excel worksheet

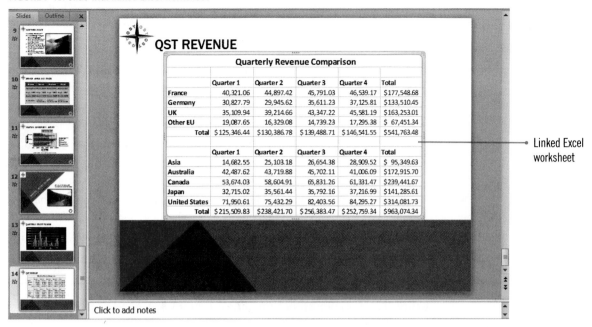

Linked Excel worksheet

FIGURE F-14: Formatted linked worksheet

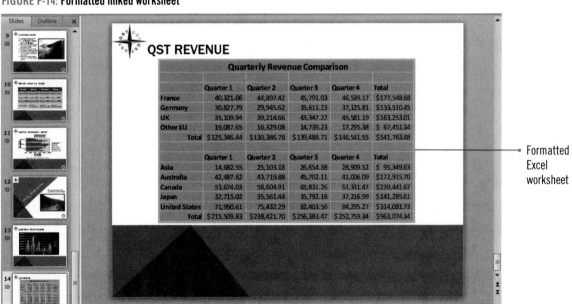

Formatted Excel worksheet

TABLE F-1: Embedding versus linking

situation	action
When you are the only user of an object and you want the object to be a part of your presentation	Embed
When you want to access the object in its source program, even if the original file is not available	Embed
When you want to update the object manually while working in PowerPoint	Embed
When you always want the latest information in your object	Link
When the object's source file is shared on a network or when other users have access to the file and can change it	Link
When you want to keep your presentation file size small	Link

Updating a Linked Excel Worksheet

To edit or change the information in a linked object, you must open the object's source file in its source program. For example, you must open Microsoft Word to edit a linked Word table, or you must open Microsoft Excel to edit a linked Excel worksheet. You can open the source program by double-clicking the linked object in the PowerPoint slide, as you did with embedded objects, or by starting the source program directly using any method you prefer. When you work on a linked object in its source program, your PowerPoint presentation can be either open or closed. If data in the linked file has changed while the presentation is closed, you will be asked to update the slides when you open the presentation. ▀▀▀ You have just received an e-mail that some of the data in the Excel worksheet is incorrect, so you update the data in the linked worksheet.

STEPS

1. **Right-click the Excel worksheet on Slide 14, point to Linked Worksheet Object, then click Edit**

   The worksheet PPT F-3.xlsx opens up in the Microsoft Excel window.

2. **Click cell D14, type 40826.76, click cell C5, type 26312.88, then press [Enter]**

   The Quarter 3 value for Japan and the Quarter 2 value for Germany change. All totals that include these values in the Total cells are updated accordingly. Compare your screen to Figure F-15.

3. **Click cell B4, press and hold [Shift], click cell E7, release [Shift], right-click in the selected cell area, then click the Accounting Number Format button $ ▾ on the Mini toolbar**

   All of the selected cells now have the accounting format and display the dollar symbol.

4. **Click cell B11, drag to cell E15, then press [F4]**

   The same accounting number format is applied to these cells.

5. **Click cell F8, press [Ctrl], click cell F16, click the Bold button B in the Font group, click the Bottom Border list arrow ▦ ▾ in the Font group, click Thick Box Border, then click a blank cell**

   The bold font attribute and a black border is added to cells F8 and F16 to highlight the overall totals.

6. **Click the Excel window Close button ✖, click Save to save your changes, then click a blank area of the slide**

   The Excel window closes. The Excel worksheet in the PPT F-QST.pptx presentation file is now updated with the new data and shows the formatting changes you made. PowerPoint automatically makes all of the changes to the linked object. Compare your screen to Figure F-16.

7. **Check the spelling, add your name as the footer to the handouts, save the presentation, then submit your presentation to your instructor**

   If your instructor requires you to print your presentation, then use the print layout setting 6 Slides Horizontal.

8. **Close the presentation, then exit PowerPoint**

FIGURE F-15: Modified Excel worksheet

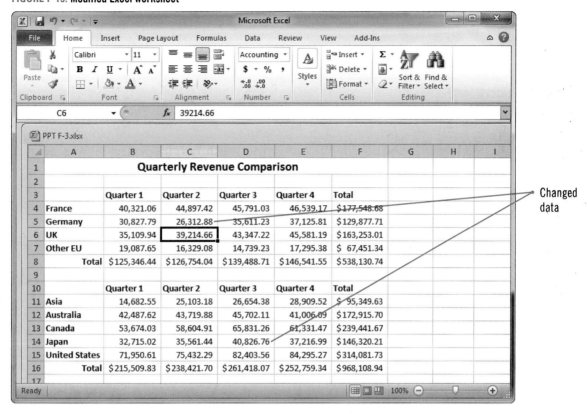

Changed data

FIGURE F-16: Slide with updated worksheet

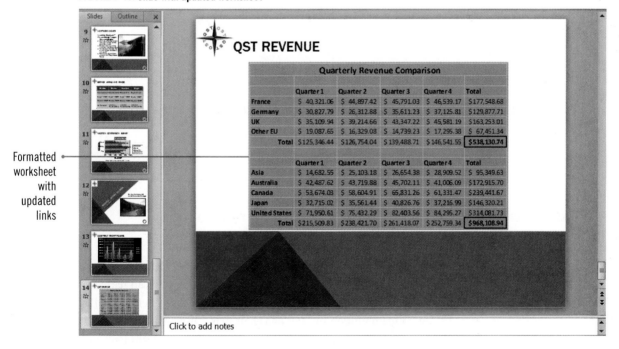

Formatted worksheet with updated links

Editing links

Once you link an object to your presentation, you have the ability to edit its link. Using the Links dialog box, you can update a link, open or change a linked object's source file, break a link, and determine if a linked object is updated manually or automatically. The Links dialog box is the only place where you can change a linked object's source file, break a link, and change the link updating method. To open the Links dialog box, click the File tab on the Ribbon, then click Edit Links to Files button under Related Documents in the right pane.

Practice

For current SAM information, including versions and content details, visit SAM Central (http://www.cengage.com/samcentral). If you have a SAM user profile, you may have access to hands-on instruction, practice, and assessment of the skills covered in this unit. Since various versions of SAM are supported throughout the life of this text, check with your instructor for the correct instructions and URL/Web site for accessing assignments.

Concepts Review

Label each of the elements of the PowerPoint window shown in Figure F-17.

FIGURE F-17

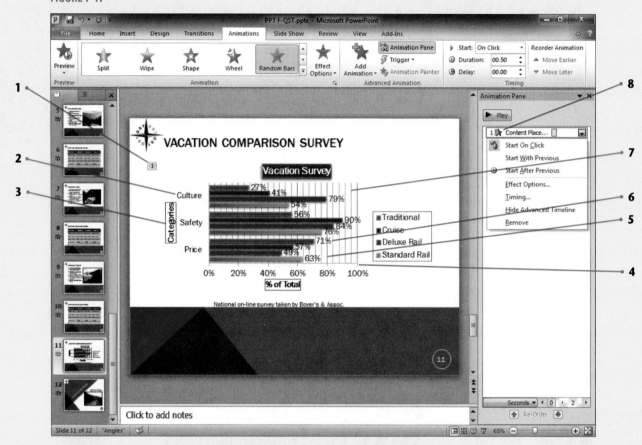

Match each of the terms with the statement that describes its function.

9. Trend
10. Major gridlines
11. Error bars
12. Source file
13. Template

a. Identifies potential data mistakes relative to each data marker in a data series
b. A chart formatting and layout that is saved so you can reuse it
c. The file that contains the embedded object you insert into a PowerPoint file
d. A main unit on the axis of a chart that is usually identified by a tick mark
e. A graphical representation of an upward or downward tendency in a data series

Select the best answer from the list of choices.

14. A(n) _____ chart displays data from one data series in proportion to the sum of all of the data series.
    a. pie
    b. doughnut
    c. surface
    d. area

15. What helps make the data easier to read in the chart and extends from the horizontal or vertical axes across the plot area?
    a. Data markers
    b. Gridlines
    c. A range of data
    d. Tick marks

16. Which animation method would you use to display each data series marker independently with the same color?
    a. By series
    b. Individually by series
    c. Individually by category
    d. By category

17. Which of the statements below is *not true* about working with charts in PowerPoint?
    a. Microsoft Graph is used to create a chart if Excel is not available.
    b. A linked chart is saved in the presentation.
    c. Document themes and effects are consistent between PowerPoint and Excel.
    d. An embedded chart's data is stored in an Excel worksheet.

18. Small lines that intersect an axis and identify categories are called _____.
    a. category markers
    b. tick marks
    c. plot layout lines
    d. chart wedges

19. You use a _____ program to create an object that you insert into PowerPoint.
    a. support
    b. destination
    c. linked
    d. source

20. To apply the styles of a presentation to an object, you would use the _____ paste method.
    a. use destination styles
    b. keep source formatting
    c. keep text only
    d. embed

Skills Review

1. **Change chart design and style.**
   a. Start PowerPoint, open the presentation PPT F-4.pptx, then save it as **PPT F-Lucio Bros** to the drive and folder where you store your Data Files.
   b. Click Slide 3 in the Slides pane, then select the chart.
   c. Open the Chart Tools Design tab, then apply Layout 7 from the Chart Layouts group.
   d. Change the label on the Vertical (Value) Axis to **Millions**, and then change the Horizontal (Category) Axis label to **Divisions**.
   e. Apply Style 28 from the Chart Styles group.
   f. Change the chart type to Clustered Cylinder. (*Hint*: A cylinder is a type of column chart.)

2. **Customize a chart layout.**
   a. Open the Chart Tools Layout tab, then change the horizontal gridlines to major gridlines and the vertical gridlines to major gridlines.
   b. Click the Chart Floor button in the Background group, click More Floor Options, click the Solid fill option button, click the Color list arrow, click Ice Blue, Text 2, then click Close.

Skills Review (continued)

    c. Right-click the value axis label, click the Shape Outline button arrow on the Mini toolbar, then click White, Text 1.

    d. Select the category axis title, then press [F4].

    e. Click a blank area of the chart, then save your changes.

3. Format chart elements.

    a. Open the Chart Tools Layout tab, click the Chart Area list arrow in the Current Selection group, then click Series "2nd Qtr."

    b. Click the Format Selection button in the Current Selection group, then drag the Gap Width slider to the left to about 150%.

    c. Click Fill in the left pane, then change the fill to a gradient fill, click the Direction list arrow, then click Linear Down.

    d. Click 3-D Format in the left pane, click the Material list arrow, click Dark Edge, then click Close.

    e. Right-click the value axis, then click Format Axis.

    f. Under Axis Options click the Major unit Fixed option button, then type **15** in the text box.

    g. Click the Major tick mark type list arrow, click Cross, click Close, then save your changes.

4. Animate a chart.

    a. Select the Animations tab, then apply the Float In Entrance animation to the chart.

    b. Click the Effect Options button, then change the animation to By Element in Category.

    c. Click the Animation Pane button, click the Object 4 list arrow in the Animation Pane, click Effect Options, then click the Chart Animation tab.

    d. Click the check box to not draw the chart background, then click OK.

    e. Change the duration to 1.50 and the delay to .75 for all the animations.

    f. Close the Animation Pane, then save your changes.

5. Embed an Excel chart.

    a. Select Slide 4, then click the Insert tab.

    b. Click the Object button in the Text group, click the Create from file option button, click Browse, locate and open the file PPT F-5.xlsx from the drive and folder where you store your Data Files, then click OK.

    c. Double-click the chart, then drag the right-middle sizing handle so the extra column next to the legend is hidden from view.

    d. Click the Chart Tools Design tab, then change the chart style to Style 40.

    e. Change the horizontal gridlines to display only major gridlines.

    f. Right-click the legend, click the Shape Outline list arrow on the Mini toolbar, click Automatic, then click a blank area of the slide.

    g. Resize the chart so it fills most of the slide, then save your changes.

6. Link an Excel worksheet.

    a. Add a new slide after the current slide with the Title Only layout.

    b. Type **Lucio Bros. Publishing**, click the Insert tab, then click the Object button in the Text group.

    c. Click the Create from file option button, locate the file PPT F-6.xlsx in the drive and folder where you store your Data Files, then link it to the slide.

    d. Resize the worksheet object by dragging its sizing handles.

    e. Right-click the worksheet, click Format Object, click the Solid fill option button, click the Color list arrow, then click Orange, Accent 3.

    f. Change the transparency to 25%, click Close, then save your changes.

Skills Review (continued)

FIGURE F-18

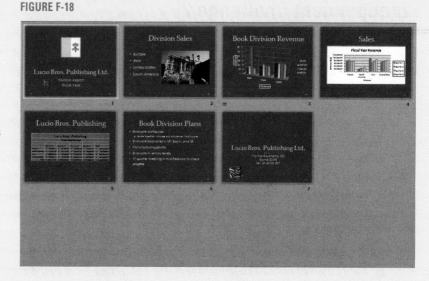

7. Update a linked Excel worksheet.

a. Double-click the worksheet.

b. Select cells B5 to F9, click the Accounting Number Format list arrow in the Number group, then click Euro.

c. Click cell F9, then click the Bold button in the Font group.

d. Click cell D5, type **72492.38**, click cell E7, then type **87253.11**.

e. Close the Excel window, then click Save to save your changes. The changes appear in the linked worksheet. Figure F-18 shows the completed presentation.

f. Add your name to the handout footer, save your work, submit your presentation to your instructor, close the presentation, and exit PowerPoint.

Independent Challenge 1

You work for Madison & Sons Inc., a business consulting company that helps businesses organize or restructure themselves to be more efficient and profitable. You are one of four consultants who work directly with clients. To prepare for an upcoming meeting with executives at a local Internet communications company, you create a brief presentation outlining typical investigative and reporting techniques, past results versus the competition, and the company's business philosophy. Use PowerPoint to customize a chart on Slide 5 of the presentation.

a. Start PowerPoint, open the presentation PPT F-7.pptx from the drive and folder where you store your Data Files, then save it as **PPT F-Madison**.

b. Select the chart on Slide 5, then apply Layout 3 from the Chart Layouts gallery.

c. Apply Style 29 from the Chart Styles gallery, then type **AMPI Rating Comparison** in the chart title text box.

d. Change the chart type to Clustered Bar, then add minor vertical gridlines to the chart.

e. Right-click the value axis, click Format Axis, click Number in the left pane, click Number in the Category list, type **1** in the Decimal Places text box, then click Close.

f. Click the Data Labels button, then show data labels using the Outside End option.

Advanced Challenge Exercise

- Right-click the value axis, click Format Axis, click the Major unit Fixed option button, then type **0.5**.
- Click the Minor unit Fixed option button, type **0.1**, then click Close
- Right-click the category axis, click Format Axis, click Alignment in the left pane, type **−25** in the Custom angle text box, then click Close.

g. Change the data labels to the Inside End option, then check the spelling in the presentation.

h. Add your name as a footer to the slides and handouts, then view the presentation in Reading View.

i. Save the presentation, submit your presentation to your instructor, close the presentation, then exit PowerPoint.

Independent Challenge 2

One of your responsibilities working in the Kansas State Schools system is to provide program performance data for educational programs designed for disabled children in the state. You need to develop and give a presentation describing the program's results at a national education forum held this year in Denver, Colorado. You have been working on the presentation, and now you need to use PowerPoint to put the finishing touches on a chart.

a. Start PowerPoint, open the presentation PPT F-8.pptx from the drive and folder where you store your Data Files, then save it as **PPT F-Kansas**.

b. Select Slide 7, select the chart, then change the chart style to Style 31.

c. Click the Chart Tools Layout tab click the 3-D Rotation button, then in the Rotation section click the X up arrow once.

d. Open the Chart Tools Format tab, select the Math data series, then change the shape fill to the gradient From Center.

e. Change the Reading data series to the Cork texture shape fill, click the Chart Tools Design tab, then change the chart layout to Layout 7.

f. Type **APCI Score** in the vertical axis label, then type **Grade Level** in the horizontal axis label.

g. Apply the Wipe Entrance animation to the chart, then change the Effect options to By Category.

h. Check the spelling in the presentation, add your name as a footer to the slides and handouts, then save the presentation.

i. View the presentation in Slide Show view, submit your presentation to your instructor, close the presentation, then exit PowerPoint.

Independent Challenge 3

Hanover Mark Industries is a large company that develops and produces medical equipment and technical machines for operating and emergency rooms throughout the United States. You are one of the client representatives in the company, and one of your assignments is to prepare a presentation for the division management meetings on the profitability and efficiency of each division in the company. Use PowerPoint to develop the presentation.

a. Open the file PPT F-9.pptx from the drive and folder where you store your Data Files, then save it as **PPT F-Hanover**.

b. Apply the Clarity theme, then add at least two graphics to the presentation.

c. Add a new slide after the title slide titled **Company Divisions**, then create a SmartArt graphic that identifies the company's seven divisions: Administration, Accounting, Sales and Marketing, Research and Development, Product Testing, Product Development, and Manufacturing.

d. Format the new SmartArt graphic using SmartArt Styles and colors.

e. Select the Division Performance slide, then insert the Excel file PPT F-10.xlsx from the drive and folder where you store your Data Files.

f. Drag the corner sizing handles of the chart so it covers most of the slide, then double-click the chart.

Advanced Challenge Exercise

- Click the Chart Tools Layout tab, click the Trendline button in the Analysis group, click Linear Trendline, click Sales, then click OK.
- Right-click the value axis, then click Format Axis.
- Click the Minor tick mark type list arrow, then click Outside, then click Close.

g. Apply the Style 42 chart style to the chart, right-click the category axis, click Format Axis, click the Axis labels list arrow, click Low, then click Close.

h. Select the Division Budgets slide, then link the Excel file PPT F-11.xlsx from the drive and folder where you store your Data Files.

i. Open the linked worksheet in Excel, select cells B5 through F12, click the Accounting Number Format button in the Number group, save the changes to the worksheet, then close Excel.

Independent Challenge 3 (continued)

j. Right-click the linked chart, click Format Object, click the Solid fill option button, change the fill color to Red, Text 2 at 25% transparency.

k. Resize the worksheet to fill the slide, add your name as a footer to the slides and handouts, check the spelling, then view your presentation in Slide Show view.

l. Submit your presentation to your instructor, close the presentation and exit PowerPoint.

Real Life Independent Challenge

You are on staff at your college newspaper. One of your jobs is to review computer games and post a presentation on the paper's Web site. The presentation identifies the top computer games based on student testing and other reviews. Use PowerPoint to create a presentation that includes research and your own information. Use the basic presentation provided as a basis to develop this presentation.

As you create this presentation, follow these guidelines:

- Include three computer games in your presentation.
- Each game has at least one defined mission or task.
- Consumer satisfaction of each game is identified on a scale of 1.0 to 10.0.
- There are three categories of games: Adventure, Action, and Strategy.
- Presentation should include at least eight slides, including the title slide.

If you have access to the Web, you can research the following topics to help you develop information for your presentation:

- Consumer or industry reviews of computer games
- Computer game descriptions and pricing

a. Connect to the Internet, then use a search engine to locate Web sites that have information on PC computer games. Review at least two Web sites that contain information about computer games. Print the home pages of the Web sites you use to gather data for your presentation.

b. Open the presentation PPT F-12.pptx from the drive and folder where you store your Data Files, then save it as **PPT F-Review**.

c. Add your name as the footer on all slides and handouts.

d. (Before you complete this step make a copy of the Data File PPT F-13.xlsx.) Link the Excel chart PPT F-13.xlsx from the drive and folder where you store your Data Files on the Game Reviews slide.

e. Resize the chart on the slide, then open the linked chart in Excel.

f. Click the Sheet 1 tab at the bottom of the Excel window, provide a name for each game, click the Sheet 2 tab, then save your changes.

g. Right-click the chart legend, click Delete on the shortcut menu, click the Page Layout tab, click the Colors button in the Themes group, then click Austin.

h. Save your changes, then exit Excel.

i. Create at least one SmartArt diagram that briefly explains the specifications of one of the games.

j. Create a table that lists the price of each game.

k. Enhance the presentation with clip art or other graphics, an appropriate design theme, and other items that improve the look of the presentation.

l. Modify the Slide Master as necessary.

m. Check the spelling in the presentation, save the presentation, then view the presentation in Slide Show view.

n. Add your name as a footer to the slides and handouts, submit your presentation to your instructor, close the presentation, then exit PowerPoint.

Visual Workshop

Create a slide that looks like the example in Figure F-19. Start a new presentation, then insert the Excel worksheet PPT F-14.xlsx from the drive and folder where you store your Data Files. (*Hint*: The worksheet is formatted with a 60% transparent dark blue fill and a gold 3 point border.) Save the presentation as **PPT F-Wise Inc**. Add your name as a footer to the slides, then submit your presentation to your instructor.

FIGURE F-19

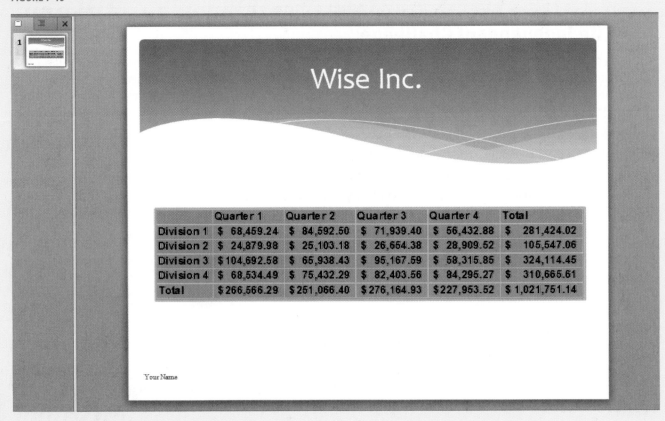

Inserting Graphics, Media, and Objects

PowerPoint provides you with many different types of illustrations to improve your presentation. From customized tables and professional-looking graphics to videos and sounds, you have a wide range of options when it comes to developing your presentation. You also have other advanced tools, such as macros, hyperlinks, and action buttons that help correlate, simplify, and assimilate information. In this unit, you work on a short presentation that describes other tour opportunities that you link to the primary Train Tour presentation you have been working on for Quest Specialty Travel. You use the advanced features in PowerPoint to customize a table and a SmartArt graphic, then you insert a video and sound that complements the information. Finally, you use a macro to insert some pictures, create action buttons, and link one presentation to another one.

OBJECTIVES

Create custom tables

Design a SmartArt graphic

Format a SmartArt graphic

Insert clip art video

Insert a sound

Use macros

Add action buttons

Insert a hyperlink

Creating Custom Tables

A table is a great way to display and organize related information. In PowerPoint, you have the ability to create dynamic-looking tables. Tables you create in PowerPoint automatically display the style as determined by the theme assigned to the slide, including color combinations and shading, line styles and colors, and other attributes. It is easy to customize the layout of a table or change how data is organized. You can delete and insert rows or columns, merge two or more cells together, or split one cell into more cells. ▨▨▨▨ You open a short presentation on Canadian Train Add-On Tours that you have been working on and finish customizing a table.

STEPS

1. **Start PowerPoint, open the presentation PPT G-1.pptm from the drive and folder where you store your Data Files, then click the Enable Content button in the Security Warning banner**

   Although this presentation looks similar to other presentations it has the file extension .pptm instead of .pptx. The .pptm file extension identifies the PowerPoint file as having macros attached to it. A **macro** is a set of actions that you use to automate tasks. You enabled the macros attached to this presentation.

2. **Save the presentation as PPT G-QST Link, click OK in the privacy warning message box, then click the Slide 2 thumbnail in the Slides tab**

   The Security Warning banner closes, and Slide 2 appears in the Slide pane.

3. **Click the table on Slide 2, click the Table Tools Design tab on the Ribbon, click the Pen Style button in the Draw Borders group, then click the dash-dot-dot style (5th style)**

   The pointer changes to ⌀, which indicates that you are in drawing mode.

4. **Click the white vertical column line that divides the Pricing and Includes columns in the first row in table, then click the vertical column line for each row in that column to the bottom of the table**

   Compare your screen to Figure G-1.

5. **Click the Draw Table button in the Draw Borders group, click the Table Tools Layout tab on the Ribbon, click the Walking Bicycle cell, then click the Split Cells button in the Merge group**

   Clicking the Draw Table button turns the drawing mode off and changes the pointer back to ⌖. Clicking the Split Cells button opens the Split Cells dialog box. The default table is 2 columns and 1 row, and the Number of columns text box is selected.

6. **Type 1 in the Number of columns text box, click the Number of rows up arrow once, then click OK**

   You split the cell to create a new row in that cell.

7. **Double-click to select the word Bicycle, click the Home tab on the Ribbon, click the Cut button ✂ in the Clipboard group, press [Backspace], click the new row, click the Paste list arrow in the Clipboard group, then click the Keep Source Formatting button 🖿**

   The words "Walking" and "Bicycle" are now in two separate rows within the Transportation column. See Table G-1 for more information on Paste button options.

8. **Repeat Steps 5–7 to split the Bicycle pricing data in the Pricing column into two rows as shown in Figure G-2**

   Now the Bicycle information is separate from the Walking information.

9. **Click outside the table, save your presentation, then click OK in the privacy warning message box**

FIGURE G-1: Table with new column line style

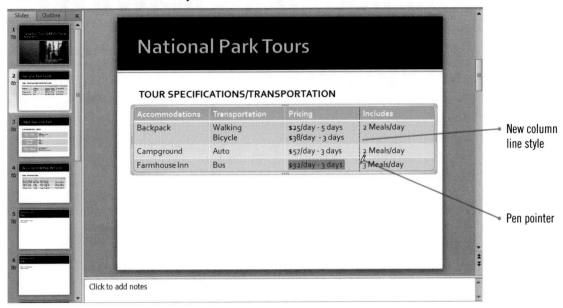

New column line style

Pen pointer

FIGURE G-2: New row with data

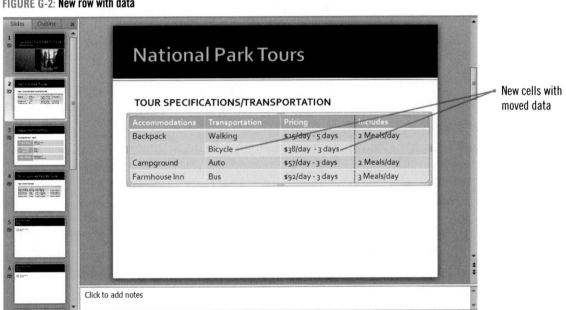

New cells with moved data

TABLE G-1: Understanding common Paste button options

symbol	button name	result
	Keep Source Formatting	Uses the formatting characteristics from the object's source file
	Use Destination Styles	Uses the current styles of the presentation
	Embed	Inserts the object as an embedded object
	Picture	Inserts the object as a picture
	Keep Text Only	Inserts the object as text only with no formatting
	Use Destination Theme	Uses the current theme of the presentation

Designing a SmartArt Graphic

Using SmartArt graphics in a presentation dramatically improves your ability to create vibrant content on slides. SmartArt allows you to easily combine your content with an illustrative diagram, improving the overall quality of your presentation. Better presentations lead to improved understanding and retention by your audience. In a matter of minutes, and with little training, you can create a SmartArt graphic using slide content that would otherwise have been placed in a simple bulleted list. 🖥️ You continue working on the Canadian Train Add-On tours presentation by changing the graphic layout, adding a shape and text to the SmartArt graphic, and then changing its color and style.

STEPS

1. **Click the** Slide 3 thumbnail **in the Slides tab, click the** Tour Sites shape **in the SmartArt graphic, then click the** SmartArt Tools Design tab **on the Ribbon**

   The Tour Sites shape is selected and displays sizing handles and a rotate handle. Each shape in the SmartArt graphic is separate and distinct from the other shapes and can be individually edited, formatted, or moved within the boundaries of the SmartArt graphic.

2. **If necessary, click the** Text Pane button **in the Create Graphic group to open the Text pane, click the** Add Bullet button **in the Create Graphic group, then type** Kamloops **in the Text pane**

   A new bullet appears in the Text pane and in the upper-right shape of the graphic. Compare your screen with Figure G-3.

3. **Click the** More button 🔽 **in the Layouts group, then click** Horizontal Picture List **(3rd row)**

   The SmartArt graphic layout changes.

4. **Click the** Add Shape list arrow **in the Create Graphic group, then click** Add Shape After

   A new shape in the same style appears and a new bullet appears in the Text pane.

5. **Type** Upgrades, **press [Enter], press [Tab], type** Add trip to Victoria BC, **press [Enter], type** Shopping in Banff, **press [Enter], then type** Personal guide

6. **Click the** More button 🔽 **in the SmartArt Styles group, click** Subtle Effect **in the Best Match section, then click the** Change Colors button **in the SmartArt Styles group**

   A gallery of color themes appears showing the current theme applied to the graphic in the Accent 1 section.

7. **Click** Colorful - Accent Colors **in the Colorful section**

   Each shape now has its own color.

8. **Click the** Text Pane button **in the Create Graphic group, then click the** Right to Left button **in the Create Graphic group**

   The graphic flips and appears as a mirror image. You prefer the original view of the graphic.

9. **Click the** Right to Left button, **click a blank area of the slide, save your changes, then click** OK **in the privacy warning message box**

   Compare your screen to Figure G-4.

FIGURE G-3: SmartArt graphic with added text

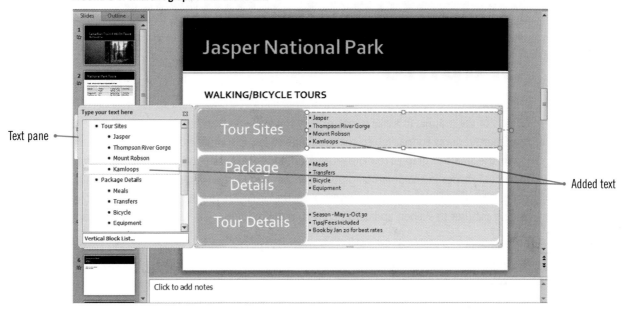

Text pane

Added text

FIGURE G-4: SmartArt graphic with new design

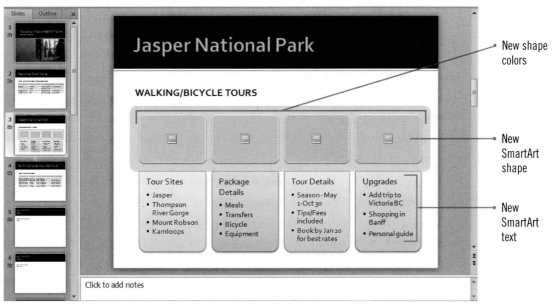

New shape colors

New SmartArt shape

New SmartArt text

Creating mathematical equations

You can insert or create mathematical equations using the Equation button in the Symbols group on the Insert tab. Click the Equation button list arrow to access nine common equations, which include the area of a circle, the Pythagorean theorem (my personal favorite), and the quadratic formula. To create your own equations click the Equation button to open the Equation Tools Design tab. To help you create equations, you have access to eight types of symbols including basic math, geometry, operators, and scripts. You also have the ability to create mathematical structures such as integrals and functions.

Formatting a SmartArt Graphic

Though you can use styles and themes to format a SmartArt graphic, you still may need to refine individual aspects of the graphic to make it look exactly the way you want it to look. You can use the commands on the SmartArt Tools Format tab to change shape styles, fills, outlines, and effects. You can also convert text within the SmartArt graphic to WordArt and format the text using any of the WordArt formatting commands. Individual shapes in the SmartArt graphic can be made larger or smaller, or altered into a different shape altogether. ▓▓▓ You continue working on the SmartArt graphic on Slide 3 by adjusting four shapes, adding pictures to shapes, and adjusting text in the graphic.

STEPS

1. **Click the SmartArt graphic, click the SmartArt Tools Format tab on the Ribbon, then click the shape above the Tour Sites shape**

   The shape behind the picture icon is selected.

2. **Click the Change Shape button in the Shapes group, then click Round Diagonal Corner Rectangle (the last shape in the Rectangles section)**

   The form of the shape changes.

3. **Click the shape above the Package Details shape, press and hold [Ctrl], click the remaining two shapes, release [Ctrl], press [F4], then click in a blank area of the SmartArt graphic**

   All four small shapes now have a new shape as shown in Figure G-5.

4. **Click the picture icon 🖼 in the first shape on the left**

   The Insert Picture dialog box opens.

5. **Locate and click the file PPT G-2.jpg in the drive and folder where you store your Data Files, then click Insert**

   The picture is placed in the shape. Notice the picture takes on the contour of the shape.

6. **Click the 🖼 above the Package Details shape, insert the file PPT G-3.jpg, click the next 🖼, insert the file PPT G-4.jpg, click the last 🖼, then insert the file PPT G-5.jpg**

   All four shapes have pictures in them.

7. **Click a blank area inside the SmartArt graphic, then drag the left or right sizing handles to center the graphic in the white space on the slide**

   The SmartArt graphic fills the white area on the slide.

8. **Click a blank area of the slide, save your work, then click OK in the privacy warning message box**

   Compare your screen with Figure G-6.

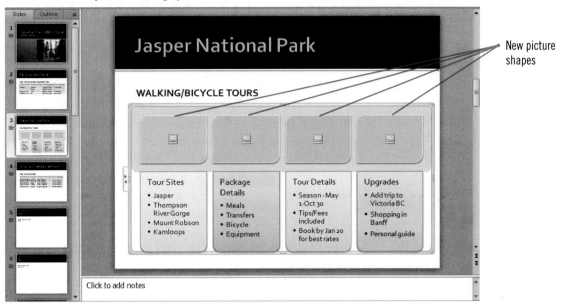

New picture shapes

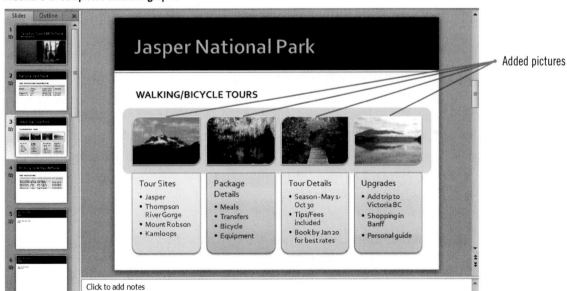

Added pictures

PowerPoint 2010

Saving a presentation in PDF and XPS file formats

In certain situations, such as when sharing sensitive or legal materials with others, you may find it necessary to save your presentation file in a fixed layout format. A **fixed layout format** is a specific file format that "locks" the file from future change and allows others only the ability to view or print the presentation. To save a presentation in one of these fixed formats, click the File tab on the Ribbon, click Save & Send, click Create PDF/XPS Document, then click Create a PDF/XPS. The Publish as PDF or XPS dialog box opens. Select the appropriate file type in the Save as type list box, choose other options (optimization), then publish your presentation in a fixed layout format. To view a fixed layout format presentation, you need appropriate viewer software that you can download from the Internet.

Inserting Graphics, Media, and Objects

Inserting Clip Art Video

In your presentation, you may want to use special effects to illustrate a point or capture the attention of your audience. You can do this by inserting an animated or digital video. Animated videos contain multiple images that stream together or move when you run a slide show to give the illusion of motion. PowerPoint animated videos, also known as **clip art videos**, are stored as Graphics Interchange Format (GIF) files in the Clip Organizer. The **Clip Organizer** contains various drawings, photographs, clip art, sounds, and animated GIFs that you can insert into your presentation. **Digital video** is live action captured in digital format by a video camera. You can embed or link a digital video file from your hard drive or link a digital video file from a Web page on the Internet. ▓▓▓▓ You continue to develop your presentation by inserting a clip art video from the Clip Organizer showing backpackers walking in the forest.

STEPS

1. **Click the** Slide 2 thumbnail **in the Slides tab, click the** Insert tab **on the Ribbon, click the** Video list arrow **in the Media group, then click** Clip Art Video

   The Clip Art task pane opens and displays clip art videos.

2. **Type** backpacking **in the Search for text box, then click** Go

   PowerPoint searches for backpacking clip art video.

3. **Scroll down the Clip Art task pane, if necessary, until you see the thumbnail of the backpackers shown in Figure G-7, then click the** thumbnail

   The backpacking clip art video appears in the center of the slide.

4. **Click the** Clip Art task pane Close button ✖

   The Clip Art task pane closes, and the Picture Tools Format tab is open on the Ribbon.

5. **Right-click the** clip art video, **then click** Size and Position **on the shortcut menu**

   The Format Picture dialog box opens.

6. **In the Scale section double-click the number** 100 **in the Height text box, type** 300, **then click** Position **in the left pane**

   The clip art video increases in size by 200 percent.

7. **Select the** number **in the Horizontal text box, type** 6.2, **press [Tab] twice, type** 5.2 **in the Vertical text box, then click** Close

   The clip art video moves to a new location at the bottom of the slide. The clip would look good with a soft edge effect from the Picture Effects gallery.

8. **Click the** Picture Effects button **in the Picture Styles group, point to** Soft Edges, **click** 25 Point, **then click a blank area of the slide**

   Compare your screen with Figure G-8. The clip art video won't begin unless you view it in Slide Show view.

9. **Click the** Slide Show button 🖵 **on the status bar, watch the video for a few seconds, press [Esc], save your work, then click** OK **in the privacy warning message box**

FIGURE G-7: Clip Organizer showing clip art video files

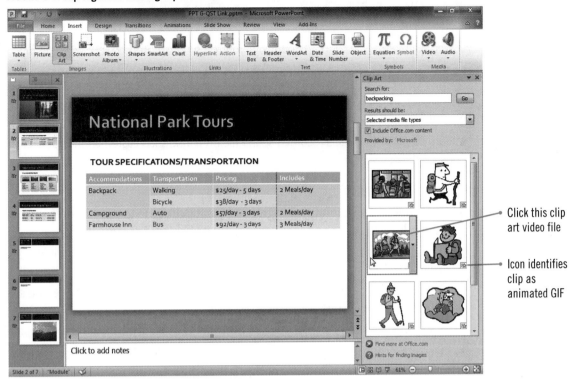

Click this clip art video file

Icon identifies clip as animated GIF

FIGURE G-8: Slide showing formatted clip art video

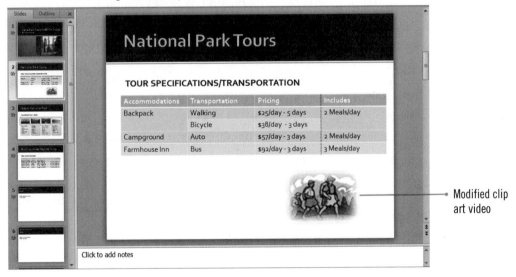

Modified clip art video

PowerPoint 2010

Inserting and editing digital video

You can insert digital videos from files you have stored on your hard drive, any storage media, the Microsoft Web site, or other sources on the Internet. To insert a video on a PowerPoint slide, click the Insert tab, then click the Video list arrow in the Media group. Click either the Video from File option or the Video from Web Site option. Clicking the Video from File option opens the Insert Video dialog box where you can locate and insert a video file. Clicking the Video from Web Site option opens the Insert Video from Web Site dialog box. Use this dialog box to paste the embed code for the video you want to link from the Internet. To link a video from the Internet you must have a video file's embed code; otherwise, you cannot link the video file to a presentation. After you watch your video, you can use editing tools to trim beginning or ending portions of the video. You can also add a timed fade effect to the start or end of the video.

Inserting a Sound

PowerPoint allows you to insert sounds in your presentation in the same way you insert clip art video or digital video. You can add sounds to your presentation from files on a disk, the Microsoft Clip Organizer, the Internet, or a network drive. The primary use of sound in a presentation is to provide emphasis to a slide or an element on the slide. For example, if you are creating a presentation about an Idaho raft tour on the Snake River, you might consider inserting a rushing water sound on a slide showing a photograph of people rafting. ▓▓▓▓ You insert a recorded sound file from a satisfied customer on Slide 3 of the presentation to enhance the message on the slide.

STEPS

QUICK TIP

To insert a sound from the Microsoft Clip Organizer, click the Audio list arrow, then click Clip Art Audio.

1. **Click the Slide 3 thumbnail in the Slides tab, click the Insert tab on the Ribbon, click the Audio list arrow in the Media group, then click Audio from File**

   The Insert Audio dialog box opens. Common sound formats you can insert into a presentation include Windows audio files (Wave Form) (wav), MP3 audio files (mp3), and Windows Media Audio files (wma).

2. **Locate and click the file PPT G-6.wma in the drive and folder where you store your Data Files, then click Insert**

   A sound icon with an audio control bar appears in the center of the slide as shown Figure G-9.

TROUBLE

If the sound does not play, see your instructor or technical support person for help.

3. **Drag the sound icon 🔊 to the right of Walking/Bicycle Tours, then click the Play/Pause button ▷ in the audio control bar**

   The sound icon is moved off the SmartArt graphic and plays one time through. After hearing the audio play, you decide to trim the start point to cut out the laughing at the beginning.

4. **Click the Audio Tools Playback tab on the Ribbon, click the Trim Audio button in the Editing group, then drag the dialog box down the slide below the sound icon**

   The Trim Audio dialog box opens as shown in Figure G-10. Notice on the audio timeline the start point (green marker) and the end point (red marker), which identify the beginning and end of the audio. The audio is 19.551 seconds long.

5. **Click the Play button ▶ in the Trim Audio dialog box, watch the audio on the sound timeline, then drag the start point 𝗂 to the right until 00:03.126 appears above the sound timeline**

   The audio will now start at this point when played. The end of the audio needs to be changed also.

6. **Click the End Time down arrow until 00:17.200 appears as shown in Figure G-11, click OK, then click ▷ in the audio control bar**

   The audio now plays between the new start and end points. By default, the audio plays when you click the sound icon during a slide show.

QUICK TIP

You can add a bookmark to an audio clip that identifies a specific point in time. You can use bookmarks to manually start or end an audio or jump to a precise point in the audio.

7. **Click the Start button in the Audio Options group, then click Automatically**

   The audio will now run automatically as soon as the slide appears in Slide Show view.

8. **Click the Slide Show button 🖳 on the status bar, then listen to the audio**

   Notice that the sound icon appears during the slide show. You can hide the sound icon during a slide show by clicking the Hide During Show check box in the Audio Options group.

9. **Press [Esc], click a blank area of the slide, then save your changes**

FIGURE G-9: Slide showing inserted sound

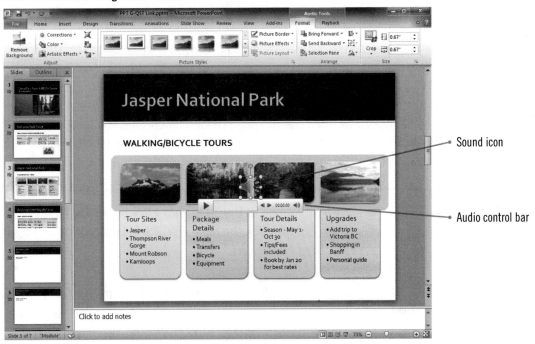

Sound icon

Audio control bar

FIGURE G-10: Trim Audio dialog box

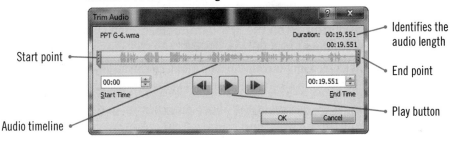

Start point

Audio timeline

Identifies the audio length

End point

Play button

FIGURE G-11: Trim Audio dialog box showing trimmed audio

Repositioned start point

Identifies new start position

Identifies new audio length

Repositioned end point

Identifies new end position

Recording a voice narration on a slide

If your computer has speakers, a sound card, and a microphone, you can record a voice narration and then play it during a slide show. To record a narration, click the Insert tab on the Ribbon, click the Audio list arrow in the Media group, then click Record Audio. The Record Sound dialog box opens. To start recording, click the Record button in the dialog box, then click the Stop button when you are finished.

A sound icon appears on the slide. Narration recordings and other sounds are embedded in the presentation and will increase the PowerPoint file size. You can preview a narration in Normal view by pointing to the sound icon on the slide, then clicking the Play/Pause button in the audio control bar.

Using Macros

As you learned in the first lesson of this unit, a macro is a recording of an action or a set of actions that you use to automate tasks. The contents of a macro consist of a series of command codes that you create in the Visual Basic for Applications programming language using Microsoft Visual Basic, which you can access through the Developer tab in PowerPoint. You can use macros to automate almost any action that you perform repeatedly when creating presentations, which saves you time and effort. Any presentation with the .pptm file extension is saved with a macro. ██████ You use macros that you already created to format and place two pictures.

STEPS

QUICK TIP

To add the Developer tab to the Ribbon, click the File tab on the Ribbon, click Options, click Customize Ribbon in the left pane, click the Developer check box in the Main Tabs list box, then click OK.

1. **Click the Slide 5 thumbnail in the Slides tab, click the Insert Picture from File icon 🖾 in the content placeholder, click the file PPT G-7.jpg in the drive and folder where you store your Data Files, then click Insert**

   A picture appears in the content placeholder.

2. **Click the View tab on the Ribbon, then click the Macros button in the Macro group**

   The Macro dialog box opens displaying the two macros attached to this presentation file.

3. **Click Module2.PictureReduction in the Macro name list, then click Edit**

   The Microsoft Visual Basic for Applications window opens displaying two small windows as shown in Figure G-12. Each window represents a separate macro. Each macro is designed to modify the size of a picture and place it in a specific place on the slide. The difference between the two macros is that the Module2 macro unlocks the aspect ratio so that pictures of any size can be modified within the designated parameters.

4. **Click the Run button ▶ on the Standard toolbar, then click the Microsoft Visual Basic for Applications window Close button ▬ X ▬**

   The macro runs and performs two functions on the picture: It modifies the size of the picture to specific width and height dimensions, and it moves the picture to precise coordinates on the slide.

5. **Click the Slide 6 thumbnail in the Slides tab, click 🖾 in the content placeholder, click the file PPT G-8.jpg in the drive and folder where you store your Data Files, then click Insert**

   A picture appears in the content placeholder.

QUICK TIP

To learn more about macros and the Visual Basic for Applications pro-gramming language, click the Visual Basic button on the Developer tab to open the Visual Basic window, then click the Help button.

6. **Click the View tab on the Ribbon, click the Macros button in the Macro group, click Module2.PictureReduction in the Macro name list, then click Run**

   The macro runs and modifies the picture size and position on the slide.

7. **Click the Picture Tools Format tab on the Ribbon, click the Artistic Effects button in the Adjust group, point to each effect in the gallery, then click Plastic Wrap**

   The picture is formatted with an artistic effect.

8. **Click the Slide 5 thumbnail in the Slides tab, click the picture, then press [F4], click the Slide 7 thumbnail in the Slides tab, click the picture, then press [F4]**

   All of the pictures at the end of the presentation now have the same artistic effect.

9. **Click a blank area of the slide, then save your work**

   Compare your screen to Figure G-13.

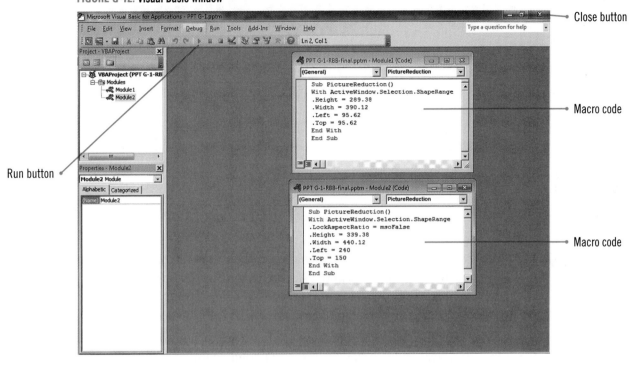

FIGURE G-12: Visual Basic window

Close button

Macro code

Run button

Macro code

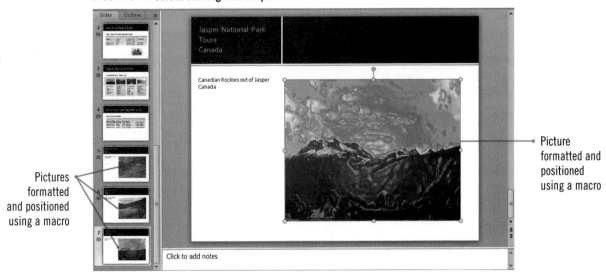

FIGURE G-13: Screen showing inserted picture

Pictures formatted and positioned using a macro

Picture formatted and positioned using a macro

Macro security

There are certain risks involved when you enable macros on your computer. The macros used in this lesson are simple commands that automate the size and relative position of a picture on a slide; however, hackers can introduce harmful viruses or other malicious programs into your computer using macros. By default, PowerPoint disables macros when you open a presentation file that includes macros to prevent possible damage to your computer. To understand PowerPoint security settings and how PowerPoint checks for harmful macros, click the Macro Security button on the Developer tab, or click the File tab, click Options, then click Trust Center in the left pane. The bottom line with macros is if you can't trust the source of the macro, do not enable them.

Adding Action Buttons

An **action button** is an interactive button that you create from the Shapes gallery to perform a specific task. For example, you can create an action button to play a video or a sound, or to link to another slide in your presentation. Action buttons can also link to an Internet address on the Web, a different presentation, or another file created in another program. You can also run a macro or another program using an action button. Action buttons are commonly used in self-running presentations and presentations published on the Web. ████ You finish working on this presentation by adding action buttons to each slide, which will allow you to move from slide to slide and back to the first slide.

STEPS

1. **Click the** Slide 1 thumbnail **in the Slides tab, then click the** Home tab **on the Ribbon**
   Slide 1 appears in the Slide pane.

2. **Click the** Shapes button **in the Drawing group to open the Shapes gallery, click** Action Button: Forward or Next ▷ **in the Action Buttons section, press and hold [Shift], drag to create a button as shown in Figure G-14, then release [Shift]**
   A small action button appears on the slide, and the Action Settings dialog box opens. Pressing [Shift] while you create a shape maintains the shape's proportions as you change its size.

3. **Make sure** Next Slide **is selected in the Hyperlink to list, then click** OK
   The dialog box closes. The action button now has an action, in this case, moving to the next slide.

4. **Click the** Drawing Tools Format tab **on the Ribbon, click the** More button ▾ **in the Shape Styles group, then click** Light 1 Outline, Colored Fill – Red, Accent 6 **in the 3rd row**
   The action button is easier to see on the slide.

5. **Drag the** action button **to the lower-left corner of the slide**

6. **Click the** Home tab **on the Ribbon, click the** Copy button ▣▾ **in the Clipboard group, click the** Slide 2 thumbnail **in the Slides tab, then click the** Paste button **in the Clipboard group**
   An exact copy of the action button, including the associated action, is placed on Slide 2.

7. **Paste a copy of the** action button **on Slides 3, 4, 5, and 6, click the** Slide 7 thumbnail **in the Slides tab, click the** Shapes button **in the Drawing group, then click** Action Button: Home ▣ **in the Action Buttons section**

8. **Use [Shift] to create a similar sized action button as you did for Slide 1, make sure** First Slide **is selected in the Hyperlink to list, click** OK, **then drag the** action button **to the lower-left corner of the slide**
   Compare your screen to Figure G-15.

9. **Click the** Slide Show button ▧ **on the status bar, click the** Home action button, **click the** action buttons **to move from slide to slide, then on Slide 7 press [Esc] to end the slide show**
   The pointer changes to 🖑 when you click each action button.

10. **Add your name to the slide footer, save your changes, submit your presentation to your instructor, click the** File tab **on the Ribbon, then click** Close **to close the presentation but do not exit PowerPoint**

FIGURE G-14: **New action button**

Action Settings
dialog box

Action button

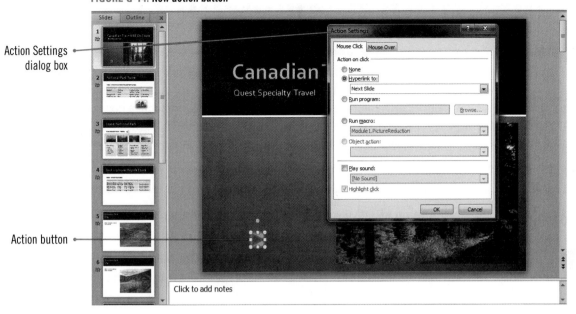

FIGURE G-15: **Last slide showing Home action button**

Home action
button

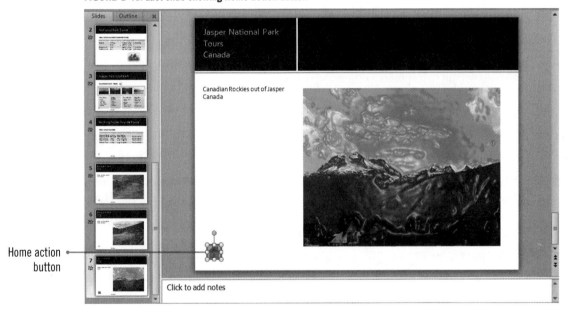

Saving slides as graphics

You can save PowerPoint slides as graphics and later use them in other presentations, in graphics programs, and on Web pages. Display the slide you want to save, click the File tab, then click Save As. In the Save As dialog box, click the Save as type list arrow, select the desired graphics format, then name the file. Graphics format choices include JPEG file Interchange Format (*.jpg), TIFF Tag Image File Format (*.tif), and Device Independent Bitmap (*.bmp). Click Save, then click the desired option when the alert box appears asking if you want to save all the slides or only the current slide.

Inserting a Hyperlink

While creating a presentation, there might be a circumstance where you want to view a document that either won't fit on the slide or is too detailed for your presentation. In these cases, you can insert a **hyperlink**, a specially formatted word, phrase, graphic, or drawn object that you click during a slide show to "jump to," or display, another slide or PowerPoint presentation in your current presentation; a document from another program, like Word; or a Web page. A hyperlinked object is similar to a linked object because you can modify the object in its source program. ▒▒▒▒▒ You add two hyperlinks to the primary presentation you have been working on that provide more detail on the Jasper bicycle tour.

STEPS

1. **Open the presentation PPT G-9.pptx from the drive and folder where you store your Data Files, then save the presentation as PPT G-Final.pptx**

QUICK TIP
Links can also be established between slides of the same presentation, a new presentation, an e-mail address, or any Web page.

2. **Click the Slide 6 thumbnail in the Slides tab, select Route highlights in the text object, click the Insert tab on the Ribbon, then click the Hyperlink button in the Links group**
   The Insert Hyperlink dialog box opens. The Existing File or Web Page button is selected in the Link to: pane, and the Current Folder button is selected in the Look in pane.

3. **Click the file PPT G-10.docx in the drive and folder where you store your Data Files, click OK, then click in a blank area of the slide**
   Now that you have made Route highlights a hyperlink to the file PPT G-10.docx, the text is formatted in a green color and is underlined, which is how a hyperlink is formatted in this theme. It's important to test any hyperlink you create.

4. **Click the Slide Show button ▣ on the status bar, point to Route highlights, notice the pointer change to 🖑, then click Route highlights**
   Microsoft Word opens, and the Word document containing a detailed description of the Vancouver-to-Calgary train tour appears, as shown in Figure G-16.

5. **Click the down scroll arrow and read the document, then click the Word window Close button ▣ ✕ ▣**
   The PowerPoint slide reappears in Slide Show view. The hyperlink is now a light brown, the color for followed hyperlinks in this theme, indicating that the hyperlink has been selected or viewed.

QUICK TIP
To edit, open, copy, or remove a hyperlink, right-click the hyperlink, then click the appropriate command on the shortcut menu.

6. **Press [Esc], click the Slide 8 thumbnail in the Slides tab, right-click the Information action button, click Hyperlink, click the Hyperlink to option button, click the Hyperlink to list arrow, click the down scroll arrow, then click Other PowerPoint Presentation**
   The Hyperlink to Other PowerPoint Presentation dialog box opens.

7. **Click the file PPT G-11.pptx in the drive and folder where you store your Data Files, then click OK**
   The Hyperlink to Slide dialog box opens. You can choose which slides you want to link to.

8. **Click OK to link to Slide 1, click OK to close the Action Settings dialog box, click ▣, click the Information action button, click the action buttons to view the slides in the presentation, press [Esc] to end the slide show, then press [Esc] again**
   The slide show ends. Both hyperlinks work correctly.

9. **Add your name to the notes and handouts footer, save your changes, then click the Slide Sorter button ▦ on the status bar**
   Compare your screen to Figure G-17.

10. **Submit your presentation to your instructor, close the presentation, then exit PowerPoint**

FIGURE G-16: Linked Word document

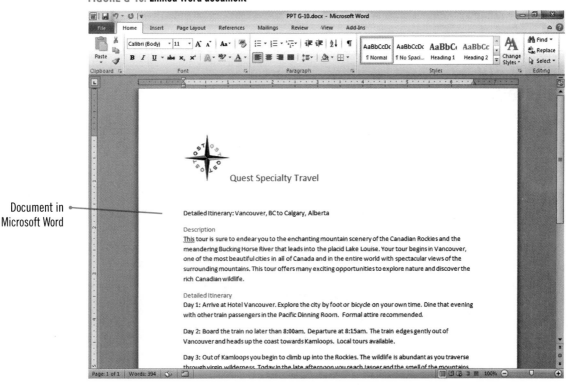

Document in
Microsoft Word

FIGURE G-17: Final presentation in Slide Sorter view

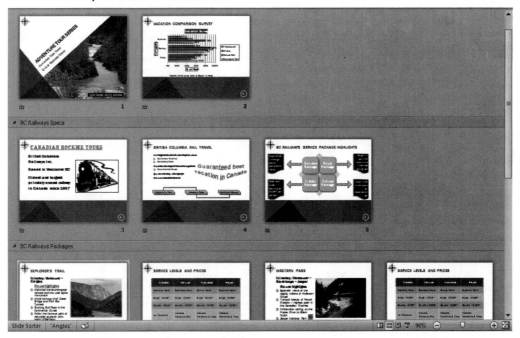

Inserting a screenshot

Using the Screenshot button in the Images group on the Insert tab, you can insert a picture, or screenshot, of an open program window or a specific part of the window. A screenshot is simply a picture of the window displayed on your screen. For example, you could use the screenshot feature to insert a picture of information you found on a Web page or found in other documents or programs that might not be easily transferable to PowerPoint. Screenshots are static and are not able to be updated if the source information changes. Only open nonminimized windows are available to be captured as a screenshot. When you click the Screenshot button all open program windows appear in the Available Windows gallery. To take a screenshot of part of a window, click the Screenshot button, then click Screen Clipping.

Inserting Graphics, Media, and Objects

Practice

For current SAM information, including versions and content details, visit SAM Central (http://www.cengage.com/samcentral). If you have a SAM user profile, you may have access to hands-on instruction, practice, and assessment of the skills covered in this unit. Since various versions of SAM are supported throughout the life of this text, check with your instructor for the correct instructions and URL/Web site for accessing assignments.

Concepts Review

Label each element of the PowerPoint window shown in Figure G-18.

FIGURE G-18

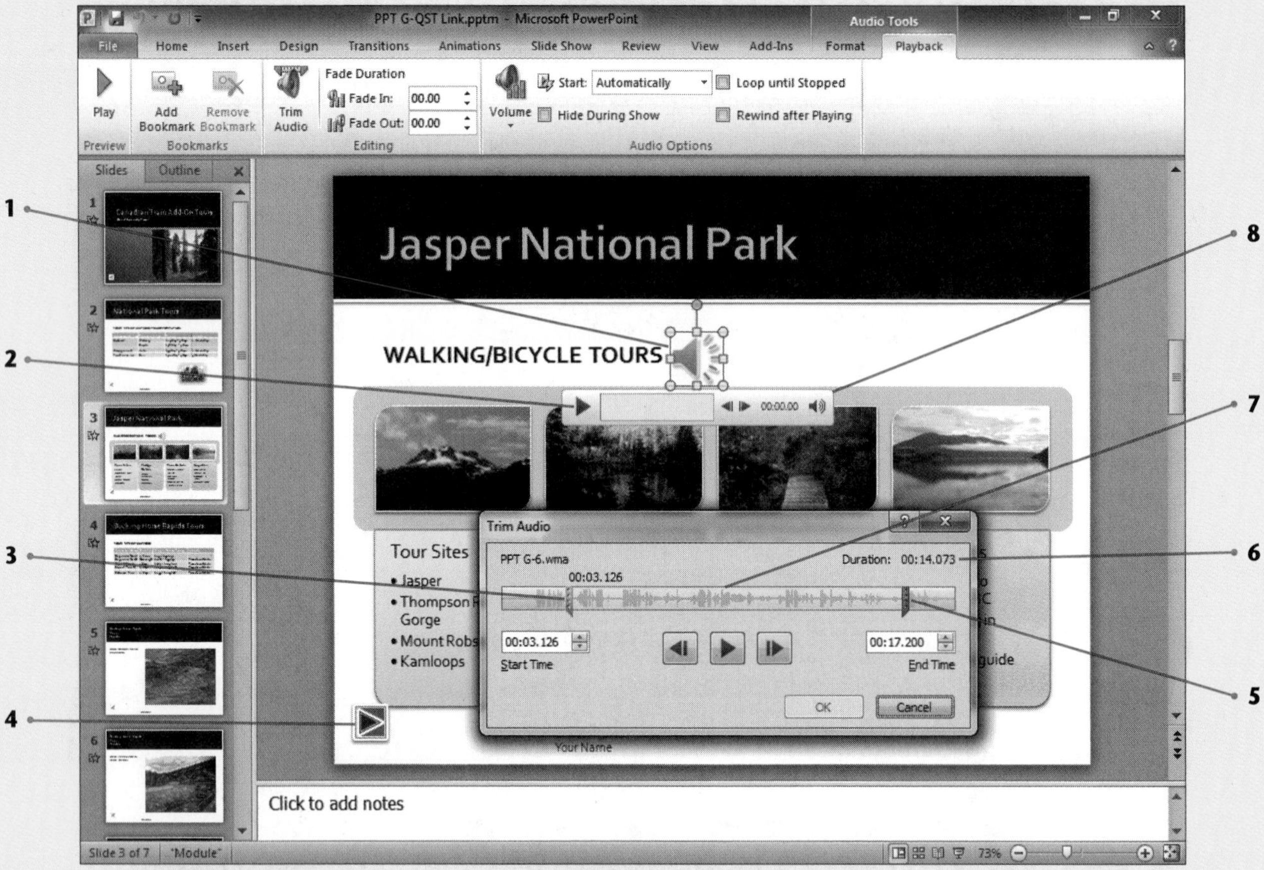

Match each of the terms with the statement that best describes its function.

9. **Equation button**
10. **.pptm**
11. **Animated video**
12. **Macro**
13. **Action button**
14. **Hyperlink**

a. Identifies a presentation file with attached macros
b. A file that contains multiple images streamed together that move during a slide show
c. Click to create mathematical integrals and functions
d. An interactive shape that performs a specific task when clicked
e. A formatted word or graphic that you can click to jump to a Web page
f. A set of actions you use to automate tasks

Select the best answer from the list of choices.

15. A _____ format is a specific file format that "locks" the file from future changes.
    - **a.** movie
    - **b.** GIF
    - **c.** macro enabled
    - **d.** fixed layout

16. Which statement best describes the function of a hyperlink in PowerPoint?
    - **a.** A button clicked in a table to start the slide show
    - **b.** Click during a slide show to display an Excel file
    - **c.** Used for animation
    - **d.** Enables a macro

17. Which of the following combines content with an illustrative diagram?
    - **a.** Hyperlink
    - **b.** Table
    - **c.** SmartArt
    - **d.** Action button

18. What is an animated GIF file?
    - **a.** Multiple images streamed together
    - **b.** A hyperlink
    - **c.** A sound
    - **d.** A digital movie

19. According to the book, a _____ is live action captured in a digital format.
    - **a.** GIF file
    - **b.** video
    - **c.** hyperlink
    - **d.** macro

20. A macro is essentially a series of _____ that you create in Visual Basic for Applications.
    - **a.** action buttons
    - **b.** file extensions
    - **c.** linked files
    - **d.** command codes

Skills Review

1. **Create custom tables.**
   a. Start PowerPoint, open the presentation PPT G-12.pptm from the drive and folder where you store your Data Files, click the Enable Content button, then save it as **PPT G-Cheese Industry**.
   b. Go to Slide 5, select the table, click the Table Tools Design tab, click the More button in the Table Styles group, then click the Medium Style 1 – Accent 3 in the Medium section.
   c. Click the Pen Weight button in the Draw Borders group, select 2¼ pt, then apply the new line style to the horizontal border for the first row.
   d. Apply the 2¼-pt line style to the vertical border lines between the cells in the first row, then click the Draw Table button.
   e. Select the table, open the Table Tools Layout tab, click the Cell Margins button in the Alignment group, then click Wide.
   f. Click anywhere in the upper-left cell, click the Select button in the Table group, click Select Row, then click the Center button in the Alignment group.
   g. Click anywhere in the bottom row, then click the Insert Below button in the Rows & Columns group.
   h. Click the left cell of the new row, type **Tomme de Savoie**, press [Tab], type **Valencay**, then save your changes.

2. **Design a SmartArt graphic.**
   a. Go to Slide 4, click the SmartArt graphic, then click the SmartArt Tools Design tab.
   b. Click the More button in the Layouts group, then click Vertical Picture Accent List in the fourth row.
   c. Open the Text pane if it is closed, click the Add Shape list arrow in the Create Graphic group, then click Add Shape After.
   d. Type **Production**, press [Enter], click the Demote button in the Create Graphic group, type **Cow cheese 1.96 million tons**, press [Enter], type **Goat cheese 0.88 million tons**, press [Enter], type **Blue cheese 0.25 million tons**.
   e. Close the Text pane, click the Change Colors button in the SmartArt Styles group, then click Colorful Range – Accent Colors 5 to 6 in the Colorful section.
   f. Click the Right to Left button in the Create Graphic group.
   g. Resize and reposition the SmartArt graphic so it is centered on the slide, then save your changes.

Skills Review (continued)

3. Format a SmartArt graphic.

    a. Click the SmartArt Tools Format tab, click the top circle shape in the SmartArt graphic, then click the Smaller button in the Shapes group.

    b. Use the Smaller button in the Shapes group to decrease the size of the two other circle shapes in the SmartArt graphic.

    c. Click the Insert picture icon in the bottom circle shape, then locate and insert the file PPT G-13.jpg from the drive and folder where you store your Data Files.

    d. Follow the above instructions and insert the file PPT G-13.jpg to the other two circle shapes, then save your changes.

4. Insert clip art video.

    a. Go to Slide 7, click the Insert tab on the Ribbon, click the Video list arrow in the Media group, then click Clip Art Video to open the Clip Art task pane.

    b. Insert a clip art video of your choosing on the slide. Type the word **e-mail** to search for an appropriate animated GIF.

    c. Resize and reposition the GIF file as necessary.

    d. Click the Picture Effects button in the Picture Styles group, then apply an effect of your choice.

    e. Preview the clip art video in Slide Show view, close the Clip Art task pane, then save your presentation.

5. Insert a sound.

    a. Go to Slide 2.

    b. Click the Insert tab, click the Audio list arrow in the Media group, then click Audio from File.

    c. Locate and insert the sound file PPT G-14.wav from the drive and folder where you store your Data Files.

    d. Preview the sound, set the sound to start automatically during a slide show, then drag the sound icon below the map graphic of France.

    e. Use the Trim Audio dialog box to change the end point of the audio clip to 00:01.700.

    f. Click the Hide During Show check box in the Audio Options group, click the Slide Show button on the status bar, review the slide, press [Esc], then save your presentation.

6. Use macros.

    a. Go to Slide 6, click the Insert tab on the Ribbon, then click the Picture button in the Images group.

    b. Locate the file PPT G-15.jpg in the drive and folder where you store your Data Files, then insert the file.

    c. Click the View tab on the Ribbon, click the Macros button, then click Run in the Macro dialog box.

    d. Drag the picture to the center of the blank area of the slide above the text at the bottom of the slide. Use the guides to help you center the picture.

    e. Click the Picture Tools Format tab on the Ribbon, click the More button in the Picture Styles group, click Metal Frame in the top row, then save your work.

7. Add action buttons.

    a. Go to Slide 1, click the Shapes button in the Drawing group, then click Action Button: Forward or Next.

    b. Draw a small button, click OK in the Action Settings dialog box, then position the button in the upper-left corner of the slide.

    c. Click the Drawing Tools Format tab on the Ribbon, click the More button in the Shape Styles group, then click Intense Effect – Light Yellow, Accent 4 in the bottom row.

    d. Copy and paste the action button on Slides 2–7.

    e. Go to Slide 8, click the Shapes button, click Action Button: Beginning, draw a small button, click OK, then drag the button to the upper-left corner of the slide.

    f. Go to Slide 7, click the action button, click the Format Painter button in the Clipboard group, click Slide 8, then click the action button.

    g. Run the slide show from Slide 1 and test the action buttons, then save your work.

8. Insert a hyperlink.

    a. Go to Slide 6, then select the words **Fredrick Amen** in the text object.

    b. Click the Insert tab on the Ribbon, click the Hyperlink button, locate the file PPT G-16.docx in the drive and folder where you store your Data Files, then click OK.

Skills Review (continued)

c. Click in the Notes pane, then type **The hyperlink opens Fred's cheese review of the 2013 French Camembert**.

d. Open Slide Show view, click the hyperlink, read the review, then click the Word window Close button.

e. Press [Esc], then add your name as a footer to the slides.

f. Check the spelling in the presentation, view the presentation in Slide Show view from Slide 1.

g. Make any necessary changes. The completed presentation is shown in Figure G-19.

h. Submit your presentation to your instructor, then save and close the presentation.

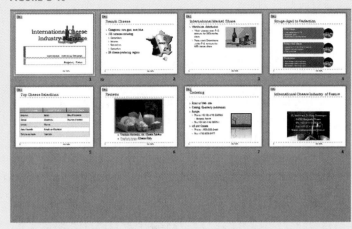

Independent Challenge 1

Milsap Brothers Engineering is a mechanical and industrial design company that specializes in designing manufacturing plants around the world. As a company financial analyst, you need to investigate and report on a possible contract to design and build a large manufacturing plant in China.

a. Open the file PPT G-17.pptx, then save it as **PPT G-China**.

b. On Slide 3, apply the table style Themed Style 1 – Accent 5, then draw a dotted line down the center of the table using the Pen Style button.

c. Click in the top row of the table, insert a row above the top row, type **Line Item** in the left cell, then type **Budget** in the right cell.

d. Click the Overhead/Benefits cell, split the cell into two columns and one row, then move the word **Benefits** to the new cell and delete the slash.

e. Create a new SmartArt graphic on Slide 4 using the following process information: **Planning and Design, Site Acquisition and Preparation, Underground Construction, Above-ground Construction**, and **Finish and Building Completion**.

f. Change the colors of the graphic to a colorful theme, then apply a 3-D style.

g. Change the shape of at least one shape in the SmartArt graphic using the Change Shape button, then click the Right to Left button in the Create Graphic group on the SmartArt Tools Design tab.

h. Add your name as a footer on the slides, then save your changes.

Advanced Challenge Exercise

- Create a new slide using the Title and Content slide layout, type **Project Organization** in the title placeholder, then create an hierarchy chart SmartArt graphic.
- Fill the text boxes with the following job titles: **Project Manager, Project Foreman, Design Manager,** and **Project Coordinator**.
- Click the top shape, click the Layout button in the Create Graphic group, then click Left Hanging.
- Format the graphic by adding a new style and color theme, make any other necessary changes, then save the presentation as **Chinese Plant ACE**.

i. Check the presentation spelling, view the presentation in Slide Show view, submit your presentation to your instructor, then close the presentation and exit PowerPoint.

Independent Challenge 2

You work for The Feldman Group, a large investment banking firm in Omaha, Nebraska. Feldman is considering buying Waxby Financial Services, a smaller investment company in Oklahoma City. As part of the company financial operations team, you need to present some projections regarding the purchase to a special committee formed by Feldman to study the proposed deal.

a. Open the file PPT G-18.pptx from the drive and folder where you store your Data Files, then save it as **PPT G-Feldman**.

b. Format the table on Slide 3 first, apply a table style from the Light Style 2 styles section of the Table Styles gallery; next draw three 1½-pt dotted vertical cell separator lines in the table, and finally, click the First Column check box in the Table Style Options group.

c. Convert the text on Slide 5 to a SmartArt graphic using one of the List layouts.

d. Format the SmartArt graphic by applying an Accent 3 color theme, and then changing the SmartArt style to Subtle Effect.

e. Insert a clip art video on Slide 3. Use the word **profits** to search for an appropriate animated GIF.

f. Select the word **Waxby** on Slide 2, click the Insert tab on the Ribbon, click the Hyperlink button in the Links group, locate the file PPT G-19.pptx from the drive and folder where you store your Data Files, then click OK.

g. Add your name as a footer on the slides, check the spelling of the presentation, then save your changes.

h. View the presentation in Slide Show view, and click the hyperlink on Slide 2.

i. Submit your presentation to your instructor, close the presentation, then exit PowerPoint.

Independent Challenge 3

You have been recently hired at Rinco Inc., a U.S. company that exports goods and services to companies in all parts of Asia, including Japan, Hong Kong, China, and the Philippines. One of your new responsibilities is to prepare short presentations on different subjects for use on the company Web site using data provided to you by others in the company.

a. Open the file PPT G-20.pptx from the drive and folder where you store your Data Files, then save it as **PPT G-Rinco**.

b. Add a design theme, background shading, or other objects to make your presentation look professional. Make adjustments to objects as necessary.

c. Convert the text on Slide 3 to a SmartArt graphic, then format the graphic using any of the formatting commands available.

d. Insert an appropriate clip art video on the last slide of the presentation.

e. Insert a sound on Slide 2. Use the word **harbor** to search for an appropriate sound.

f. Change the layout and format the charts on Slides 4 and 5.

g. Create, format, and position Forward action buttons on Slides 1–5.

h. Create, format, and position Back action buttons on Slides 2–6, then create, format, and position a Home action button on Slide 6.

Advanced Challenge Exercise *(Requirements: connected microphone, sound card, and speakers)*

- Prepare a narration for one or more slides, then produce a narration by using one of the following steps.
- **One slide:** To add a narration to one slide, go to the slide, click the Insert tab, click the Audio list arrow, click Record Audio, click the Record button in the Record Sound dialog box, record your narration, then click the Stop button to end the recording.
- **Multiple slides:** To add a narration to multiple slides while viewing a slide show, click the Slide Show tab, click the Record Slide Show button in the Set Up group, click Start Recording, record your narration, then click [Esc] to end the recording.

Independent Challenge 3 (continued)

i. Add your name as a footer to the slides, check the spelling of the presentation, save your changes, then view the presentation in Slide Show view. See Figure G-20.

j. Submit your presentation to your instructor, close the presentation, then exit PowerPoint.

FIGURE G-20

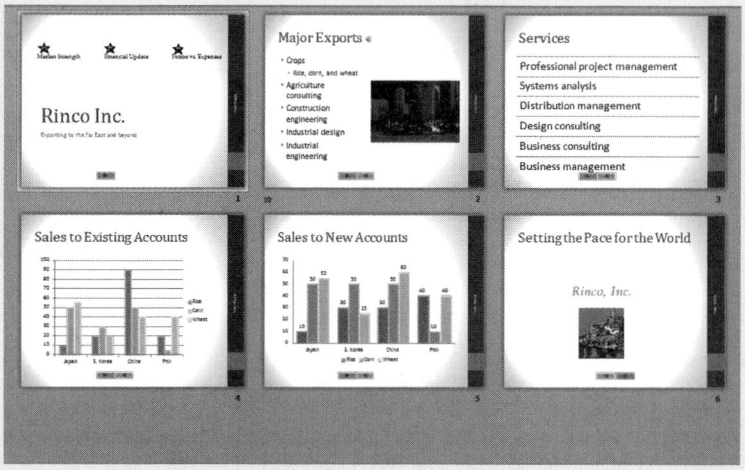

Real Life Independent Challenge

One of the assignments in your business course at the university is to give a 15-minute presentation on any subject to the class. The goal of the assignment is for you to persuade the class (and your instructor) to make an informed decision about the subject you are presenting based on your ability to communicate the facts. You decide to create a presentation using pictures and other media to play in the background while you give your presentation.

To develop the content of this presentation:

- Choose your own subject matter, for example, a favorite hobby or sport.
- Use your own media clips (pictures, sounds, or video) on your computer. If you don't have your own media clips, you can search the Clip Organizer for appropriate clips.

a. Open the file PPT G-21.pptm from the drive and folder where you store your Data Files, then save it as **PPT G-Business**. Click the Enable Content button. The file PPT G-21.pptm has no content, but is macro-enabled.

b. Add your name, the date, and the slide number as the footer on all slides, except the title slide.

c. Decide on a presentation subject, then think about what results you want to see and what information you will need to create the slide presentation.

d. Insert one picture (your own or one from the Clip Organizer) on each slide, run the available macro for each picture, then move the picture to the center of the slide.

e. Insert one or more appropriate sounds from your computer; you can record a sound, or use one from the Clip Organizer.

f. Insert one or more appropriate videos from your computer or the Clip Organizer.

g. Give each slide a title, and add text where appropriate. Create additional slides as necessary.

h. Apply an appropriate design theme.

i. Check the spelling of the presentation, view the final presentation in Slide Show view, save the final version, then submit the presentation to your instructor. See Figure G-21.

j. Close the presentation, then exit PowerPoint.

FIGURE G-21

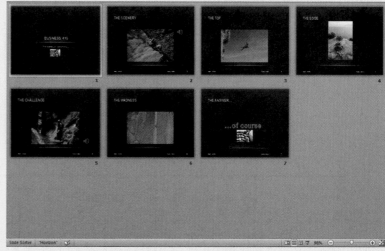

Visual Workshop

Create a slide that looks like the example in Figure G-22. The SmartArt is created using the Horizontal Bullet List layout with the Cartoon style and the colored Gradient Loop – Accent 1 color. Save the presentation as **PPT G-California**. Add your name as a footer on the slide, save the presentation, then submit the presentation to your instructor.

FIGURE G-22

Using Advanced Features

After your work on a presentation is complete, PowerPoint provides you with several options for preparing and distributing your final presentation. For example, you can send the presentation out for review and receive comments and changes, which you then incorporate into your presentation. At this stage in the process, you can also create customized slide shows and use advanced options to set up and deliver a slide show. You also use PowerPoint to create albums to organize and share your photographs. Before you distribute the Canadian train tour presentation, you need to have other people in the company review it. Once others have reviewed your presentation, you can incorporate their changes and comments. You then create a custom slide show, change slide show options, and prepare the presentation for distribution. You end your day by creating a photo album of your relatives that have worked in the railroad industry and learning about broadcasting a presentation on the Internet.

OBJECTIVES

Send a presentation for review

Combine reviewed presentations

Set up a slide show

Create a custom show

Prepare a presentation for distribution

Use templates and add comments

Create a photo album

Broadcast a presentation

Sending a Presentation for Review

When you finish creating a presentation, it is often helpful to have others look over the slides for accuracy and clarity. If you are not in the same location as the reviewers, and you have Microsoft Outlook on your computer, you can open Outlook directly from PowerPoint and send a presentation file as an attachment in an e-mail. A reviewer can open the presentation on their computer, make changes and comments, and then e-mail it back to you. Use Outlook to send the presentation to your supervisor for her comments and suggestions.

STEPS

1. **Start PowerPoint, open the presentation PPT H-1.pptx from the drive and folder where your Data Files are stored, then save it as PPT H-QST**

2. **Click the File tab on the Ribbon, click Save & Send, then click the Send as Attachment button in the Send Using E-mail section**

   Microsoft Outlook opens in a new message window as shown in Figure H-1. The subject text box includes the name of the presentation and the Attached text box shows the presentation is automatically attached to the e-mail.

3. **Click the To button in the Outlook message window**

   The Select Names: Contacts dialog box opens. If you have added Contacts to the address book in Outlook, you can use this dialog box to select e-mail addresses for the people you want to review the presentation.

4. **Click Cancel, then type your e-mail address in the To text box**

   Your e-mail address appears in the To text box in the Outlook window.

5. **Click in the message body, then type Please review and get back to me. Thanks.**

   The e-mail is ready to send. Compare your screen to Figure H-2.

6. **Click the Send button in the Outlook message window**

   Outlook sends the e-mail message with the attached presentation file, and the Outlook message window closes.

7. **Start Outlook, click the Send/Receive tab on the Ribbon, then click the Send/Receive All Folders button in the Send & Receive group**

   You may have to wait a short time before the e-mail message you sent to yourself arrives in the Inbox with the PowerPoint file attachment. If the e-mail message is selected, it appears in the Reading pane.

8. **Click the Outlook Close button** ❌

   Outlook closes and the PowerPoint window appears.

FIGURE H-1: Outlook message window

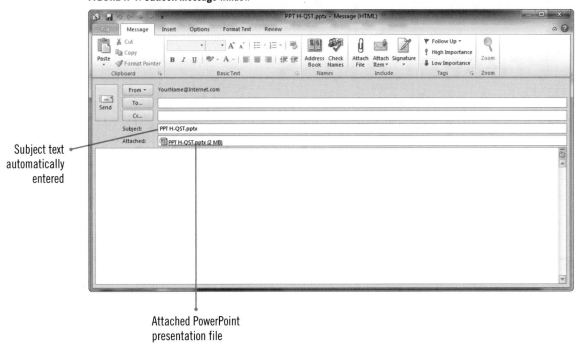

Subject text
automatically
entered

Attached PowerPoint
presentation file

FIGURE H-2: Completed Outlook message window

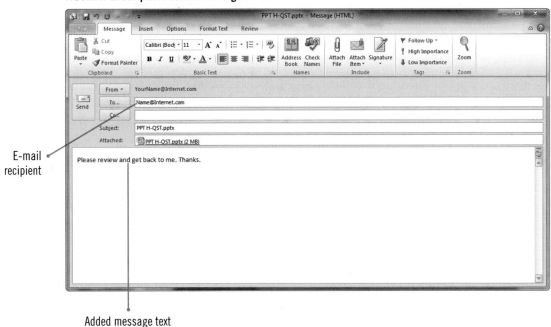

E-mail
recipient

Added message text

Packaging a presentation

Before you copy and distribute one or more presentations, you should always inspect the presentations for personal or confidential information. Once you are ready to save the presentations to a CD or folder, open a presentation, click the File tab, then click Save & Send. Click Package Presentation for CD, then click the Package for CD button. The Package for CD dialog box opens with the current open presentation shown in the list of files to be copied. At this point

you can add or remove presentations that you want packaged together. All linked and embedded objects are included in the package. In the Package for CD dialog box, click the Copy to Folder button to save the presentations to a folder on your computer or network, or insert a CD into your computer and click the Copy to CD button. Follow the instructions, then click Close when the saving process is completed.

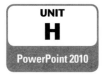

Combining Reviewed Presentations

Once a reviewer has completed their review of your presentation and sends it back, you can merge the changes in the reviewer's presentation into your original presentation using the Compare command on the Review tab. You can accept individual changes, changes by slides, changes by reviewer if there is more than one reviewer, or all changes to the presentation. You also have the option or rejecting some or all of the changes and ending the review without making all of the changes. ▇▇▇▇▇ You sent the QST presentation to your supervisor who has reviewed the presentation and sent it back to you. You are now ready to combine the reviewed presentation with your original one.

STEPS

1. **Click the Review tab on the Ribbon, then click the Compare button in the Compare group**
   The Choose File to Merge with Current Presentation dialog box opens.

2. **Locate the presentation PPT H-2.pptx in the drive and folder where you store your Data Files, click PPT H-2.pptx, then click Merge**
   The reviewed presentation is merged with your original one. The Revisions task pane opens on the right side of the screen. It is divided into two tabs: the Slides tab and the Details tab. The Slides tab displays a thumbnail of the current slide and shows what the slide would look like if the suggested changes were made. The Details tab displays individual changes by reviewer for the current slide. The first change is to the text object on Slide 4 and is identified by a reviewer marker as shown in Figure H-3.

> **QUICK TIP**
> To accept all changes on the current slide or in the whole presentation, click the Accept list arrow, then click the appropriate option.

3. **Click the All changes to Content Placeholder 2 check box, then review the text change in the text object**
   "Easy" replaces "Quick and easy" in the third first-level bullet in the text object. The reviewer marker and all three check boxes now have check marks in them indicating that the change has been accepted.

4. **Click the Next button in the Compare group, click the Review comment thumbnail RBB2 at the top of the slide, then read the comment**
   Slide 9 appears in the Slide pane showing one reviewer marker and one review comment thumbnail labeled RBB2.

5. **Click the Delete button in the Comments group, click the reviewer marker on the slide, then click the Inserted TextBox 2 check box**
   A new formatted text box appears on the slide with information about meals. You decide to reject this change, but will create a slide that discusses meals at a later time.

6. **Click the Inserted TextBox 2 check box to remove the check mark, click the Next button in the Compare group, then click Continue in the message dialog box**
   All of the changes are reviewed. Slide 4 appears in the Slide pane showing the accepted change to the text object.

7. **Click the Next button in the Comments group, then click Continue in message dialog box**
   Slide 1 appears and displays a comment as shown in Figure H-4.

> **QUICK TIP**
> To reject all changes on the current slide or in the whole presentation, click the Reject list arrow, then click the appropriate option.

8. **Click the Delete list arrow in the Comments group, click Delete All Markup in this Presentation, then click Yes in the message dialog box**
   All of the comments in the presentation are now deleted.

9. **Click the End Review button in the Compare group, read the message dialog box, click Yes, then save your work**
   The Revisions task pane closes.

Using Advanced Features

FIGURE H-3: Screen showing open Revisions pane

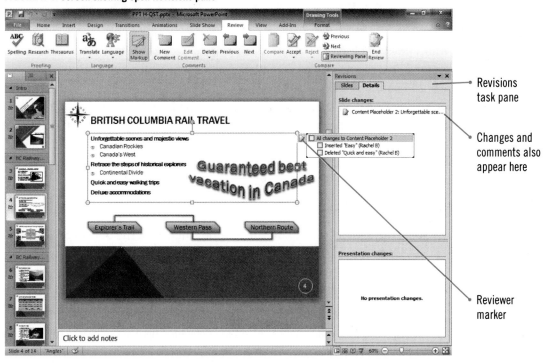

Revisions task pane

Changes and comments also appear here

Reviewer marker

FIGURE H-4: Slide with comment

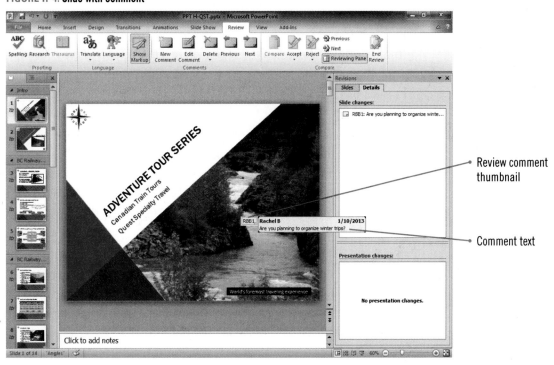

Review comment thumbnail

Comment text

PowerPoint 2010

Coauthoring a presentation

Using collaboration software, such as SharePoint Foundation 2010, Microsoft SharePoint Server 2010, or Microsoft Office Live Workspace, you have the ability to work with others on a presentation over the Internet at the same time. To set up a presentation to be coauthored with you as the original author, click the File tab, click Save & Send, then click Save to SharePoint. Choose a SharePoint location or server to store a primary copy of your presentation, then click the Save As button. All changes made to the presentation are recorded, including who is working on the presentation and where in the presentation they are working. To use this feature, all authors must have PowerPoint 2010 installed on their computers.

Setting Up a Slide Show

With PowerPoint, you can create a self-running slide show that plays without user intervention. For example, you can set up a presentation so viewers can watch a slide show on a stand-alone computer, in a small booth or **kiosk**, at a convention, mall, or some other public place. You can also create a self-running presentation on a CD, DVD, or Flash drive for others to watch. You have a number of options when designing a self-running presentation; for example, you can include hyperlinks or action buttons to assist your audience as they move through the presentation. You can also add a synchronized voice that narrates the presentation, and set either manual or automatic slide timings. ⬛⬛⬛ You prepare the presentation so it can be self-running.

STEPS

1. **Click the Slide Show tab on the Ribbon, then click the Set Up Slide Show button in the Set Up group**

   The Set Up Show dialog box has options you can set to specify how the show will run.

2. **Click the Browsed at a kiosk (full screen) option button in the Show type section of the Set Up Show dialog box**

   This option allows you to have a self-running presentation that can be viewed without a presenter.

QUICK TIP
You must use automatic timings, navigation hyperlinks, or action buttons when you use the kiosk option; otherwise, you will not be able to progress through the slides.

3. **Make sure the All option button is selected in the Show slides section, then make sure the Using timings, if present option button is selected in the Advance slides section**

   These settings include all the slides in the presentation and enable PowerPoint to advance the slides at time intervals you set. See Figure H-5.

4. **Click OK, click the Transitions tab on the Ribbon, click the On Mouse Click check box in the Timing group to remove the check mark, click the After up arrow until 00:10.00 appears, then click the Apply To All button in the Timing group**

   Each slide in the presentation now will now be displayed for 10 seconds before the slide show advances automatically to the next slide.

5. **Click the Slide Show button 🖵 on the status bar, view the show, let it start again, press [Esc], then click the Slide Show tab on the Ribbon**

   PowerPoint advances the slides automatically at 10-second intervals. After the last slide, the slide show starts over because the kiosk slide show option loops the presentation until someone presses [Esc].

6. **Click the Set Up Slide Show button in the Set Up group, click the Presented by a speaker (full screen) option button, then click OK**

   The slide show options are back to their default settings.

QUICK TIP
To view a hidden slide while in Slide Show view, right-click the current slide, click Go to Slide, then click the hidden slide.

7. **Click the Slide 1 thumbnail in the Slides tab, click the Hide Slide button in the Set Up group, click the From Beginning button in the Start Slide Show group, then press [Esc]**

   The slide show begins with Slide 2. Notice that Slide 1 in the Slides tab is dimmed and has a hidden slide icon on its number indicating it is hidden, as shown in Figure H-6.

8. **Right-click the Slide 1 thumbnail in the Slides tab, click Hide Slide in the shortcut menu, then save your changes**

   Slide 1 is no longer hidden, or dimmed, and the hidden slide icon is removed.

FIGURE H-5: Set Up Show dialog box

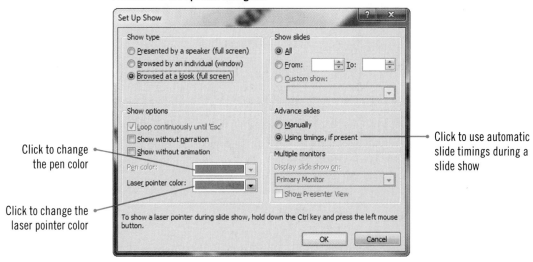

Click to change the pen color

Click to change the laser pointer color

Click to use automatic slide timings during a slide show

FIGURE H-6: Slide 1 is a hidden slide

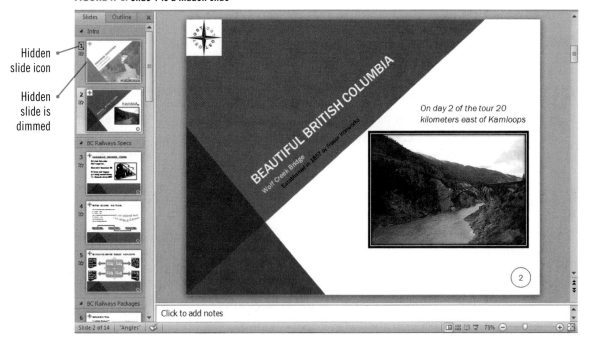

Hidden slide icon

Hidden slide is dimmed

Using Presenter view

Presenter view is a special PowerPoint view that permits you to run a presentation through two monitors; one monitor that you see on your computer and a second monitor that your audience views. Running a presentation through two monitors provides you more control over your presentation, allowing you to click thumbnails of slides to jump to specific slides and run other programs, if necessary. Presenter view is designed with large icons, buttons, and other tools, which help you easily navigate through a presentation. Speaker notes, not visible to the audience, are easy to read for the presenter. To use this feature, your computer must have multiple monitor capacity, and you need to turn on multiple monitor support and Presenter view. To turn on multiple monitor support, click the Use Presenter View check box in the Monitors group on the Slide Show tab and follow the instructions.

Creating a Custom Show

A custom show gives you the ability to adapt a presentation for use in different circumstances or with different audiences. For example, you might have a 25-slide presentation that you show to new customers, but only 12 of those slides are necessary for a presentation for existing customers. PowerPoint provides two types of custom shows: basic and hyperlinked. A basic custom show is a separate presentation or a presentation that includes slides from the original presentation. A hyperlinked custom show is a separate (secondary) presentation that is linked to a primary custom show or presentation. You have been asked to create a version of the Canadian Train Tours presentation for a staff meeting, so you create and view a custom slide show containing only the slides appropriate for that audience. You also learn to use the laser pointer during a slide show.

STEPS

1. **Click the Slide Show tab on the Ribbon, click the Custom Slide Show button in the Start Slide Show group, click Custom Shows to open the Custom Shows dialog box, then click New**

   The Define Custom Show dialog box opens. The slides that are in your current presentation are listed in the Slides in presentation list box.

2. **Press and hold [Ctrl], click Slide 1, click Slides 3–12, release [Ctrl], then click Add**

   The 11 slides you selected move to the Slides in custom show list box, indicating that they will be included in the new presentation. See Figure H-7.

3. **Click 3. British Columbia Rail Travel in the Slides in custom show list, then click the Slide Order up arrow button 🔼 once**

   The slide moves from third place to second place in the list. You can arrange the slides in any order in your custom show by clicking the Slide order up and down arrows.

4. **Click 11. Vacation Comparison Survey, click Remove, drag to select the existing text in the Slide show name text box, type Brief Train Presentation, then click OK**

   The Custom Shows dialog box lists your custom presentation. The custom show is not saved as a separate presentation file on your computer even though you assigned it a new name. To view a custom slide show, you must first open the presentation you used to create the custom show in Slide Show view. You then can open the custom show from the Custom Shows dialog box.

5. **Click Show, view the Brief Train Presentation slide show, then press [Esc] to end the slide show**

   The slides in the custom show appear in the order you set in the Define Custom Show dialog box. At the end of the slide show, you return to the presentation in Normal view.

6. **Click the From Beginning button in the Start Slide Show group, right-click the screen, point to Custom Show, then click Brief Train Presentation**

   The Brief Presentation custom show appears in Slide Show view.

7. **When Slide 3 appears, press and hold [Ctrl], press and hold the left mouse button, move the laser pointer around the slide as shown in Figure H-8, release [Ctrl], release the mouse button, then view the presentation**

   You can use the laser pointer in any presentation on any slide during a slide show.

8. **Press [Esc] at any point to end the slide show, then save your changes**

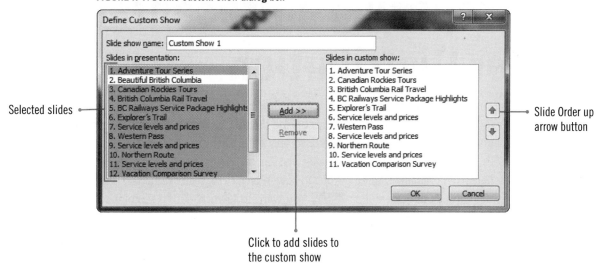

Selected slides

Click to add slides to the custom show

Slide Order up arrow button

FIGURE H-8: Screen showing slide 3 in the custom slide show

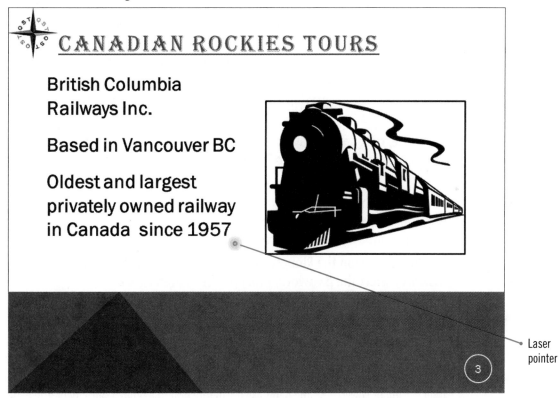

Laser pointer

Link to a custom slide show

You can use action buttons to switch from the "parent" show to the custom show. Click the Shapes button in the Drawing group on the Home tab, then click an action button. Draw an action button on the slide. Click the Hyperlink to list arrow, click Custom Show, click the custom show you want to link, then click OK. Now when you run a slide show you can click the action button you created to run the custom show. You can also create an interactive table of contents using custom shows. Create your table of contents entries on a slide, then hyperlink each entry to the section it refers to using a custom show for each section.

Preparing a Presentation for Distribution

Reviewing and preparing your presentation before you share it with others is an essential step, especially with so many security and privacy issues on the Internet today. One way to help secure your PowerPoint presentation is to set a security password, so only authorized people can view or modify its content. If you plan to open a presentation in an earlier version of PowerPoint, it is a good idea to determine if the presentation is compatible. Some features in PowerPoint 2010, such as SmartArt graphics, are not compatible in earlier versions of PowerPoint. 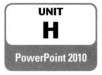 You want to learn about PowerPoint security and compatibility features so you can use them on presentations and other documents.

STEPS

1. **Click the Slide 1 thumbnail in the Slides tab, click the File tab on the Ribbon, click the Protect Presentation button, then click Encrypt with Password**

   The Encrypt Document dialog box opens.

2. **Type 123abc**

   As you type the password, solid black symbols appear in the text box, which makes it unreadable, as shown in Figure H-9. If anyone is looking at your screen while you type, this helps protect the confidentiality of your password.

   > **TROUBLE**
   > If you mistype the password in the Confirm Password dialog box, an alert dialog box opens.

3. **Click OK to open the Confirm Password dialog box, type 123abc, then click OK**

   The presentation is now set with a password. Once the presentation is closed, this password must be entered in a Password dialog box to open the presentation. The presentation is **encrypted**, protected from unauthorized users.

4. **Click Close, click Save to save changes, click the File tab, click Recent, then click PPT H-QST.pptx on the Recent Presentations list to open the file**

   The Password dialog box opens.

   > **QUICK TIP**
   > To set other password options, open the Save As dialog box, click Tools, then click General Options.

5. **Type 123abc, then click OK**

   The presentation opens. Be aware that if you don't remember your password, there is no way to retrieve it from the presentation or from Microsoft, and you will not be able to open or view your presentation.

6. **Click the File tab on the Ribbon, click the Protect Presentation button, click Encrypt with Password, select the password, press [Delete], then click OK**

   The password is removed and is no longer needed to open the presentation.

   > **QUICK TIP**
   > The Check Accessibility feature checks for potential issues that might be difficult for people with disabilities to read. Click the File tab, click the Check for Issues button, then click Check Accessibility to open the Accessibility Checker task pane.

7. **Click the Check for Issues button, then click Check Compatibility**

   The Compatibility Checker analyzes the presentation, then the Microsoft PowerPoint Compatibility Checker dialog box opens, as shown in Figure H-10. Each item in the dialog box represents a feature that is not supported in earlier versions of PowerPoint. This means that if you try to run this presentation using an earlier version of PowerPoint, the items listed will function in a limited capacity or not at all.

8. **Click the down scroll arrow, read all of the items in the dialog box, click OK, add your name to the notes and handouts footer, then click the Slide Sorter button 🔲 on the status bar**

   The dialog box closes. Compare your screen to Figure H-11.

9. **Save your work, submit your presentation to your instructor, then close the presentation but do not exit PowerPoint**

Encrypted password

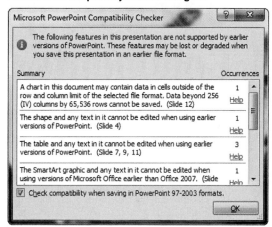

FIGURE H-11: **Final presentation in Slide Sorter view**

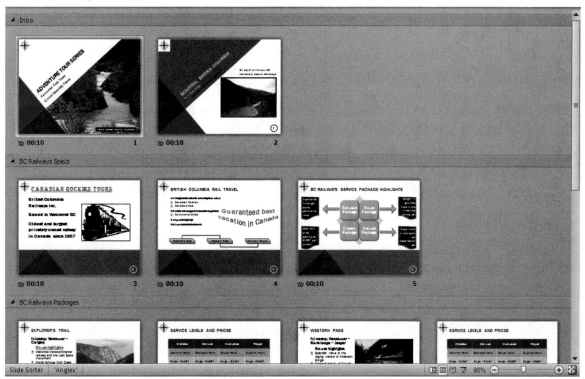

Creating a strong password

Creating a strong password is a vital part of securing your presentations, other sensitive documents, Internet accounts, and personal information. The strongest password is a random complex string of lowercase and uppercase characters and numbers. For example, the password used in this lesson, 123abc, is a weak password. Though it has both numbers and lowercase letters, it is an easy sequential password that someone could guess. Here are some simple guidelines to making a good password: (1) make the password long by using eight or more characters; (2) use a variety of uppercase and lowercase letters, symbols, and numbers; (3) if possible use words or phrases that you can remember that are difficult for others to guess; (4) keep your password secret and never reveal it in an e-mail; and (5) regularly change your password.

PowerPoint 2010

Using Templates and Adding Comments

PowerPoint offers you a variety of ways to create a presentation including beginning with a blank presentation, a theme, a template, or an existing presentation. A **template** is a type of presentation that contains custom design information made to the slide master and slide layouts. A template can contain theme colors, theme fonts, theme effects, background styles, and even content. PowerPoint installs a number of templates on your computer that include the standard Blank presentation and Sample templates. You also have access to templates online from the Office.com Web site that you can download. 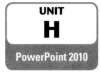 You need to review available PowerPoint templates that could be used to display pictures of upcoming tour specials for the company Web site.

STEPS

1. **Click the File tab on the Ribbon, then click New**
   The Available Templates and Themes pane opens in Backstage view. Blank Presentation is selected.

2. **Click Sample templates, click each template thumbnail to view it in the Preview pane, then click Contemporary Photo Album**
   These templates are installed on your computer and are available for you to use. Each template comes with sample content including graphics and text. See Figure H-12.

3. **Click the Create button in the Preview pane, click the Save button 🔲 on the Quick Access toolbar, then save the file as PPT H-Sample Album to the drive and folder where you store your Data Files**
   A new presentation with six slides appears in the program window.

   QUICK TIP
   You can copy the text of a comment to the slide by clicking the review comment thumbnail, then dragging the comment text to a blank area on the slide.

4. **Click the Review tab on the Ribbon, click the New Comment button in the Comments group, then type This sample photo album might work for our next photo proposal.**
   A new comment text box appears next to the review comment thumbnail on the slide, as shown in Figure H-13.

5. **Click the Slide 5 thumbnail in the Slides tab, click the middle photograph, click the New Comment button in the Comments group, then type The use of different picture styles looks great.**
   A new comment appears on Slide 5 next to the middle photograph.

   QUICK TIP
   Double-click the review comment thumbnail to open the comment text box to add to or edit the comment text.

6. **Click the Previous button in the Comments group, click the Edit Comment button in the Comments group, then type I really like this picture style.**
   The comment text box opens. To add or edit comment text, you need to open the comment text box.

7. **Click the Show Markup button in the Comments group**
   The review comment thumbnail and comment text box on Slide 1 are hidden. The Show Markup button is a toggle button, which alternates between showing and hiding comments.

8. **Click the Next button in the Comments group, then click the Show Markup button in the Comments group, add your name to the slide footer, then save your work**
   The review comment thumbnail is visible again. After you save the presentation, the review comment thumbnail changes to A2 identifying the comment as the second comment made by the author of the presentation.

9. **Submit your presentation to your instructor, then close the presentation but do not exit PowerPoint**

FIGURE H-12: Screen showing sample templates

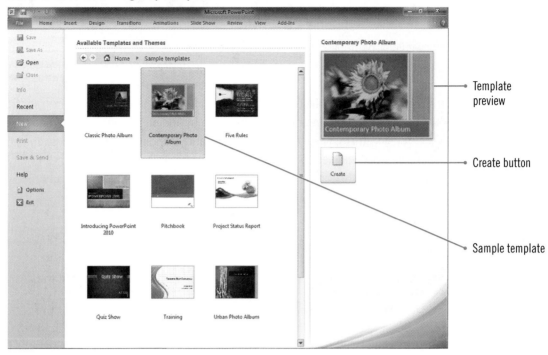

Template preview

Create button

Sample template

FIGURE H-13: Slide showing applied template and new comment

Review comment thumbnail

New template with sample content appears on six slides

Today's date appears here

New comment

Comment text box

Contemporary Photo Album

Saving a presentation to SkyDrive on Windows Live

SkyDrive is a free password-protected online storage service provided by Microsoft at the Windows Live Web site on the Internet. Files you upload and store on SkyDrive can be opened from any computer in the world that has access to the Internet. You can store up to 25 GB on SkyDrive, and you have the capability of sharing files with others you are connected with on your Windows Live network. To take

advantage of this service you need to first have a Windows Live ID, which you can get from the Windows Live Web site. Then, to save a presentation file to SkyDrive, click the File tab on the Ribbon, click Save & Send, click Save to Web, click the Sign In button, then follow the directions.

Creating a Photo Album

A PowerPoint photo album is a special presentation designed specifically to display photographs. You can add pictures to a photo album from any storage device such as a hard drive, flash drive, digital camera, scanner, or Web camera. As with any presentation, you can customize the layout of a photo album presentation by adding title text to slides, applying frames around the pictures, and applying a theme. You can also format the pictures of the photo album by adding a caption, converting the pictures to black and white, rotating them, applying artistic effects, and changing their brightness and contrast. ▰▰▰▰▰ On a break from work, you decide to create a personal photo album showing some of your relatives who worked for the railroad in the early and mid-20th century.

STEPS

1. **Click the Insert tab on the Ribbon, click the Photo Album list arrow in the Images group, then click New Photo Album**

   The Photo Album dialog box opens.

2. **Click File/Disk, select the file PPT H-3.jpg from the drive and folder where you store your Data Files, then click Insert**

   The photograph appears in the Preview box and is listed in the Pictures in album list, as shown in Figure H-14. The buttons below the Preview box allow you to rotate the photo or change its contrast or brightness.

   QUICK TIP
   You can make appearance changes to photographs by clicking the Brightness and Contrast buttons in the Photo Album dialog box.

3. **Click File/Disk, click the file PPT H-4.jpg, press and hold [Shift], click the file PPT H-7.jpg, release [Shift], then click Insert**

   Four more photographs appear in the dialog box.

4. **Click Create, save the presentation as PPT H-Photo Album to the drive and folder where you store your Data Files, then change the slide title to Family Railroad Engineers**

   A new presentation opens. PowerPoint creates a title slide along with a slide for each photograph that you inserted. The computer user name appears in the subtitle text box by default.

5. **Click the Photo Album list arrow in the Images group, then click Edit Photo Album**

   The Edit Photo Album dialog box opens. You can use this dialog box to format the photographs and slide layout of your photo album presentation.

6. **Click PPT H-3.jpg in the Pictures in album list, press and hold [Shift], click PPT H-7.jpg, release [Shift], click the Picture layout list arrow in the Album Layout section, click 1 picture with title, click the Frame shape list arrow, click Center Shadow Rectangle, then click Update**

   All of the slides now have a title text placeholder, and the photographs are formatted with a shadow and centered on each slide.

7. **Referring to Figure H-15, click each slide thumbnail in the Slides pane, add the corresponding title to each slide, then click the Slide Sorter view button 🖿 on the status bar**

   All of the slides now have a title.

8. **Drag the Zoom Slider ▽ on the status bar until your screen looks similar to Figure H-15, then add your name to the slides footer**

9. **Save your changes, submit your presentation to your instructor, close the presentation, then exit PowerPoint**

FIGURE H-14: Photo Album dialog box

File/Disk button

Up and Down buttons

Brightness buttons

Contrast buttons

Rotate buttons

FIGURE H-15: Completed photo album

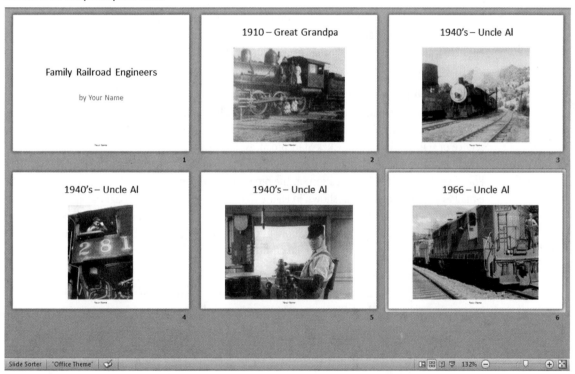

Recording a slide show

With the Record Slide Show feature you have the ability to record and save audio narrations, slide and animation timings, and laser pointer gestures for each slide during a slide show. This feature is great to use if you want to record audience comments so that people who were unable to attend the presentation live can view and listen to it later. To record a slide show, click the Slide Show tab, click the Record Slide Show list arrow in the Set Up group, then start the recording from the beginning of the current slide. You then have to choose which elements you want to record during the slide show. If you choose to record audio narrations, you must have a microphone, a sound card, and speakers. A sound icon appears on every narrated slide.

Broadcasting a Presentation

Being able to assemble everyone in the same room for a presentation can be difficult, which is why the PowerPoint broadcasting feature provides a way to share your presentation to a remote audience. You can use PowerPoint to broadcast a presentation to an audience over the Internet in real time using a Web browser. In preparation for hosting a presentation broadcast to others in your company, you learn the basics of broadcasting from PowerPoint.

DETAILS

- **Broadcast overview**

  Using the Broadcast Slide Show feature in PowerPoint, you can present a slide show to anyone on the Internet. To view the presentation broadcast, audience members need to have an Internet address (URL) link so they can access your broadcast on the Internet. You can e-mail your audience members the URL for your slide show before or during the broadcast without interfering with the broadcast. You are required to have a network service to host a broadcast, like the PowerPoint Broadcast Service, which is available to anyone on the Internet with a Windows Live ID. You can also use a broadcast service provided by your company or organization that has Microsoft Office Web Apps installed.

- **Prepare a presentation for a broadcast**

  Before you attempt to broadcast a presentation slide show, make sure you are connected to the Internet or an organization server with a broadcast site and Office Web Apps installed. To host a broadcast, you need to use one of the supported Web browsers: Internet Explorer, Firefox, or Safari. Not all PowerPoint features are supported for broadcasting, and some features are altered. For example, slide transitions in your presentation are converted to Fade and sounds, including narrations, or videos are not transmitted. Also, you cannot annotate or markup slides during a broadcast, and hyperlinks are not shown to your audience. Keep in mind too that the broadcast service you use might impose file size limitations on broadcasted presentation files.

- **Broadcast a presentation**

  To broadcast a presentation, click the Broadcast Slide Show button in the Start Slide Show group on the Slide Show tab. The Broadcast Slide Show dialog box opens as shown in Figure H-16. You can change the broadcast service or start the broadcast. Click Start Broadcast to open a Windows Security dialog box, where you enter your user name and password to access the broadcast site. After you enter your user name and password, PowerPoint sets up the URL location on the broadcast server and displays the URL link that you can copy or e-mail to audience members as shown in Figure H-17. A Broadcast View message bar appears below the Ribbon in the PowerPoint window and alerts you that you are currently broadcasting and cannot make any changes to the presentation. Click Start Slide Show in the dialog box to open the presentation in Slide Show view. Click the End Broadcast button in the Broadcast group to end the broadcast.

- **View a presentation broadcast**

  To view a broadcast as an audience member, you need to open the Internet address (URL) provided by the host of the broadcast. The URL can be sent to audience members in an e-mail or copied and sent. When an audience member clicks the slide show URL link, the slide show opens in their Web browser. The audience follows along live as you present the slide show broadcast.

FIGURE H-16: Broadcast Slide Show dialog box

Current broadcast service

Click to change broadcast services

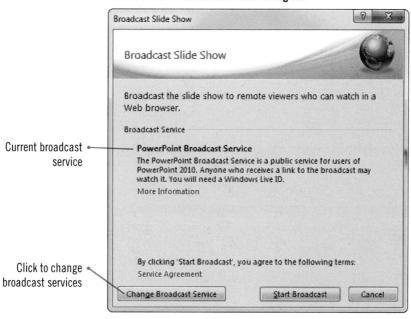

FIGURE H-17: Screen showing presentation broadcast

Broadcast tab commands

Broadcast View message bar

URL link

Click to send the URL link using e-mail

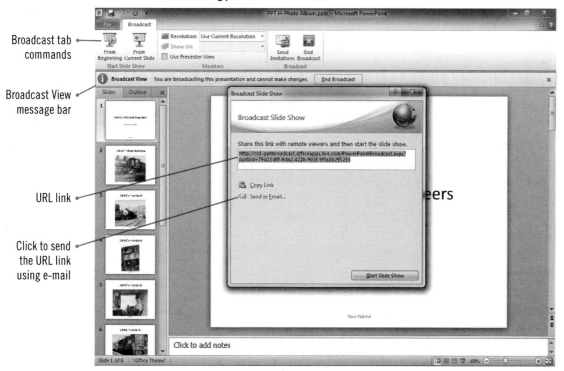

Publish slides to a Slide Library

If your computer is connected to a network server running Office SharePoint Server 2007 or Office SharePoint Server 2010 software, you can store slides in a folder called a **Slide Library** for others to access, modify, and use. Using a Slide Library, others can make changes to your slides, and you in turn can track and review all changes and have access to the latest version of your slides. To

publish slides from PowerPoint to a Slide Library (after a Slide Library is created on a server), click the File tab, click Save & Send, click Publish Slides, then click the Publish Slides button. The Publish Slides dialog box opens. Use Browse in the dialog box to select the Slide Library location you are going to use. To add slides to a Slide Library, click the check box next to each slide, then click Publish.

Practice

For current SAM information, including versions and content details, visit SAM Central (http://www.cengage.com/samcentral). If you have a SAM user profile, you may have access to hands-on instruction, practice, and assessment of the skills covered in this unit. Since various versions of SAM are supported throughout the life of this text, check with your instructor for the correct instructions and URL/Web site for accessing assignments.

Concepts Review

Label each element of the PowerPoint window shown in Figure H-18.

FIGURE H-18

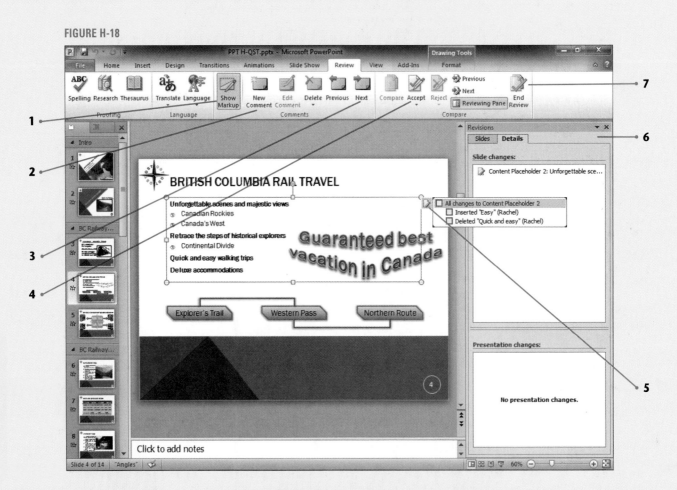

Match each term with the statement that best describes its function.

8. Slide Library
9. Hyperlinked custom show
10. Basic custom show
11. Kiosk
12. Template

a. A separate presentation that is connected to a custom show
b. A folder on a network server that stores slides for others to access and modify
c. A special slide show created from selected slides in a presentation
d. A small booth for a stand-alone computer that can run a slide show without user intervention
e. A type of presentation that contains custom design and content

Select the best answer from the list of choices.

13. When you combine two presentations together, you are _____ all the changes from one presentation into your original presentation.
    - **a.** linking
    - **b.** merging
    - **c.** removing
    - **d.** hyperlinking

14. Which view allows you to view a presentation using two monitors?
    - **a.** Multiple Monitor view
    - **b.** Reading view
    - **c.** Presenter view
    - **d.** Theater view

15. Which of the following statements is *not* true about a presentation set to run at a stand-alone computer?
    - **a.** You don't have to be present to run the slide show.
    - **b.** You can use action buttons to progress through the slides.
    - **c.** The presentation can loop continuously.
    - **d.** The presentation works best with manual slide timings.

16. What do you create when you want to show specific slides in a presentation to a specific audience?
    - **a.** Encrypted file
    - **b.** Broadcast
    - **c.** Template
    - **d.** Custom show

17. Creating a _____ helps keep your presentation secure.
    - **a.** password
    - **b.** hyperlink
    - **c.** shared server
    - **d.** Slide Library

18. A _____ is a special presentation designed specifically to display pictures.
    - **a.** broadcast
    - **b.** picture template
    - **c.** photo album
    - **d.** Slide Library

19. Which of the following identifies features that might not work in earlier versions of PowerPoint?
    - **a.** SkyDrive Server
    - **b.** Compatibility Checker
    - **c.** Kiosk
    - **d.** Document Inspector

20. You can use PowerPoint to _____ a presentation to a remote audience over the Internet.
    - **a.** broadcast
    - **b.** publish
    - **c.** package
    - **d.** review

Skills Review

1. **Send a presentation for review.**
    - **a.** Start PowerPoint, open the file PPT H-8.pptx from the drive and folder where you store your Data Files, then save it as **PPT H-NY Cafe**. (*Note*: You need to have Outlook set up to complete the next three steps.)
    - **b.** Click the File tab, click Save & Send, then click the Send as Attachment button.
    - **c.** Type a brief message in the e-mail message, then send the presentation to yourself.
    - **d.** Open Microsoft Outlook, open the message you sent to yourself, then close Outlook.

2. **Combine reviewed presentations.**
    - **a.** Click the Review tab, then click the Compare button in the Compare group.
    - **b.** Locate the presentation PPT H-9.pptx from the drive and folder where you store your Data Files, click PPT H-9.pptx, then click Merge.
    - **c.** Read the comment on the slide, delete the comment, then click the check box to accept the changes on Slide 3.
    - **d.** Click the Next button in the Compare group, then click Continue in the message dialog box.
    - **e.** Click the Slide 1 thumbnail in the Slides tab, click the Next button in the Comments group, read the comment on Slide 2, then delete the comment.
    - **f.** End the review, click Yes to save the review changes, then save your work.

Skills Review (continued)

3. **Set up a slide show.**
   a. Click the Slide Show tab, click the Set Up Slide Show button, set up a slide show that will be browsed at a kiosk, using automatic slide timings, then click the Transitions tab.
   b. Remove the check mark from the On Mouse Click check box, set a slide timing of 5 seconds to all the slides, run the slide show all the way through once, then press [Esc] to end the slide show.
   c. Change the slide show options to run using manual slide timings and presented by a speaker.
   d. Run through the slide show from Slide 1 using the action buttons at the bottom of the slides. Move forward and backward through the presentation, watching the animation effects as they appear, then press [Esc] when you are finished.
   e. Hide Slide 5, run through the slide show, then unhide Slide 5.
   f. When you have finished viewing the slide show, reset the slide timings to automatic, then save your changes.

4. **Create a custom show.**
   a. Create a custom show called **Goals** which includes Slides 2, 3, 4, and 5.
   b. Move Slide 3 Performance Series above Slide 2 Lecture Series.
   c. View the show from within the Custom Shows dialog box, then press [Esc] to end the slide show.
   d. Go to Slide 1, begin the slide show, then, when Slide 1 appears, go to the Goals custom show.
   e. View the custom slide show, return to Normal view, then save your changes.

5. **Prepare a presentation for distribution.**
   a. Click the File tab, click Protect Presentation, then click Encrypt with Password.
   b. Type 12345, then type the same password in the Confirm Password dialog box.
   c. Close the presentation, save your changes, open the presentation, then type **12345** in the Password dialog box.
   d. Open the Encrypt Document dialog box again, then delete the password.
   e. Click the File tab, click Check for Issues, click Check Compatibility, read the information, then close the dialog box.
   f. Save your work, add your name to the notes and handouts footer, then check the spelling in the presentation. The completed presentation is shown in Figure H-19.
   g. Submit your presentation to your instructor, then close the presentation.

   FIGURE H-19

6. **Use templates and add comments.**
   a. Click the File tab, click New, click Sample templates, click Classic Photo Album, then click Create.
   b. Save the presentation as **PPT H-Classic Photo Album** to the drive and folder where you store your Data Files.
   c. Click the Review tab on the Ribbon, click the New Comment button, type **What do you think of this design for our new photo series?**, then go to Slide 3.
   d. Add a new comment, type **This is an interesting photo layout.**, click the Previous button, then click the Edit Comment button.
   e. Type **I like this title slide design.**, add your name to the slide footer, then save your work.
   f. Submit your presentation to your instructor, then close the presentation.

Skills Review (continued)

7. Create a photo album.

  a. Create a photo album presentation, then from the drive and folder where you store your Data Files, insert the files PPT H-10.jpg, PPT H-11.jpg, PPT H-12.jpg, PPT H-13.jpg, PPT H-14.jpg, PPT H-15.jpg, PPT H-16.jpg, and PPT H-17.jpg.

  b. Move picture PPT H-15.jpg so it is second in the list, move PPT H-12.jpg so it is last in the list, create the photo album, then save it as **PPT H-Vacation** to the drive and folder where you store your Data Files.

  c. Change the title on the title slide to **My Vacation in the West**, then type your name in the subtitle text box.

  d. Open the Edit Photo Album dialog box, change the picture layout to 1 picture, change the frame shape to Simple Frame, White, then update the presentation.

  e. Apply a solid black background (Design tab) to all the slides, add your name to the slide footer on all slides except the title slide, then save your changes. The completed photo album is shown in Figure H-20.

  f. Submit your presentation to your instructor, close the presentation, then exit PowerPoint.

FIGURE H-20

Independent Challenge 1

You work for Island Getaways, Inc., an international tour company that provides specialty tours to destinations throughout Asia and the Pacific. You have to develop presentations that the sales force can use to highlight different tours at conferences and meetings. To complete the presentation, you need to create at least two of your own slides. Assume that Island Getaways has a special (20% off regular price) on tours to Fiji and the Cook Islands during the spring of 2013. Also assume that Island Getaways offers tour packages to the Philippines, Japan, Australia, and New Zealand.

  a. Start PowerPoint, open the presentation PPT H-18.pptx, then save it as **PPT H-Islands** to the drive and folder where you store your Data Files.

  b. Open the Review tab on the Ribbon, use the Next button in the Comments group to view each comment, read the comment, then delete the last comment on the Departing Cities slide.

  c. Use the Previous button in the Comments group to move back to slides that have comments, write a new comment in response to each of the original comments, then move each review comment thumbnail next to the original review comment thumbnails.

  d. Use the Compatibility Checker on the presentation.

  e. Use the information provided above to help you develop additional content for two new slides.

  f. Insert at least three different media clips (pictures, clip art videos, videos, clip art, or sounds). Use clips from PowerPoint or from other approved legal media sources.

  g. Apply slide transitions, timings, and animations to all the slides in the presentation.

Independent Challenge 1 (continued)

h. Apply a saved design theme. On the Design tab, click the Themes More button, click Browse for Themes, then apply the PPT H-19.thmx theme from the drive and folder where you store your Data Files.

i. Convert the text on Slide 2 to a SmartArt diagram, then format the diagram using the techniques you learned in this book.

j. Use the Compatibility Checker again on the presentation. Note any differences, then view in Slide Show view.

k. Add your name as a footer on all notes and handouts, then check the spelling in the presentation.

l. Submit your presentation to your instructor, close the presentation, then exit PowerPoint.

Independent Challenge 2

You work in Monterey, California, at the State Agricultural Statistics Agency. Part of your job is to compile agricultural information gathered from the counties of California and create presentations that display the data for public viewing. You are currently working on a summary presentation that will be made public on the agency Web site.

a. Start PowerPoint, open the presentation PPT H-20.pptx, then save it as **PPT H-Ag Report** to the drive and folder where you store your Data Files.

b. Convert the information on Slide 5 to a SmartArt diagram using one of the Picture list layouts. Insert the file PPT H-21.jpg from the drive and folder where you store your Data Files for all of the pictures in the SmartArt graphic.

c. Format the SmartArt diagram using the commands on the SmartArt Tools Design and Format tabs.

d. Format the table on Slide 4. Change the table layout so the table displays the information properly, split the Cattle and Calves cell into two cells, then format the table.

e. Create a custom slide show that displays any four slides from the presentation.

f. Insert appropriate media clips on at least two slides.

Advanced Challenge Exercise *(requires Internet connection and instructor approval)*

- Write at least two comments in the presentation, then send the presentation as an e-mail attachment to another student in your class.
- The reviewing student should create and insert his or her own comments, and make at least one text change, then send it back to you.
- Once you get the presentation back, review the comments, then make adjustments to the presentation.

g. Save the presentation, add your name as the footer on all notes and handouts, check the spelling of the presentation, then view the presentation in Slide Show view.

h. Submit your presentation to your instructor, close the presentation, then exit PowerPoint.

Independent Challenge 3

You are the assistant director of operations at NorthWest Container, Inc., an international marine shipping company based in Seattle, Washington. NorthWest handles 45 percent of all the trade between Asia, the Middle East, and the West Coast of the United States. You need to give a quarterly presentation to the company's operations committee outlining the type and amount of trade NorthWest handled during the previous quarter.

Plan a presentation with at least six slides that details the type of goods NorthWest carries. Create your own content, but assume the following:

- NorthWest hauls automobiles from Tokyo to San Francisco. Northwest can usually haul between 2,800 and 3,500 automobiles in a quarter.
- NorthWest hauls large equipment made by Caterpillar Tractor and John Deere Tractor from the United States.
- NorthWest hauls common household goods that include electronic equipment, appliances, toys, and furniture.
- NorthWest owns 10 cargo ships that can operate simultaneously. All 10 ships were in operation during the last quarter.
- NorthWest hauled a total of 3.8 million tons during the last quarter.

Independent Challenge 3 (continued)

a. Start PowerPoint, create a new presentation based on a template or theme in the New Presentation dialog box, then save it as **PPT H-NorthWest**.

b. Use the information provided to help develop the content for your presentation. If you have Internet access, use the Internet to research the shipping business.

c. Use at least two different media clips to enhance your presentation.

d. Set transitions and animations, and rehearse slide timings.

e. View the presentation in Slide Show view.

Advanced Challenge Exercise *(requires Internet connection and instructor approval)*

- Create a personal Windows Live ID account on the Microsoft Web site.
- Click the Slide Show tab on the Ribbon, then click the Broadcast Slide Show button in the Start Slide Show group.
- Follow the instructions to invite one or more attendees to view the broadcast, then broadcast your presentation.
- End the broadcast.

f. Check the spelling of the presentation, add your name as a footer on all notes and handouts, then save your work.

g. Submit your presentation to your instructor, close the presentation, then exit PowerPoint.

Real Life Independent Challenge

Your assignment for your American history class is to create a photo album based on your personal life and family history. You must use your own pictures of past and present family members, pets, a family home, a family business, or any other type of family activity that help tell the story of your personal family life and history.

a. Start PowerPoint, create a photo album presentation, insert your pictures to the presentation, then save it as **PPT H-My Family History** to the drive and folder where you store your Data Files.

b. Add your name to the title slide and as the footer on the handouts.

c. Use the Edit Photo Album dialog box to format the pictures. An example of a family photo album is shown in Figure H-21.

d. Check the spelling of the presentation, save your changes, then view the final presentation in Slide Show view.

e. Submit your presentation to your instructor, close the presentation, then exit PowerPoint.

FIGURE H-21

Visual Workshop

Create the slide shown in Figure H-22. Save the presentation as **PPT H-National Parks**. The SmartArt graphic uses the Vertical Curved List layout. Apply the Insert SmartArt Style, apply a transition to the slide, apply a slide timing of 12 seconds, then apply entrance and exit animations to each object in the SmartArt graphic. Add your name to the slide footer, then submit your presentation to your instructor.

FIGURE H-22

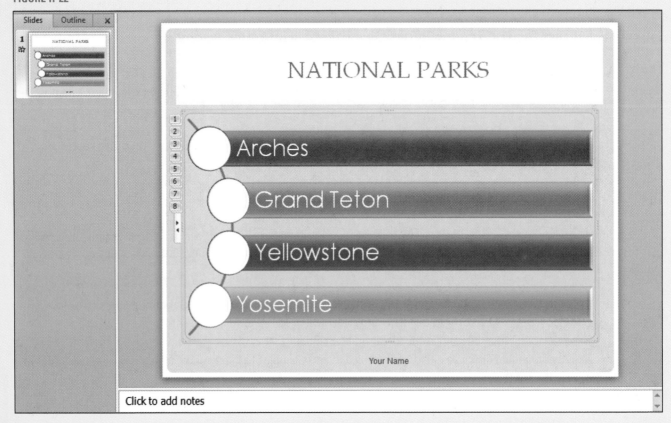

Working with Windows Live and Office Web Apps

If the computer you are using has an active Internet connection, you can go to the Microsoft Windows Live Web site and access a wide variety of services and Web applications. For example, you can check your e-mail through Windows Live, network with your friends and coworkers, and use SkyDrive to store and share files. From SkyDrive, you can also use Office Web Apps to create and edit Word, PowerPoint, Excel, and OneNote files, even when you are using a computer that does not have Office 2010 installed. ▰▰▰ You work in the Vancouver branch of Quest Specialty Travel. Your supervisor, Mary Lou Jacobs, asks you to explore Windows Live and learn how she can use SkyDrive and Office Web Apps to work with her files online.

(*Note*: SkyDrive and Office Web Apps are dynamic Web pages, and might change over time, including the way they are organized and how commands are performed. The steps and figures in this appendix were accurate at the time this book was published.)

OBJECTIVES

Explore how to work online from Windows Live

Obtain a Windows Live ID and sign in to Windows Live

Upload files to Windows Live

Work with the PowerPoint Web App

Create folders and organize files on SkyDrive

Add people to your network and share files

Work with the Excel Web App

Exploring How to Work Online from Windows Live

You can use your Web browser to upload your files to Windows Live from any computer connected to the Internet. You can work on the files right in your Web browser using Office Web Apps and share your files with people in your Windows Live network. ▰▰▰ You review the concepts and services related to working online from Windows Live.

DETAILS

- **What is Windows Live?**

  Windows Live is a collection of services and Web applications that you can use to help you be more productive both personally and professionally. For example, you can use Windows Live to send and receive e-mail, to chat with friends via instant messaging, to share photos, to create a blog, and to store and edit files using SkyDrive. Table WEB-1 describes the services available on Windows Live. Windows Live is a free service that you sign up for. When you sign up, you receive a Windows Live ID, which you use to sign in to Windows Live. When you work with files on Windows Live, you are cloud computing.

- **What is Cloud Computing?**

  The term **cloud computing** refers to the process of working with files online in a Web browser. When you save files to SkyDrive on Windows Live, you are saving your files to an online location. SkyDrive is like having a personal hard drive in the cloud.

- **What is SkyDrive?**

  SkyDrive is an online storage and file sharing service. With a Windows Live account, you receive access to your own SkyDrive, which is your personal storage area on the Internet. On your SkyDrive, you are given space to store up to 25 GB of data online. Each file can be a maximum size of 50 MB. You can also use SkyDrive to access Office Web Apps, which you use to create and edit files created in Word, OneNote, PowerPoint, and Excel online in your Web browser.

- **Why use Windows Live and SkyDrive?**

  On Windows Live, you use SkyDrive to access additional storage for your files. You don't have to worry about backing up your files to a memory stick or other storage device that could be lost or damaged. Another advantage of storing your files on SkyDrive is that you can access your files from any computer that has an active Internet connection. Figure WEB-1 shows the SkyDrive Web page that appears when accessed from a Windows Live account. From SkyDrive, you can also access Office Web Apps.

- **What are Office Web Apps?**

  Office Web Apps are versions of Microsoft Word, Excel, PowerPoint, and OneNote that you can access online from your SkyDrive. An Office Web App does not include all of the features and functions included with the full Office version of its associated application. However, you can use the Office Web App from any computer that is connected to the Internet, even if Microsoft Office 2010 is not installed on that computer.

- **How do SkyDrive and Office Web Apps work together?**

  You can create a file in Office 2010 using Word, Excel, PowerPoint, or OneNote and then upload the file to your SkyDrive. You can then open the Office file saved to SkyDrive and edit it using your Web browser and the corresponding Office Web App. Figure WEB-2 shows a PowerPoint presentation open in the PowerPoint Web App. You can also use an Office Web App to create a new file, which is saved automatically to SkyDrive while you work. In addition, you can download a file created with an Office Web App and continue to work with the file in the full version of the corresponding Office application: Word, Excel, PowerPoint, or OneNote. Finally, you can create a SkyDrive network that consists of the people you want to be able to view your folders and files on your SkyDrive. You can give people permission to view and edit your files using any computer with an active Internet connection and a Web browser.

FIGURE WEB-1: SkyDrive on Windows Live

Browser window

SkyDrive - Windows Live tab

By default, one folder is available on SkyDrive; you can create additional folders

The name of the person who signed into Windows Live and SkyDrive appears here

Monitors the amount of space still available on your SkyDrive

FIGURE WEB-2: PowerPoint presentation open in the PowerPoint Web App

Browser window

Ribbon available in PowerPoint Web App

The presentation in PowerPoint Web App maintains the same look and feel as the same presentation in the desktop version of PowerPoint

Name of PowerPoint presentation open in PowerPoint Web App

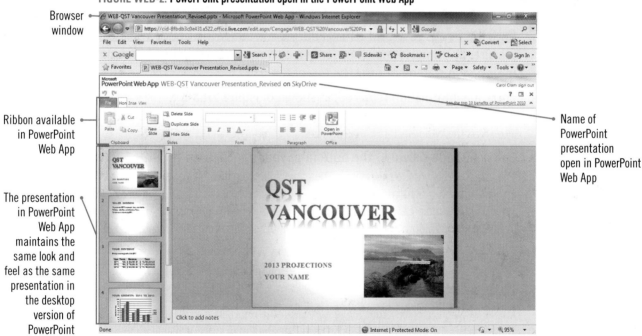

TABLE WEB-1: Services available via Windows Live

service	description
E-mail	Send and receive e-mail using a Hotmail account
Instant Messaging	Use Messenger to chat with friends, share photos, and play games
SkyDrive	Store files, work on files using Office Web Apps, and share files with people in your network
Photos	Upload and share photos with friends
People	Develop a network of friends and coworkers, then use the network to distribute information and stay in touch
Downloads	Access a variety of free programs available for download to a PC
Mobile Device	Access applications for a mobile device: text messaging, using Hotmail, networking, and sharing photos

Web Apps

Obtaining a Windows Live ID and Signing In to Windows Live

To work with your files online using SkyDrive and Office Web Apps, you need a Windows Live ID. You obtain a Windows Live ID by going to the Windows Live Web site and creating a new account. Once you have a Windows Live ID, you can access SkyDrive and then use it to store your files, create new files, and share your files with friends and coworkers. ░░░░ Mary Lou Jacobs, your supervisor at QST Vancouver, asks you to obtain a Windows Live ID so that you can work on documents with your coworkers. You go to the Windows Live Web site, create a Windows Live ID, and then sign in to your SkyDrive.

STEPS

QUICK TIP

If you already have a Windows Live ID, go to the next lesson and sign in as directed using your account.

1. **Open your Web browser, type home.live.com in the Address bar, then press [Enter]**

   The Windows Live home page opens. From this page, you can create a Windows Live account and receive your Windows Live ID.

2. **Click the Sign up button** *(Note: You may see a Sign up link instead of a button)*

   The Create your Windows Live ID page opens.

3. **Click the Or use your own e-mail address link under the Check availability button or if you are already using Hotmail, Messenger, or Xbox LIVE, click the Sign in now link in the Information statement near the top of the page**

4. **Enter the information required, as shown in Figure WEB-3**

   If you wish, you can sign up for a Windows Live e-mail address such as yourname@live.com so that you can also access the Windows Live e-mail services.

TROUBLE

The code can be difficult to read. If you receive an error message, enter the new code that appears.

5. **Enter the code shown at the bottom of your screen, then click the I accept button**

   The Windows Live home page opens. The name you entered when you signed up for your Windows Live ID appears in the top right corner of the window to indicate that you are signed in to Windows Live. From the Windows Live home page, you can access all the services and applications offered by Windows Live. See the Verifying your Windows Live ID box for information on finalizing your account set up.

6. **Point to Windows Live, as shown in Figure WEB-4**

   A list of options appears. SkyDrive is one of the options you can access directly from Windows Live.

TROUBLE

Click I accept if you are asked to review and accept the Windows Live Service Agreement and Privacy Statement.

7. **Click SkyDrive**

   The SkyDrive page opens. Your name appears in the top right corner, and the amount of space available is shown on the right side of the SkyDrive page. The amount of space available is monitored, as indicated by the gauge that fills with color as space is used. Using SkyDrive, you can add files to the existing folder and you can create new folders.

8. **Click sign out in the top right corner under your name, then exit the Web browser**

   You are signed out of your Windows Live account. You can sign in again directly from the Windows Live page in your browser or from within a file created with PowerPoint, Excel, Word, or OneNote.

FIGURE WEB-3: Creating a Windows Live ID

Click to sign in using a Hotmail, Messenger, or Xbox Live account

Once your registration is complete, you will be asked to verify your ID

A different code will appear on your screen

Type your e-mail address

You can choose to get a Windows Live e-mail address

Enter the information required

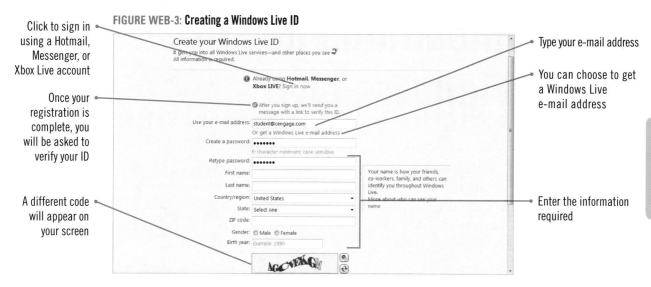

FIGURE WEB-4: Selecting SkyDrive

SkyDrive in the list of Windows Live options

Information about your Windows Live network

Your name appears here

Click to quickly add people to your network

An advertisement appropriate for your location appears here

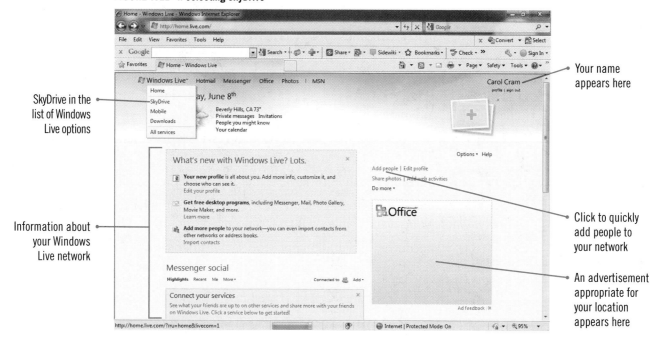

Verifying your Windows Live ID

As soon as you accept the Windows Live terms, an e-mail is sent to the e-mail address you supplied when you created your Windows Live ID. Open your e-mail program, and then open the e-mail from Microsoft with the Subject line: Confirm your e-mail address for Windows Live. Follow the simple, step-by-step instructions in the e-mail to confirm your Windows Live ID. When the confirmation is complete, you will be asked to sign in to Windows Live, using your e-mail address and password. Once signed in, you will see your Windows Live Account page.

Uploading Files to Windows Live

Once you have created your Windows Live ID, you can sign in to Windows Live directly from Word, PowerPoint, Excel, or OneNote and start saving and uploading files. You upload files to your SkyDrive so you can share the files with other people, access the files from another computer, or use SkyDrive's additional storage. ▨▨▨▨ You open a PowerPoint presentation, access your Windows Live account from Backstage view, and save a file to SkyDrive on Windows Live. You also create a new folder called Cengage directly from Backstage view and add a file to it.

STEPS

1. **Start PowerPoint, open the file** WEB-1.pptx **from the drive and folder where you store your Data Files, then save the file as** WEB-QST Vancouver Presentation

2. **Click the** File tab, **then click** Save & Send
   The Save & Send options available in PowerPoint are listed in Backstage view, as shown in Figure WEB-5.

3. **Click** Save to Web

4. **Click** Sign In, **type your e-mail address, press [Tab], type your** password, **then click** OK
   The My Documents folder on your SkyDrive appears in the Save to Windows Live SkyDrive information area.

5. **Click** Save As, **wait a few seconds for the Save As dialog box to appear, then click** Save
   The file is saved to the My Documents folder on the SkyDrive that is associated with your Windows Live account. You can also create a new folder and upload files directly to SkyDrive from your hard drive.

6. **Click the** File tab, **click** Save & Send, **click** Save to Web, **then sign in if the My Documents folder does not automatically appear in Backstage view**

7. **Click the** New Folder **button in the Save to Windows Live SkyDrive pane, then sign in to Windows Live if directed**

8. **Type** Cengage **as the folder name, click** Next, **then click** Add files

9. **Click** select documents from your computer, **then navigate to the location on your computer where you saved the file WEB-QST Vancouver Presentation in Step 1**

10. **Click** WEB-QST Vancouver Presentation.pptx **to select it, then click** Open
    You can continue to add more files; however, you have no more files to upload at this time.

11. **Click** Continue
    In a few moments, the PowerPoint presentation is uploaded to your SkyDrive, as shown in Figure WEB-6. You can simply store the file on SkyDrive or you can choose to work on the presentation using the PowerPoint Web App.

12. **Click the** PowerPoint icon 🖼 **on your taskbar to return to PowerPoint, then close the presentation and exit PowerPoint**

FIGURE WEB-5: Save & Send options in Backstage view

PowerPoint file

Save & Send area
in Backstage view

Save to Web
option

FIGURE WEB-6: File uploaded to the Cengage folder on Windows Live

Browser
window

Path to file

Current folder
menu bar

Uploaded file

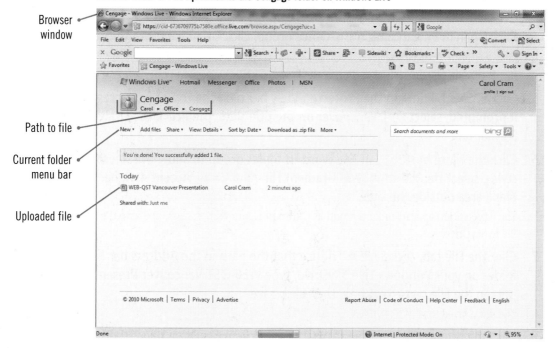

Working with the PowerPoint Web App

Once you have uploaded a file to SkyDrive on Windows Live, you can work on it using its corresponding Office Web App. **Office Web Apps** provide you with the tools you need to view documents online and to edit them right in your browser. You do not need to have Office programs installed on the computer you use to access SkyDrive and Office Web Apps. From SkyDrive, you can also open the document directly in the full Office application (for example, PowerPoint) if the application is installed on the computer you are using. ⬛⬛⬛ You use the PowerPoint Web App to make some edits to the PowerPoint presentation. You then open the presentation in PowerPoint and use the full version to make additional edits.

STEPS

TROUBLE

Click the browser button on the task-bar, then click the Windows Live SkyDrive window to make it the active window.

1. **Click the WEB-QST Vancouver Presentation file in the Cengage folder on SkyDrive**

   The presentation opens in your browser window. A menu is available, which includes the options you have for working with the file.

2. **Click Edit in Browser, then if a message appears related to installing the Sign-in Assistant, click the Close button ✖ to the far right of the message**

   In a few moments, the PowerPoint presentation opens in the PowerPoint Web App, as shown in Figure WEB-7. Table WEB-2 lists the commands you can perform using the PowerPoint Web App.

QUICK TIP

The changes you make to the presentation are saved automatically on SkyDrive.

3. **Enter your name where indicated on Slide 1, click Slide 3 (New Tours) in the Slides pane, then click Delete Slide in the Slides group**

   The slide is removed from the presentation. You decide to open the file in the full version of PowerPoint on your computer so you can apply WordArt to the slide title. You work with the file in the full version of PowerPoint when you want to use functions, such as WordArt, that are not available on the PowerPoint Web App.

4. **Click Open in PowerPoint in the Office group, click OK in response to the message, then click Allow if requested**

   In a few moments, the revised version of the PowerPoint slide opens in PowerPoint on your computer.

5. **Click Enable Editing on the Protected View bar near the top of your presentation window if prompted, select QST Vancouver on the title slide, then click the Drawing Tools Format tab**

QUICK TIP

Use the ScreenTips to help you find the required WordArt style.

6. **Click the More button ▾ in the WordArt Styles group to show the selection of WordArt styles, select the WordArt style Gradient Fill - Blue-Gray, Accent 4, Reflection, then click a blank area outside the slide**

   The presentation appears in PowerPoint as shown in Figure WEB-8. Next, you save the revised version of the file to SkyDrive.

7. **Click the File tab, click Save As, notice that the path in the Address bar is to the Cengage folder on your Windows Live SkyDrive, type WEB-QST Vancouver Presentation_Revised. pptx in the File name text box, then click Save**

   The file is saved to your SkyDrive.

TROUBLE

The browser opens to the Cengage folder but the file is not visible. Follow Step 8 to open the Cengage folder and refresh the list of files in the folder.

8. **Click the browser icon on the taskbar to open your SkyDrive page, then click Office next to your name in the SkyDrive path, view a list of recent documents, then click Cengage in the list to the left of the recent documents list to open the Cengage folder**

   Two PowerPoint files now appear in the Cengage folder.

9. **Exit the Web browser and close all tabs if prompted, then exit PowerPoint**

FIGURE WEB-7: Presentation opened in the PowerPoint Web App from Windows Live

Browser window

Name of Web App

PowerPoint Web App Ribbon

URL is the file location

FIGURE WEB-8: Revised PowerPoint presentation

PowerPoint title bar

PowerPoint Ribbon

Presentation title enhanced using full version of PowerPoint

Name added using PowerPoint Web App

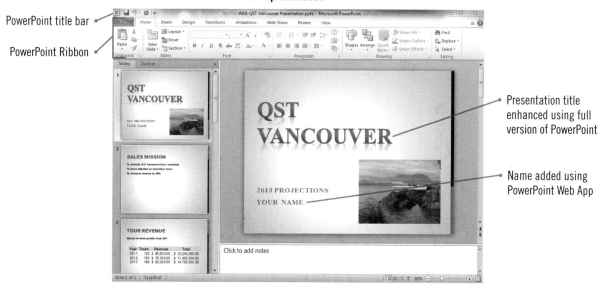

TABLE WEB-2: Commands on the PowerPoint Web App

tab	commands available
File	• Open in PowerPoint: select to open the file in PowerPoint on your computer • Where's the Save Button?: when you click this option, a message appears telling you that you do not need to save your presentation when you are working on it with PowerPoint Web App. The presentation is saved automatically as you work. • Print • Share • Properties • Give Feedback • Privacy • Terms of Use • Close
Home	• Clipboard group: Cut, Copy, Paste • Slides group: Add a New Slide, Delete a Slide, Duplicate a Slide, and Hide a Slide • Font group: Work with text: change the font, style, color, and size of selected text • Paragraph group: Work with paragraphs: add bullets and numbers, indent text, align text • Office group: Open the file in PowerPoint on your computer
Insert	• Insert a Picture • Insert a SmartArt diagram • Insert a link such as a link to another file on SkyDrive or to a Web page
View	• Editing view (the default) • Reading view • Slide Show view • Notes view

Web Apps

Creating Folders and Organizing Files on SkyDrive

As you have learned, you can sign in to SkyDrive directly from the Office applications PowerPoint, Excel, Word, and OneNote, or you can access SkyDrive directly through your Web browser. This option is useful when you are away from the computer on which you normally work or when you are using a computer that does not have Office applications installed. You can go to SkyDrive, create and organize folders, and then create or open files to work on with Office Web Apps. You access SkyDrive from your Web browser, create a new folder called Illustrated, and delete one of the PowerPoint files from the My Documents folder.

STEPS

TROUBLE
Go to Step 3 if you are already signed in.

1. **Open your Web browser, type home.live.com in the Address bar, then press [Enter]**

   The Windows Live home page opens. From here, you can sign in to your Windows Live account and then access SkyDrive.

TROUBLE
Type your Windows Live ID (your e-mail) and password, then click Sign in if prompted to do so.

2. **Sign into Windows Live as directed**

   You are signed in to your Windows Live page. From this page, you can take advantage of the many applications available on Windows Live, including SkyDrive.

3. **Point to Windows Live, then click SkyDrive**

   SkyDrive opens.

4. **Click Cengage, then point to WEB-QST Vancouver Presentation.pptx**

   A menu of options for working with the file, including a Delete button to the far right, appears to the right of the filename.

5. **Click the Delete button ☒, then click OK**

   The file is removed from the Cengage folder on your SkyDrive. You still have a copy of the file on your computer.

6. **Point to Windows Live, then click SkyDrive**

   Your SkyDrive screen with the current selection of folders available on your SkyDrive opens, as shown in Figure WEB-9.

7. **Click New, click Folder, type Illustrated, click Next, click Office in the path under Add documents to Illustrated at the top of the window, then click View all in the list under Personal**

   You are returned to your list of folders, where you see the new Illustrated folder.

8. **Click Cengage, point to WEB-QST Vancouver Presentation_Revised.pptx, click More, click Move, then click the Illustrated folder**

9. **Click Move this file into Illustrated, as shown in Figure WEB-10**

   The file is moved to the Illustrated folder.

FIGURE WEB-9: Folders on your SkyDrive

Current location

Folders currently available

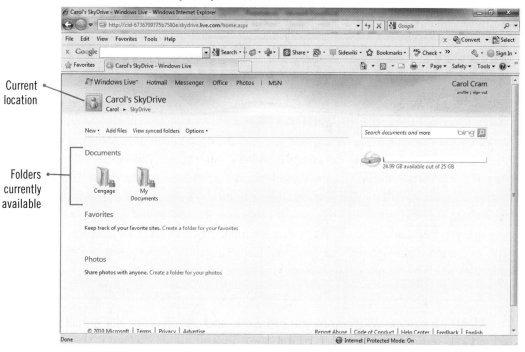

FIGURE WEB-10: Moving a file to the Illustrated folder

Click to move file to this location

Be sure to rename a file before moving it if you are moving it to a location where another copy of the same file exists

Name of file to be moved

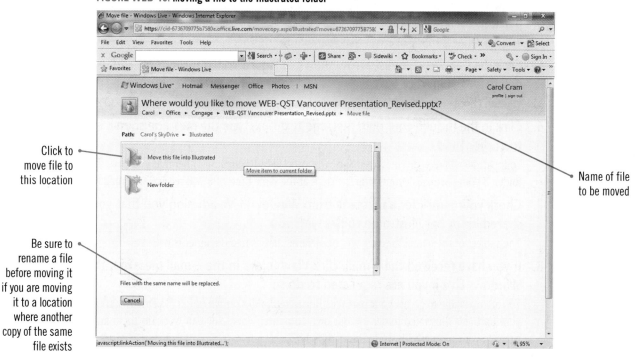

Adding People to Your Network and Sharing Files

One of the great advantages of working with SkyDrive on Windows Live is that you can share your files with others. Suppose, for example, that you want a colleague to review a presentation you created in PowerPoint and then add a new slide. You can, of course, e-mail the presentation directly to your colleague, who can then make changes and e-mail the presentation back. Alternatively, you can save time by uploading the PowerPoint file directly to SkyDrive and then giving your colleague access to the file. Your colleague can edit the file using the PowerPoint Web App, and then you can check the updated file on SkyDrive, also using the PowerPoint Web App. In this way, you and your colleague are working with just one version of the presentation that you both can update. ▓▓▓ You have decided to share files in the Illustrated folder that you created in the previous lesson with another individual. You start by working with a partner so that you can share files with your partner and your partner can share files with you.

STEPS

1. **Identify a partner with whom you can work, and obtain his or her e-mail address; you can choose someone in your class or someone on your e-mail list, but it should be someone who will be completing these steps when you are**

2. **From the Illustrated folder, click** Share

3. **Click** Edit permissions

   The Edit permissions page opens. On this page, you can select the individual with whom you would like to share the contents of the Illustrated folder.

4. **Click in the** Enter a name or an e-mail address text box, **type the** e-mail address **of your partner, then press** [Tab]

   You can define the level of access that you want to give your partner.

5. **Click the** Can view files list arrow **shown in Figure WEB-11, click** Can add, edit details, and delete files, **then click** Save

   You can choose to send a notification to each individual when you grant permission to access your files.

6. **Click in the** Include your own message text box, **type the message shown in Figure WEB-12, then click** Send

   Your partner will receive a message from Windows Live advising him or her that you have shared your Illustrated folder. If your partner is completing the steps at the same time, you will receive an e-mail from your partner.

7. **Check your e-mail for a message from Windows Live advising you that your partner has shared his or her Illustrated folder with you**

   The subject of the e-mail message will be "[Name] has shared documents with you."

8. **If you have received the e-mail, click** View folder **in the e-mail message, then sign in to Windows Live if you are requested to do so**

   You are now able to access your partner's Illustrated folder on his or her SkyDrive. You can download files in your partner's Illustrated folder to your own computer where you can work on them and then upload them again to your partner's Illustrated shared folder.

9. **Exit the browser**

FIGURE WEB-11: Editing folder permissions

Folder permissions will be changed for the Illustrated folder

Click to select network permission options

Type email address to continue to add people

Person whose permission status will change

Click to select person from list of contacts

Click to select permission option

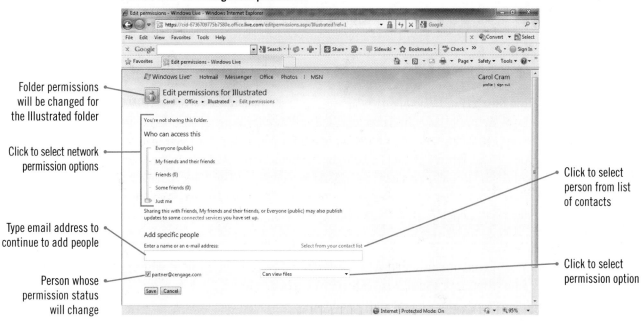

FIGURE WEB-12: Entering a message to notify a person that file sharing permission has been granted

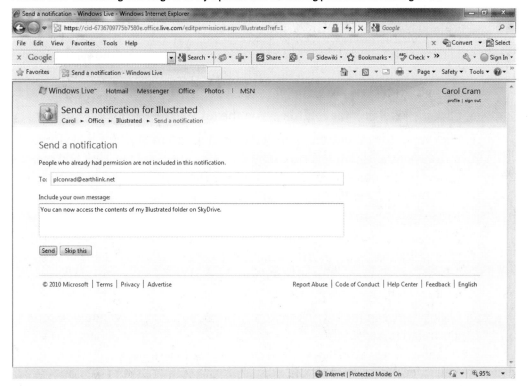

Sharing files on SkyDrive

When you share a folder with other people, the people with whom you share a folder can download the file to their computers and then make changes using the full version of the corresponding Office application.

Once these changes are made, each individual can then upload the file to SkyDrive and into a folder shared with you and others. In this way, you can create a network of people with whom you share your files.

Working with the Excel Web App

You can use the Excel Web App to work with an Excel spreadsheet on SkyDrive. Workbooks opened using the Excel Web App have the same look and feel as workbooks opened using the full version of Excel. However, just like the PowerPoint Web App, the Excel Web App has fewer features available than the full version of Excel. When you want to use a command that is not available on the Excel Web App, you need to open the file in the full version of Excel. ▓▓▓▓ You upload an Excel file containing a list of the tours offered by QST Vancouver to the Illustrated folder on SkyDrive. You use the Excel Web App to make some changes, and then you open the revised version in Excel 2010 on your computer.

STEPS

1. **Start Excel, open the file WEB-2.xlsx from the drive and folder where you store your Data Files, then save the file as WEB-QST Vancouver Tours**
   The data in the Excel file is formatted using the Excel table function.

TROUBLE
If prompted, sign in to your Windows Live account as directed.

2. **Click the File tab, click Save & Send, then click Save to Web**
   In a few moments, you should see three folders to which you can save spreadsheets. My Documents and Cengage are personal folder that contains files that only you can access. Illustrated is a shared folder that contains files you can share with others in your network. The Illustrated folder is shared with your partner.

3. **Click the Illustrated folder, click the Save As button, wait a few seconds for the Save As dialog box to appear, then click Save**

QUICK TIP
Alternately, you can open your Web browser and go to Windows Live to sign in to SkyDrive.

4. **Click the File tab, click Save & Send, click Save to Web, click the Windows Live SkyDrive link above your folders, then sign in if prompted**
   Windows Live opens to your SkyDrive.

5. **Click the Excel program button 🗷 on the taskbar, then exit Excel**

6. **Click your browser button on the taskbar to return to SkyDrive if SkyDrive is not the active window, click the Illustrated folder, click the Excel file, click Edit in Browser, then review the Ribbon and its tabs to familiarize yourself with the commands you can access from the Excel Web App**
   Table WEB-3 summarizes the commands that are available.

7. **Click cell A12, type Gulf Islands Sailing, press [TAB], type 3000, press [TAB], type 10, press [TAB], click cell D3, enter the formula =B3*C3, press [Enter], then click cell A1**
   The formula is copied automatically to the remaining rows as shown in Figure WEB-13 because the data in the original Excel file was created and formatted as an Excel table.

8. **Click SkyDrive in the Excel Web App path at the top of the window to return to the Illustrated folder**
   The changes you made to the Excel spreadsheet are saved automatically on SkyDrive. You can download the file directly to your computer from SkyDrive.

9. **Point to the Excel file, click More, click Download, click Save, navigate to the location where you save the files for this book, name the file WEB-QST Vancouver Tours_Updated, click Save, then click Close in the Download complete dialog box**
   The updated version of the spreadsheet is saved on your computer and on SkyDrive.

10. **Exit the Web browser**

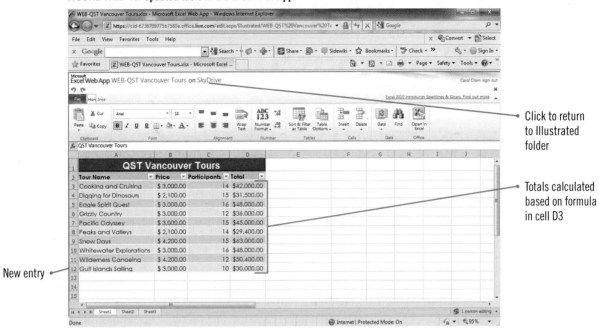

Click to return to Illustrated folder

Totals calculated based on formula in cell D3

New entry

TABLE WEB-3: **Commands on the Excel Web App**

tab	commands available
File	• Open in Excel: select to open the file in Excel on your computer • Where's the Save Button?: when you click this option, a message appears telling you that you do not need to save your spreadsheet when you are working in it with Excel Web App; the spreadsheet is saved automatically as you work • Save As • Share • Download a Snapshot: a snapshot contains only the values and the formatting; you cannot modify a snapshot • Download a Copy: the file can be opened and edited in the full version of Excel • Give Feedback • Privacy Statement • Terms of Use • Close
Home	• Clipboard group: Cut, Copy, Paste • Font group: change the font, style, color, and size of selected labels and values, as well as border styles and fill colors • Alignment group: change vertical and horizontal alignment and turn on the Wrap Text feature • Number group: change the number format and increase or decrease decimal places • Tables: sort and filter data in a table and modify Table Options • Cells: insert and delete cells • Data: refresh data and find labels or values • Office: open the file in Excel on your computer
Insert	• Insert a Table • Insert a Hyperlink to a Web page

Exploring other Office Web Apps

Two other Office Web Apps are Word and OneNote. You can share files on SkyDrive directly from Word or from OneNote using the same method you used to share files from PowerPoint and Excel. After you upload a Word or OneNote file to SkyDrive, you can work with it in its corresponding Office Web App. To familiarize yourself with the commands available in an Office Web App, open the file and then review the commands on each tab on the Ribbon. If you

want to perform a task that is not available in the Office Web App, open the file in the full version of the application.

In addition to working with uploaded files, you can create files from new on SkyDrive. Simply sign in to SkyDrive and open a folder. With a folder open, click New and then select the Web App you want to use to create the new file.

Windows Live and Microsoft Office Web Apps Quick Reference

To Do This	Go Here
Access Windows Live	From the Web browser, type **home.live.com**, then click Sign In
Access SkyDrive on Windows Live	From the Windows Live home page, point to Windows Live, then click SkyDrive
Save to Windows Live from Word, PowerPoint, or Excel	File tab | Save & Send | Save to Web | Select a folder | Save As
Create a New Folder from Backstage view	File tab | Save & Send | Save to Web | New Folder button
Edit a File with a Web App	From SkyDrive, click the file, then click Edit in Browser
Open a File in a desktop version of the application from a Web App: Word, Excel, PowerPoint	Click Open in [Application] in the Office group in each Office Web App
Share files on Windows Live	From SkyDrive, click the folder containing the files to share, click Share on the menu bar, click Edit permissions, enter the e-mail address of the person to share files with, click the Can view files list arrow, click Can add, edit details, and delete files, then click Save

Microsoft Office Specialist Skills Appendix

Files You Will Need:

No files needed.

Certification is an established trend in the Information Technology industry that helps match skilled people who want jobs with employers who are hiring skilled workers. Typically, a software or hardware company creates and gives exams that test competence on using specific programs or products. People who pass the exam demonstrate their ability to use the software or hardware effectively. By passing an exam, a person becomes "certified" and can his or her competence and knowledge of the software or hardware to prospective employers and colleagues. As a potential employee, you may have a better chance of landing a job if you are certified in the skills required for the job. As an employer, certification is another way to screen for qualified employees. This Appendix provides you with information to help you understand the Microsoft Office Specialist Certification program. It also provides a grid that lists the Microsoft Office Specialist Exam skills for Microsoft PowerPoint 2010 and provides page references for where each skill is covered in this book. This Appendix also includes a reference section on PowerPoint 2010 Microsoft Office Specialist Exam skills that are not covered in the lesson material in the book.

OBJECTIVES

Understand the Microsoft Office Specialist Certification program

Learn the Microsoft Office Specialist Certification process

Learn the Microsoft Office Specialist Certification levels

Get ready to take the exam

Take the exam

REFERENCES

Microsoft Office Specialist Exam skills: PowerPoint 2010

Additional skills for Microsoft PowerPoint 2010

REFERENCES

Review these skills which are not covered in the lessons in the book to be fully prepared for the exam.

Understanding the Microsoft Office Specialist Certification Program

The Microsoft Office Specialist program is the only comprehensive, performance-based certification program approved by Microsoft to validate desktop computer skills using the Microsoft Office 2010 programs.

What is the Microsoft Office Specialist Program?

The Microsoft Office Specialist program provides computer program literacy by identifying important skills, measures proficiency by testing the skills, and identifies opportunities for skill enhancement through courseware. Candidates who pass an exam receive a certificate that sets them apart from their peers in the competitive job market. The certificate is a valuable credential, recognized worldwide as proof that an individual has the desktop computing skills needed to work productively and efficiently. Certification is a valuable asset to individuals who want to begin or advance their computer careers. Exams are available for: Microsoft Word, Microsoft Excel®, Microsoft Access™, Microsoft PowerPoint®, Microsoft Outlook®, and Microsoft SharePoint®.

Who Gives the Exam?

The Microsoft Office Specialist exams are developed, marketed, and administered by Certiport, Inc., a company that has an exclusive license from Microsoft for the exams. The exams are available in a variety of languages. Exams must be taken at an authorized Certiport Center, which gives exams in a quiet room with the proper hardware and software. Trained personnel manage and proctor the exams.

What are the Benefits of Getting Certified?

Getting certified as a Microsoft Office Specialist in one or several of the Microsoft Office 2010 programs can be beneficial to you and your current or prospective employer. Earning certification acknowledges that you have the expertise to work with Microsoft Office programs. Individuals who are Microsoft Office Specialist certified report increased competence and productivity with Microsoft Office programs. They are also more highly regarded and have increased credibility with their employers, co-workers, and clients. Certification sets you apart in today's competitive job market, bringing employment opportunities, greater earning potential and career advancement, and increased job satisfaction.

For example, if you have passed the Microsoft PowerPoint 2010 certification exam you have an advantage when interviewing for a job that requires knowledge and use of PowerPoint to complete business-related tasks. Certification lets your prospective employer know that you not only have the necessary skills to perform that aspect of the job, but that you also have the initiative to prepare for, sign up for, pay for, and take an exam. Certification can help you increase your productivity within your current job and is a great way to enhance your skills without taking courses to obtain a new degree. More information about the benefits of getting certified can be found on the Certiport Web site.

> **QUICK TIP**
> Microsoft certification lets you access a member Web site, career-building tools, and training.

Learning the Microsoft Office Specialist Certification Process

As with any process, there are steps. If you are organized, the process can be simple and you will achieve your goals. Getting a Microsoft Office Specialist certification credential is a process. After you take a course and learn the program, you can pursue certification. This book provides you with comprehensive coverage of the features and skills for using Microsoft PowerPoint 2010. If you complete the units and lessons, including the end of unit exercises, and if you review the reference material on additional exam skills at the end of this Appendix, then you should have the necessary skills to pass the PowerPoint 2010 Microsoft Office Specialist exam and get certified.

Get Organized

The steps to successfully completing Microsoft Office Specialist certification are outlined in Table 1 and discussed in the remainder of this appendix. Once you have decided that you want to be certified, there are many tools, Web sites, and professionals to guide you towards to your goal.

QUICK TIP
Web addresses may change. If you cannot find what you are looking for, go to *www.microsoft.com* or *www.certiport.com* and do a search using keywords on the topic.

Steps to getting certified

what to do	how to do it
1. Choose an exam	Choose from one of the following exams, based on your skills and interests: • Microsoft Office Word 2010 • Microsoft Office Word 2010 Expert • Microsoft Office Excel 2010 • Microsoft Office Excel 2010 Expert • Microsoft Office PowerPoint 2010 • Microsoft Office Outlook 2010 • Microsoft Office Access 2010 • Microsoft Office SharePoint 2010
2. Find a testing center	Find an authorized testing center near you using the Certiport Center locator at *www.certiport.com/Portal/Pages/LocatorView.aspx*.
3. Prepare for the exam	Select the method that is appropriate for you, including taking a class or purchasing self-study materials.
4. Take a practice test	It is recommended that candidates take a Practice Test before taking an exam. • To view the practice tests available, go to *www.certiport.com/portal*. • Follow the online instructions for purchasing a voucher and taking the practice test.
5. Take the exam	• Contact the Certiport Center and make an appointment for the exam you want to take. Check the organization's payment and exam policies. • Purchase an exam voucher at *www.certiport.com/portal*. • Go to the Certiport Center to take the test, and bring a printout of the exam voucher, your Certiport username and password, and a valid picture ID.
6. Receive exam results	You will find out your results immediately. If you pass, you will receive your certificate two to three weeks after the date of the exam.

Choose an Exam

The Microsoft Office Specialist certification program offers exams for the main applications of Microsoft Office 2010, including Word, Excel, Access, PowerPoint, Outlook, and SharePoint. You can also take a Microsoft Office Specialist exam for expert levels of Word and Excel that cover more advanced skills. You can earn the highest level of certification, Microsoft Office Specialist Master, by passing three required exams—Word 2010 Expert, Excel 2010 Expert, and PowerPoint 2010—and one elective exam—Access 2010 or Outlook 2010. Choose one or more applications that will help you in your current position or job search, or one that tests skills that match your abilities and interests.

- **To learn more about the exams:**

1. Go to www.microsoft.com/learning, click the link for Certification, then click the link for Microsoft Office. You can read valuable information about the different exams and the benefits of being certified. You can even find the list of skills covered in each exam on the exam Web site. Refer to Figure 1.

FIGURE 1: Microsoft Office Specialist Certification page

- **To see the skills for a specific exam:**

1. Go to http://www.microsoft.com/learning/en/us/certification/mos.aspx, click the MOS Certifications tab, search for an exam in the application you want to explore, then click the exam number link for the exam you want to take to display more detailed information, as shown in Figure 2.

FIGURE 2: Microsoft Office Specialist exam information

Learning the Microsoft Office Specialist Certification Levels

The Microsoft Office Specialist certification program provides exams in two levels: Core and Expert. There is also a Master level which requires completion of more than one exam. As part of the process of deciding which exam you should take, you also need to decide the level of certification that best meets your needs.

Microsoft Office Specialist Core Certification

The core-level user should be able to create professional-looking documents for a variety of business, school, and personal situations. The core-level user should be able to use about 80% of the features of the program. You can achieve the Microsoft Office Specialist core certification by passing any one of the following exams: Word 2010, Excel 2010, PowerPoint 2010, Access 2010, Outlook 2010, or SharePoint 2010.

Microsoft Office Specialist Expert Certification

The expert user should be able to perform many of the advanced skills in the program at the expert level. Each test covers performance-based objectives and is designed to assess the candidates' hands-on skills using Microsoft Office. The Microsoft Office Specialist Expert Certification exams specify 75 unique performance-based tasks. You can earn the Microsoft Office Expert certification by passing one of the following exams: Word 2010 Expert and Excel 2010 Expert.

Microsoft Office Specialist Master Certification

To achieve the Microsoft Office Master certification, you need to pass three required exams and one elective exam.

Required
- Microsoft Office Word 2010 Expert
- Microsoft Office Excel 2010 Expert
- Microsoft Office PowerPoint 2010

Elective
- Microsoft Office Access 2010

or

- Microsoft Office Outlook 2010

More information about the Microsoft Office Specialist 2010 certification series can be found at *http://www.microsoft.com/learning/en/us/certification/mos.aspx#mastercert* or on the Certiport Web site at *www.certiport.com/portal*, as shown in Figure 3.

FIGURE 3: Certiport certification information

Getting Ready to Take the Exam

You have finished your studies and feel confident that you can achieve certification in one of the Microsoft Office 2010 applications. At this point you should know the program that you want to be certified in; for example, Word, Excel, PowerPoint, or Access. You also should know the level that you want to achieve, Core or Expert. Next, you need to find a test center and prepare to take the test.

Find a Testing Center

You must take Microsoft Office Specialist certification exams at an authorized testing center, called a Certiport Center. Certiport Centers are located in educational institutions, corporate training centers, and other such locations. You can find a testing center near you using the Certiport Center locator at *www.certiport.com/portal/Pages/LocatorView.aspx*, as shown in Figure 4.

QUICK TIP

Certiport Centers are located in the United States and in several countries around the world.

FIGURE 4: **Certiport Center locator**

What is the Test Like?

Completing the exercises in this book using Microsoft PowerPoint will help you prepare for the exam. Using SAM (Skills Assessment Manager) 2010 with the book is especially helpful because SAM provides performance-based assessment on the application, similar to a Microsoft Office Specialist Exam. Learning by using both the book and SAM not only teaches you the program, but it also prepares you for the exams. The exams are primarily performance-based. Exam candidates are asked to perform a series of tasks to clearly demonstrate their skills. Each exam takes approximately 50 minutes and includes approximately 30–35 questions. As you take the test, you will be asked to complete steps in a simulated environment to show that you know the steps necessary to perform the task at hand. For example, in the Word exam you might have to balance newspaper column lengths or keep text together in columns, and it will appear as though you are actually working in the Word program as you take the test. In the Excel exam, you might have to find the sum of a column of numbers or create a pie chart, and it will appear as though you are actually working in the Excel program as you take the test. In the PowerPoint exam, you may have to change the layout of a slide or change the slide background.

Prepare for the Exam: Take a Class

Reading through the exam objectives and taking a practice test can help you determine where you may need extra practice. If you are new to an Office program, you might want to take an introductory class and learn the program in its entirety. If you are already familiar with the program, you may only need to purchase study materials and learn unfamiliar skills on your own.

Taking a class—such as one that uses this book—is a good way to help you prepare for a certification exam, especially if you are a beginner. If you are an experienced user and know the basics, consider taking an advanced class. The benefits of taking a class include having an instructor as a resource, having the support of your classmates, and receiving study materials such as a lab book. Your local community college, career education center, or continuing education programs will most likely offer such courses. You can also check the Certiport Center in your area.

Purchase Materials for Self-Study

You can prepare on your own to take an exam by purchasing materials at your local bookstore or from an online retailer. To ensure that the study materials you are purchasing are well-suited to your goal of passing the Microsoft Office Specialist certification exam, you should consider the following: favorable reviews (reviews are often available when purchasing online); a table of contents that covers the skills you want to master; and the Microsoft Office Specialist Approved Courseware logo, as shown in Figure 5. This logo indicates that Microsoft and Certiport have reviewed the book and recognize it as being an adequate tool for certification preparation.

FIGURE 5: Microsoft Office Specialist Approved Courseware logo

Take a Practice Test

Consider taking an online practice test if one is available for the certification exam that you want to take. A practice test lets you determine the areas you should brush up on before taking the certification exam and helps you become familiar with the structure and format of the exam so you'll know what to expect. It is a self-assessment tool that tests you on the exam objectives and lets you know your level of proficiency. You can view the available practice tests from Certiport and register and pay for a practice test voucher at *www.certiport.com/portal*.

Is Microsoft Office Specialist the same as Microsoft Certified Application Specialist?

If you have earned a Microsoft Certified Application Specialist certification in Microsoft Office 2007, it is still valid. The name has just been changed to Microsoft Office Specialist. You can request an updated certificate from Microsoft that contains the new name.

Taking the Exam

The Microsoft Office Specialist exams are highly regarded and therefore strictly regulated. To take an exam, you must plan ahead and follow specific rules and regulations. These policies are in place to protect you, as the test taker, as well as those that will hire you based on the results of your test. If you follow these simple steps, you will see that they are easy to do.

Make an Appointment and Get Information

The locations of Certiport Centers are clearly available through their Web site. You should use the Certiport Center locator on their Web site at: *http://www.certiport.com/Portal/Pages/LocatorView.aspx*. Typically, the search results will offer a few choices. Once you find a center that is near you, and convenient, you should contact them. The locator also gives you a phone number so you can call them directly and ask questions. The Certiport Center staff can answer any questions you may have about scheduling, vouchers, and exam administration. Make an appointment for the exam you want to take. Be sure to ask about and verify the materials that you should bring with you when you take the exam.

Purchase an Exam Voucher

If your Certiport Center verifies that you need a voucher to take the test, go online to their Web site and purchase a voucher from Certiport. The voucher is your proof that you registered and paid for the exam in advance.

- **To pay for the exam and obtain a voucher:**

1. Go to *www.certiport.com/portal*, click the Login link, then create a user account with a username and password of your choice.
2. At the MyCertiport screen, click the Purchase Exam Voucher button, then follow the onscreen instructions to purchase a voucher, as shown in Figure 6.

FIGURE 6: Purchase an exam voucher

Take the Exam

You probably have been hearing this since you began your education, but it is worth repeating... if at all possible, get a good night's sleep the night before the exam! If the test is in the morning, eat a good breakfast! If the test is during the day or evening, be sure you have had something to eat so you can focus on the test. Being rested and feeling well will help you perform well on the test. You should also prepare whatever materials you need the day before the test. Running around to find your registration materials the day of the test will not help you do well. If you are late or forget any of these required items, you may not be permitted to take the exam, and may need to reschedule your test for another time.

NOTE: You must bring the following to the Certiport Center on the day of the test:

- **Your voucher, which is a printout of the electronic document you received when you paid for the test online. You will need to enter the voucher number when you log in to the test. If necessary, check with the Certiport Center to see if bringing just the voucher number, rather than a printout, is acceptable.**

- **Your Certiport username and password, which you will also have to enter at test login. You will have created a username and password when you paid for the voucher online.**

- **A valid picture ID (driver's license or valid passport).**

You may not bring any study or reference materials into the exam. You may not bring writing implements, calculators, or other materials into the test room.

Receive Exam Results

So you have taken the test, what happens next? Exam results appear on the screen as soon as you complete the exam, so you'll know your score right away. You will receive a printout of your score to take with you. If you need additional copies, go to *www.certiport.com/portal*, and then log in and go to MyCertiport, where you can always access your exam results. If you pass the exam, you will receive an official certificate in the mail in approximately two to three weeks.

If you do not pass, refunds will not be given. But keep in mind that the exams are challenging. Do not become discouraged. If you purchased a voucher with a retake, a second chance to take the exam might be all you need to pass. Study your exam results and note areas you need to work on. Check your Certiport Center's exam retake policies for more information.

> **QUICK TIP**
> The exam results are confidential.

What's it going to be like when I take the test?

Each exam is administered within a functional copy of the Microsoft program corresponding to the exam that you are taking. The exam tests your knowledge of the program by requiring you to complete specific tasks in the program. The exam is "live in the program," which means that you will work with an actual document, spreadsheet, presentation, etc., and must perform tasks on that document. You cannot use Office Online Help during the exam. The Help feature is disabled during the exam. The overall exam is timed, although there is no time limit for each question. Most exams take up to 50 minutes, but the allotted time depends on the subject and level.

Microsoft Office Specialist Exam Skills: PowerPoint 2010

Managing the PowerPoint Environment

Skill	Page Where Covered
Adjust views	
Adjust views by using the Ribbon	14 (Step 7)
Adjust views by status bar commands	14 (Steps 3–5)
Manipulate the PowerPoint window	
Work with multiple presentation windows simultaneously	51 (Clues)
Configure the Quick Access toolbar	
Show the Quick Access toolbar below the ribbon	Office 12
Configure PowerPoint file options	
Use PowerPoint Proofing	40 (Steps 1, 4)
Use PowerPoint Save options	65 (Clues), 151 (Clues), 170 (Step 2), 171 (Clues), 173 (Clues), 181 (Clues), 185 (Clues)

Creating a Slide Presentation

Skill	Page Where Covered
Construct and edit photo album	
Add captions to picture	Appendix 26
Insert text	Appendix 26
Insert images in black and white	Appendix 27
Reorder pictures in an album	Appendix 27
Adjust image	
Rotation	Appendix 26 (Tip)
Brightness	182 (Tip)
Contrast	182 (Tip)
Apply slide size and orientation settings	
Set up a custom size	123 (Clues)
Change the orientation	112 (Step 7), 123 (Clues)
Add and remove slides	
Insert an outline	50 (Step 3)
Reuse slides from a saved presentation	51 (Clues)
Reuse slides from a slide library	185 (Clues)
Duplicate selected slides	132 (Tip), Appendix 20 (Tip)
Delete multiple slides simultaneously	Appendix 20
Include noncontiguous slides in a presentation	51 (Clues), Appendix 20

Creating a Slide Presentation (Continued)

Skill	Page Where Covered
Format slides	
Format sections	50 (Tip), 86 (Steps 5–6)
Modify themes	12 (Steps 2, 4, 6)
Switch to a different slide layout	10 (Step 7)
Apply a formating to a slide	
Fill color	76 (Step 2)
Gradient	91 (Step 2b)
Picture	Appendix 21
Texture	Appendix 21
Pattern	Appendix 21
Set up slide footers	38 (Steps 2, 4)
Enter and format text	
Use text effects	28 (Steps 2, 4–8)
Change text format	
Indentation	108 (Steps 3–4)
Alignment	110 (Steps 5–6)
Line spacing	110 (Step 7)
Direction	111 (Clues)
Change the formatting of bulleted and numbered lists	106 (Steps 2–6)
Enter text in a placeholder text box	8 (Steps 3, 5, 6)
Convert text to SmartArt	30 (Step 1)
Copy and paste text	40 (Tip), 68 (Step 7d), Appendix 18 (Tip)
Use Paste Special	89 (Clues)
Use Format Painter	100 (Steps 1, 8)
Format text boxes	
Apply formatting to text box	
Fill color	Appendix 18
Gradient	115 (Step 2b)
Picture	100 (Tip)
Texture	100 (Tip)
Pattern	Appendix 18
Change the outline of a text box	
Color	Appendix 19
Weight	100 (Step 7)
Style	Appendix 19
Change the shape of a text box	32 (Steps 3, 5), 56 (Step 8)

Creating a Slide Presentation (Continued)

Skill	Page Where Covered
Apply effects	100 (Steps 4–6)
Set the alignment	110 (Steps 5–6)
Create columns in a text box	101 (Clues)
Set internal margins	110 (Steps 3–4)
Set the current text box formatting as the default for new text boxes	Appendix 19 (Clues)
Adjust text in a text box	
Wrap	56 (Steps 2–3)
Size	28 (Step 7)
Position	56 (Step 8)
Use AutoFit	8 (Steps 6–7)

Working with Graphical and Multimedia Elements

Skill	Page Where Covered
Manipulate graphical elements	
Arrange graphical elements	36 (Step 4)
Position graphical elements	36 (Steps 4–6)
Resize graphical elements	34 (Steps 2, 4)
Apply effects to graphical elements	44 (Steps 4d–4e), 152 (Step 8)
Apply styles to graphical elements	32 (Step 6)
Apply borders to graphical elements	32 (Step 7), 54 (Step 5)
Add hyperlinks to graphical elements	160, (Steps 2–3)
Manipulate images	
Apply color adjustments	52 (Step 7), 68 (Step 3d)
Apply image corrections	
Sharpen	54 (Step 6)
Soften	54 (Step 6)
Brightness	Appendix 22
Contrast	Appendix 22
Add artistic effects to an image	156 (Step 7)
Remove a background	Appendix 22
Crop a picture	54 (Steps 3–4)
Compress selected pictures or all pictures	54 (Step 8)
Change a picture	Appendix 23
Reset a picture	52 (Tip)
Modify WordArt and shapes	
Set the formatting of the current shape as the default for future shapes	Appendix 25 (Tip)

Working with Graphical and Multimedia Elements (Continued)

Skill	Page Where Covered
Change the fill color or texture	32 (Step 6), 64 (Step 4)
Change the WordArt	64 (Steps 4–6)
Convert Word Art to SmartArt	Appendix 25
Manipulate SmartArt	
Add and remove shapes	148 (Step 2)
Change SmartArt styles	148 (Step 6)
Change the SmartArt layout	148 (Step 3)
Reorder shapes	148 (Steps 8–9)
Convert a SmartArt graphic to text	30 (Tip)
Convert SmartArt to shapes	Appendix 25
Make shapes larger or smaller	164 (Step 3b)
Promote bullet levels	148 (Tip)
Demote bullet levels	148 (Tip)
Edit video and audio content	
Apply a style to video or audio content	152 (Step 8)
Adjust video or audio content	153 (Clues), 154 (Steps 6–7)
Arrange video or audio content	153 (Step 3)
Size video or audio content	152 (Steps 5–6)
Adjust playback options	154 (Steps 4–6)

Creating Charts and Tables

Skill	Page Where Covered
Construct and modify tables	
Draw a table	63 (Clues)
Insert a Microsoft Excel spreadsheet	133 (Clues), 134 (Step 3)
Set table style options	62 (Steps 5–9)
Add shading	Appendix 24
Add borders	146 (Step 3)
Add effects	62 (Step 8)
Columns and rows	
Change the alignment	62 (Step 7)
Resize	62 (Tip)
Merge	Appendix 24
Split	146 (Step 5)
Distribute	62 (Step 8)
Arrange	Appendix 24 (Tip)

Creating Charts and Tables (Continued)

Skill	Page Where Covered
Insert and modify charts	
Select a chart type	58 (Steps 3–4)
Enter chart data	60 (Steps 3–4)
Change the chart type	124 (Step 7)
Change the chart layout	124 (Step 3)
Switch row and column	60 (Step 6)
Select data	60 (Steps 2–3)
Edit data	60 (Steps 2–3)
Apply chart elements	
Use chart labels	124 (Step 4)
Use axes	128 (Steps 5–6)
Use gridlines	126 (Steps 1–2)
Use backgrounds	134 (Steps 5–7)
Manipulate chart layouts	
Select chart elements	128 (Steps 1, 4, 7)
Format selections	128 (Steps 2, 3, 5, 6, 8)
Manipulate chart elements	
Arrange chart elements	126 (Steps 3–5)
Specify a precise position	126 (Step 5)
Apply effects	130 (Steps 3–4)
Resize chart elements	140 (Steps 5g, 6d)
Apply Quick Styles	132 (Step 6)
Apply a border	128 (Step 8)
Add hyperlinks	Appendix 25 (Clues)

Applying Transitions and Animations

Skill	Page Where Covered
Apply built-in and custom animations	
Use More Entrance effects	82 (Step 2)
Use More Emphasis effects	92 (Step 5c)
Use More Exit effects	130 (Tip)
Use More Motion paths	82 (Step 7)
Apply effect and path options	
Set timing	82 (Step 3)
Set start options	102 (Steps 3–4), 103 (Clues)

Applying Transitions and Animations (Continued)

Skill	Page Where Covered
Manipulate animations	
Change the direction of an animation	102 (Step 3)
Attach a sound to an animation	Appendix 23 (Clues)
Use Animation Painter	102 (Steps 5–6)
Reorder animation	116 (Step 3h)
Select text options	82 (Step 6)
Apply and modify transitions between slides	
Modify a transition effect	80 (Step 3)
Add a sound to a transition	80 (Tip)
Modify transition duration	80 (Steps 5–6)
Set up manual or automatically timed advance options	80 (Step 6), 81 (Clues)

Collaborating on Presentations

Skill	Page Where Covered
Manage comments in presentations	
Insert and edit comments	180 (Steps 4–6)
Show or hide markup	180 (Steps 7–8)
Move to the previous or next comment	180 (Steps 6–8)
Delete comments	172 (Steps 5, 8)
Apply proofing tools	
Use Spelling and Thesaurus features	40 (Steps 1–2), 127 (Clues)
Compare and combine presentations	172 (Steps 1–2)

Preparing Presentations for Delivery

Skill	Page Where Covered
Save presentations	
Save the presentation as a picture presentation	Appendix 21
Save the presentation as a PDF	151 (Clues)
Save the presentation as an XPS	151 (Clues)
Save the presentation as an outline	Appendix 21
Save the presentation as an OpenDocument	Appendix 21
Save the presentation as a show (.ppsx)	Appendix 21
Save a slide or object as a picture file	159 (Clues)
Share presentations	
Package a presentation for CD delivery	171 (Clues)
Create video	65 (Clues)

Preparing Presentations for Delivery (Continued)

Skill	Page Where Covered
Create handouts (send to Microsoft Word)	113 (Clues)
Compress media	54 (Step 8)
Print presentations	
Adjust print settings	16 (Step 3)
Protect presentations	
Set a password	178 (Steps 1–3)
Change a password	178 (Steps 4–6)
Mark a presentation as final	84 (Step 6)

Delivering Presentations

Skill	Page Where Covered
Apply presentation tools	
Add pen and highlighter annotations	78 (Steps 4–7)
Change the ink color	175 (Figure H-5)
Erase an annotation	78 (Steps 7–8)
Discard annotations upon closing	92 (Step 3f)
Retain annotations upon closing	78 (Step 8)
Set up slide shows	
Set up a slide show	174 (Steps 1–3)
Play narrations	183 (Clues)
Set up Presenter view	175 (Clues)
Use timings	174 (Steps 3–4)
Show media controls	78 (Steps 4, 9)
Broadcast presentations	184
Create a custom slide show	176 (Steps 1–4)
Set presentation timing	
Rehearse timings	81 (Clues)
Keep timings	80 (Step 6)
Adjust a slide's timing	80 (Step 6), 92 (Step 4c)
Record presentations	
Start recording from the beginning of a slide show	183 (Clues)
Start recording from the current slide of the slide show	183 (Clues)

Additional Skills for Microsoft PowerPoint 2010

Files You Will Need:

No files needed.

The units in this book cover nearly all of the skills that are specified in Microsoft's standards for the Microsoft Office Specialist Certification exam for PowerPoint 2010. However, there are some skills that are not covered in the units. This section of the Appendix provides reference materials for the exam skills that are not covered in the units in the book. All of these skills are cross referenced in the Exam Skills Grid that precedes this page. Be sure to review this section as you prepare for the PowerPoint 2010 Core exam.

OBJECTIVES

Format text objects

Work with slides and the slide background

Modify pictures in PowerPoint

Work with tables, SmartArt, and WordArt

Edit a photo album

Formatting Text Objects

Formatting text and text objects in PowerPoint helps you develop a creative-looking presentation. Text objects can be different sizes and shapes, and you can format a text object's background (fill) and its border (outline). PowerPoint allows you the flexibility to emphasize text. You can fill a text object with color, or patterns, and format the border color and line style without changing the formatting characteristics of the text.

Apply a fill color to a text object

1. Click the Home tab on the Ribbon, click the text object you want to format, then click the Shape Fill list arrow in the Drawing Group.
2. Click a fill color from the Theme or Standard Colors palette.

QUICK TIP

To change the transparency of a text object already filled with a color, right-click the text object, click Format Shape on the shortcut menu, then drag the Transparency Slider in the Fill section of the Format Shape dialog box.

Click a color from either palette

Click to open the Colors dialog box for more colors

Apply a pattern fill to a text object

1. Right-click the text object you want to format, then click Format Shape on the shortcut menu to open the Format Shape dialog box.
2. Click the Pattern Fill option button, then click a pattern.

QUICK TIP

To copy text, select the text, click the Home tab, click the Copy button in the Clipboard group, place the insertion point where you want to paste the text, then click the Paste button in the Clipboard group.

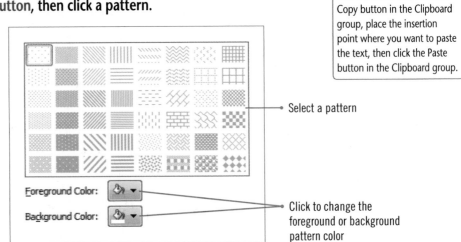

Select a pattern

Click to change the foreground or background pattern color

3. Click the Foreground Color list arrow or the Background Color list arrow .
4. Click Close.

Change the outline color, width, and style of text box

1. Click the text object you want to format, then click the Drawing Tools Format tab.
2. Click the Shape Outline list arrow in the Shape Styles group, then click a color from the Theme or Standard Colors palette.

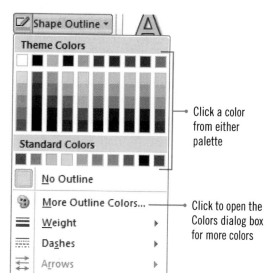

Click a color from either palette

Click to open the Colors dialog box for more colors

3. Click the Shape Outline list arrow, point to Weight, then click a line weight.
4. Click the Shape Outline list arrow, point to Dashes, then click a line style.

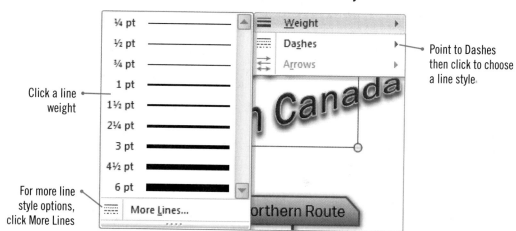

Click a line weight

For more line style options, click More Lines

Point to Dashes then click to choose a line style

Changing text box defaults

You can change the default formatting characteristics of text boxes you create using the Text Box button on the Insert tab. To change the formatting defaults for text boxes, select an existing formatted text box, or create a new one and format it as desired using any of PowerPoint's formatting commands. When you are ready to change the text box defaults, press [SHIFT], right-click the formatted text box, release [SHIFT], then click Set as Default Text Box on the shortcut menu. Any new text boxes you create will display the formatting characteristics of this formatted text box.

Working with Slides and the Slide Background

Occasionally you need to copy or delete multiple slides within the presentation. When these slides are non-contiguous (those that are not adjacent to one another), you can easily select them in the Slide Sorter view and then delete or copy and paste them where you want in the presentation. Modifying the slide background with a picture or texture can enhance your slides when you want your presentation to have a particular design. When you are ready to save your presentation, you have a number of different file format options from which to choose. To select a file format, click the File tab, then click Save or Save As to open the Save As dialog box. See the table below for an explanation of some common file format options.

Copy non-contiguous slides

1. Open the presentation from which you want to copy slides.
2. Click the Slide Sorter button ▦ on the status bar, then click the first slide thumbnail you want to copy.
3. Press and hold [CTRL], click each additional slide thumbnail you want to copy, then release [CTRL].
4. Click the Copy button ▥ in the Clipboard group, then click to place the insertion point in Slide Sorter view where you want to paste the new slides.

> **QUICK TIP**
> You can also copy and paste multiple slides using the Slides tab in Normal view.

> **QUICK TIP**
> To duplicate one or more slides, select the slides, click the Copy list arrow, then click Duplicate to paste the slides at the end of the presentation.

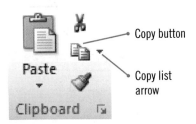

Copy button

Copy list arrow

5. Click the Paste button ▥ in the Clipboard group.

Delete multiple slides

1. In the Slides tab, click the first slide you want to delete, press and hold [CTRL], then click each additional slide you want to delete (scroll up or down if needed).
2. Release [CTRL], right-click one of the selected slides, then click Delete Slide in the shortcut menu.

> **QUICK TIP**
> To select contiguous slides, click the first slide, press and hold [SHIFT], click the last slide you want to select, then release [SHIFT].

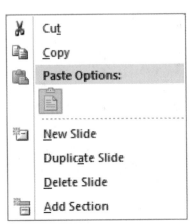

Format the slide background with a texture, or a picture

1. Click the Design tab on the Ribbon, click the Background Styles button in the Background group, then click Format Background.

QUICK TIP

To apply a pattern to a slide background, right-click the slide background, click Format Background, click the Pattern option button, click a pattern, then click Close.

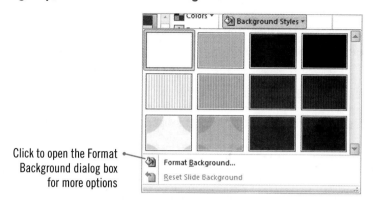

Click to open the Format Background dialog box for more options

2. Click the Picture or texture fill option button in the Format Background dialog box.

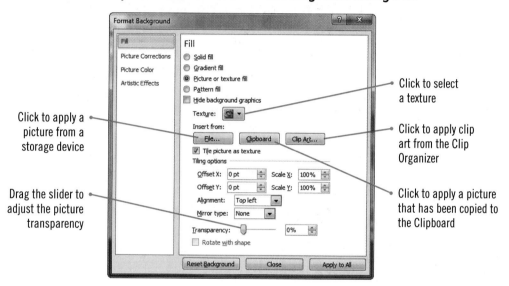

Click to apply a picture from a storage device

Click to select a texture

Click to apply clip art from the Clip Organizer

Click to apply a picture that has been copied to the Clipboard

Drag the slider to adjust the picture transparency

3. To apply a texture, click the Texture list arrow, then click a texture from the gallery.
or
To apply a picture, click the File button in the Insert from section, locate the picture, then click Insert.

4. Click Close.

File formats supported in PowerPoint 2010

save as file type	extension	description
PowerPoint presentation	.pptx	A PowerPoint 2007 or 2010 presentation (XML-enabled by default)
PowerPoint design template	.potx	A PowerPoint 2007 or 2010 presentation template that you can use to format future presentations
PowerPoint Show	.pps; .ppsx	A presentation that always opens up in Slide Show view
Outline/RTF	.rtf	A presentation that is a text-only document
OpenDocument presentation	.odp	A saving format that allows you to open a presentation in other applications that use the OpenDocument Presentation format
PowerPoint picture presentation	.pptx	A PowerPoint 2007 or 2010 presentation where each slide is converted into a picture

Appendix: PowerPoint 2010

Modifying Pictures in PowerPoint

PowerPoint has powerful basic formatting features that allow you to modify specific aspects of a picture directly on the slide without having to use a separate picture-editing program. For example, you can correct minor brightness and contrast flaws in a picture, which will make the picture stand out in your presentation. You can also modify a picture by removing its background or replace it with a different one while preserving the formatting and size of the original picture.

Correct the brightness and contrast of a picture

1. Click the picture you want to modify, then click the Picture Tools Format tab on the Ribbon.

2. Click the Corrections buttton in the Adjust group.

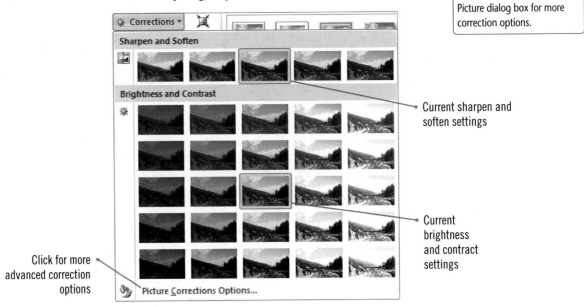

Click for more advanced correction options

Current sharpen and soften settings

Current brightness and contract settings

3. Click a brightness and contrast option in the gallery.

Remove a picture background

1. Click the picture you want to modify, click the Picture Tools Format tab on the Ribbon, then click the Remove Background button in the Adjust group to open the Background Removal tab on the Ribbon.

Background Removal tab

2. Click the Mark Areas to Keep button in the Refine group, then draw lines on the picture to mark the areas you want to keep.

3. Click the Mark Areas to Remove button, then draw lines on the picture to mark the areas you want to remove.

QUICK TIP

Click the Delete Mark button in the Refine group, then click lines you have drawn to remove marked areas of a picture.

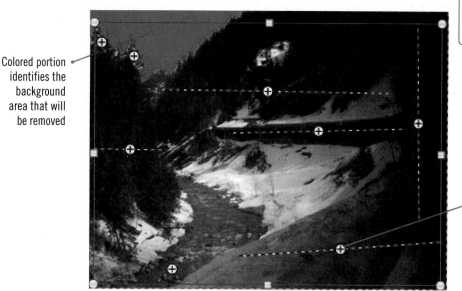

Colored portion identifies the background area that will be removed

Plus symbol identifies a portion of the picture you want to save

4. Click the Keep Changes button in the Close group to retain all of your changes or click the Discard All Changes button to remove all changes.

Change a picture

1. Right-click the picture you want to exchange for another, then click Change Picture on the shortcut menu to open the Insert Picture dialog box.

2. Locate a new picture, select the picture, then click Insert. The inserted picture will assume the size and formatting of the original picture.

QUICK TIP

If the Picture Tools Format tab is already open, you can replace a picture with another one by clicking the Change Picture button in the Adjust group.

Attaching a sound to an animation

Text or objects that have animation applied can be customized further by attaching a sound for extra emphasis. First, select the animated object, then click the Animation Pane button in the Advanced Animation group. In the Animation Pane, click the animation you want to apply the sound to, click the Animation list arrow, then click Effect Options to open the animation effect's dialog box. In the Enhancements section, click the Sound list arrow, then choose a sound. Click OK when you are finished. Now, when you run the slide show, the sound you applied will play with the animation.

Working with Tables, SmartArt, and WordArt

Using a table helps you compare and organize related information in rows and columns. PowerPoint makes it easy to insert and format tables using shading or other color attributes to help identify the information in the table. If you need to combine row or column information in a table, you can merge data from multiple cells into one cell. Sometimes objects that you use in a presentation do not function as you originally intended. So that you do not have to recreate the data, objects like SmartArt and WordArt can be converted into other objects so you can manipulate them differently.

Shade the background of a table

1. Click the table to select it, then click the Table Tools Design tab on the Ribbon.
2. Click the Shading list arrow in the Table Styles group, then choose a color from the palette.

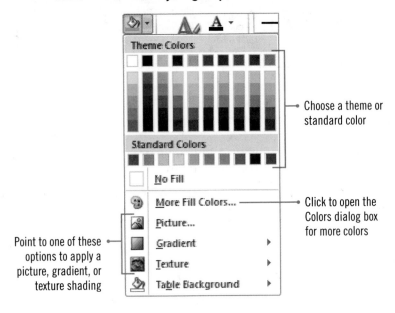

Choose a theme or standard color

Click to open the Colors dialog box for more colors

Point to one of these options to apply a picture, gradient, or texture shading

Merge data in a table

1. Click the table, then select the cells you want to merge.
2. Click the Table Tools Layout tab on the Ribbon.
3. Click the Merge Cells button in the Merge group.

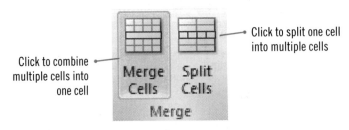

Click to split one cell into multiple cells

Click to combine multiple cells into one cell

Convert a WordArt object to SmartArt

1. Right-click the WordArt object, point to Convert to SmartArt on the shortcut menu, then choose a SmartArt layout.

QUICK TIP

You can also click the WordArt object, click the Home tab in the Paragraph group, click the Convert to SmartArt Graphic button, then choose a SmartArt graphic.

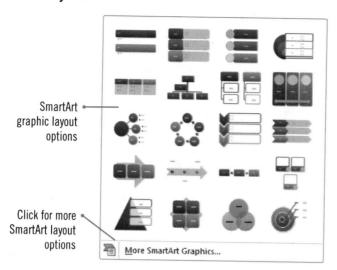

SmartArt graphic layout options

Click for more SmartArt layout options

More SmartArt Graphics...

Convert a SmartArt object to individual shapes

1. Click the SmartArt object, then click the SmartArt Tools Design tab on the Ribbon.
2. Click the Convert button in the Reset group, then click Convert to Shapes.

QUICK TIP

To convert a SmartArt object to individual shapes, you can also right-click a blank area of the SmartArt object, then click Convert to Shapes on the shortcut menu.

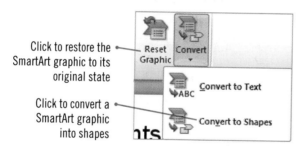

Click to restore the SmartArt graphic to its original state

Click to convert a SmartArt graphic into shapes

Reset Graphic

Convert

Convert to Text

Convert to Shapes

QUICK TIP

To set the formatting of a shape as the default, right-click the shape, then click Set as Default Shape on the shortcut menu.

3. Click the Drawing Tools Format tab on the Ribbon, then click the Group button in the Arrange group.
4. Click Ungroup.

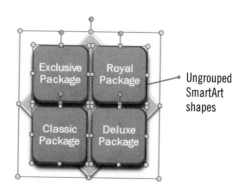

Ungrouped SmartArt shapes

Adding a hyperlink to a chart

You can add a hyperlink to any object in PowerPoint, even a chart. Select the chart, then click the Insert tab on the Ribbon. Click the Hyperlink button in the Links group, if linking to another file, click the Existing File or Web Page button, locate the file you want to link to the chart, then click OK. To link to another slide in the presentation, click the Place in The Document button, then click the slide in the list. Now, during a slide show you can click the chart to open the linked object. To remove the link, click the chart, click the Hyperlink button in the Links group, then click Remove Link.

Appendix: PowerPoint 2010

Editing a Photo Album

The Photo Album feature in PowerPoint allows you to develop a presentation based on a set of pictures. Each slide in a photo album presentation holds one picture, or you can place up to four pictures on a slide. There are seven different picture layouts from which to choose, including the Fit to slide layout and the 4 pictures layout. You can add a text caption to the pictures when you use any picture layout except the fit to slide layout option. You also have the ability to edit pictures you place in the photo album presentation by changing a picture's rotation or color. In addition, you have the flexibility to change the order of pictures in the presentation, as well as remove pictures you decide not to use. If you want your presentation to have a specific look and design, you can apply a theme to the presentation.

Add captions to pictures

1. Open the photo album presentation, click the Insert tab on the Ribbon, click the Photo Album list arrow in the Images group, then click Edit Photo Album to open the Edit Photo Album dialog box.

QUICK TIP

You can also rotate pictures in a photo album by selecting the pictures in the albums list, then clicking the Rotate buttons below the Preview box in the Edit Photo Album dialog box.

Click to edit your photo album

2. Click the Picture layout list arrow, then choose any picture layout except Fit to slide.

3. Click the Captions below ALL pictures check box under Picture Options.

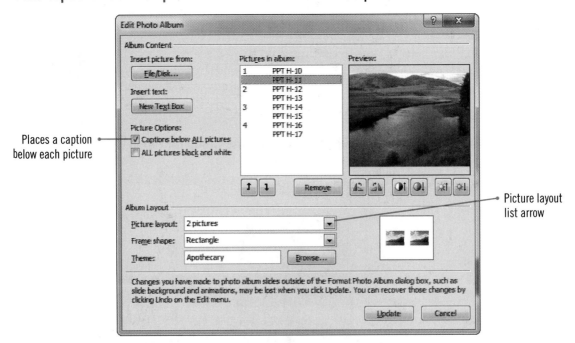

Places a caption below each picture

Picture layout list arrow

4. Click Update, then click each slide and enter caption text for each picture.

Insert a text box and enter text

1. Open the photo album presentation, click the Insert tab on the Ribbon, click the Photo Album list arrow in the Images group, then click Edit Photo Album.

2. Click the picture in the Pictures in album list, then click New Text Box.

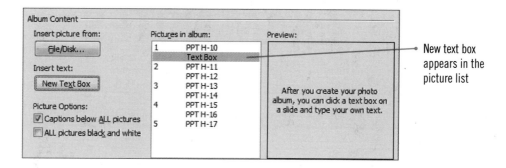

New text box appears in the picture list

3. Click Update, select the slide with the new text box, click the text box, then enter text.

Reorder pictures in a photo album

1. Open the photo album presentation, click the Insert tab on the Ribbon, click the Photo Album list arrow in the Images group, then click Edit Photo Album.

2. Click the picture in the Pictures in album list you want to move, then click the Up arrow button or the Down arrow button to reorder the picture in the album.

QUICK TIP

Use the Edit Photo Album dialog box to remove pictures from the presentation; click Remove below the Pictures in album list.

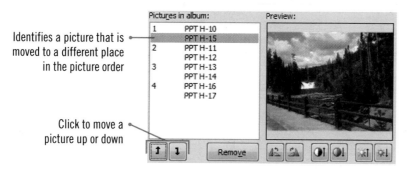

Identifies a picture that is moved to a different place in the picture order

Click to move a picture up or down

3. Click Update.

Work with themes and black and white color

1. Open the photo album presentation, click the Insert tab on the Ribbon, click the Photo Album list arrow in the Images group, then click Edit Photo Album.

2. Click Browse in the Album Layout section, choose a theme, then click Open.

3. Click the ALL pictures black and white check box in the Picture Options section to convert all pictures in the presentation to black and white.

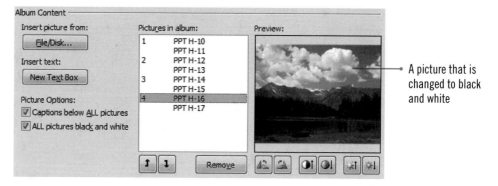

A picture that is changed to black and white

4. Click Update.

EXAM NOTES

EXAM NOTES

EXAM NOTES

EXAM NOTES

EXAM NOTES

Glossary

Action button An interactive button that you click in Slide Show view to perform an activity, such as advancing to the next slide.

Active The currently available document, program, or object; on the taskbar, when more than one program is open, the button for the active program appears slightly lighter.

Active cell A selected cell in an Excel worksheet.

Adjustment handle A small yellow diamond that changes the appearance of an object's most prominent feature.

Align To place objects' edges or centers on the same plane.

Animation tag Identifies the order an object is animated on a slide during a slide show.

Annotate A freehand drawing on the screen made by using the pen or highlighter tool. You can annotate only in Slide Show view.

Axis label Text in the first row and column of a worksheet that identifies data.

Background The area behind the text and graphics on a slide.

Background graphic An object placed on the slide master.

Backstage view The view that appears when you click the File tab. Use this view to manage a presentation file.

Backward-compatible Software feature that enables documents saved in an older version of a program to be opened in a newer version of the program.

.bmp The file extension for the bitmap graphics file format.

Broadcast Present a slide show to an audience over the Internet in real time using a Web browser.

Bullet A small graphic symbol, usually a round or square dot, often used to identify items in a list.

Category axis The horizontal axis in a chart.

Cell The intersection of a column and row in a worksheet, datasheet, or table.

Chart A graphical representation of numerical data from a worksheet. Types include 2-D and 3-D column, bar, pie, area, and line charts.

Chart template A special file (.crtx) that stores a chart's formatting and layout characteristics in the Charts Template folder.

Clip art Predesigned graphic images you can insert in any document or presentation to enhance its appearance.

Clip art video The illusion of making a static object appear to move. Some graphics such as an animated .gif (Graphics Interchange Format) file has motion when you run the slide show.

Clip Organizer A library of art, pictures, sounds, video clips, and animations that all Office applications share.

Cloud computing When data, applications, and resources are stored on servers accessed over the Internet or a company's internal network rather than on users' computers.

Collections The folders in the Clip Organizer where the clip art is stored.

Column heading The gray box containing the column letter on top of the columns in the worksheet.

Comment A note you attach to a slide or an object on a slide.

Compatibility The ability of different programs to work together and exchange data.

Compatibility Checker Finds potential compatibility issues between a PowerPoint 2010 presentation and earlier versions of PowerPoint.

Connection site An anchor point to attach a line or an arrow on a shape.

Content placeholder A placeholder that is used to enter text or objects such as clip art, charts, or pictures.

Crop To hide part of an object, such as clip art using the Cropping tool or to delete a part of a picture.

Data series A column or row in a datasheet.

Data series marker A graphical representation of a data series, such as a bar or column.

Destination file The file an object is embedded into, such as a presentation.

Digital signature A way to authenticate a presentation files using computer cryptography. A digital signature is not visible in a presentation.

Digital video Live action captured in digital format by a movie camera.

Distribute To evenly divide the space horizontally or vertically between objects relative to each other or the slide edges.

Document Inspector A PowerPoint feature that examines a presentation for hidden data or personal information.

Embedded object An object that is created in one application and inserted to another. Embedded objects remain connected to the original program file in which they were created for editing.

Encryption A security process that protects a file from unauthorized access by use of a password.

Error bars Identify potential error amounts relative to each data marker in a data series.

Exception A change you make directly to text on the slide, which does not match the theme fonts on the slide master.

File format A file type, such as .pptx, .bmp, .jpg, or .gif.

Fixed layout format A specific file format that locks the file from future change.

Gallery A visual collection of choices you can browse through to make a selection. Often available with Live Preview.

.gif The file extension for the graphics interchange format.

graphics format The type of graphics file, for example, Joint Photographic Experts Group Format (*.jpg), TIFF Tag Image Format (*.tif), or Bitmap (*.bmp).

Group To combine multiple objects into one object.

Handout master view The master view for printing handouts.

Hanging indent The first line of a paragraph begins to the left of all subsequent lines of text.

Hyperlink An object or link (a filename, word, phrase, or graphic) that, when clicked, "jumps to" another location in the current file or opens another PowerPoint presentation, a Word, Excel, or Access file, or an address on the World Wide Web.

Indent levels Text levels in the master text placeholder. Each level is indented a certain amount from the left margin, and you control their placement by dragging indent markers on the ruler.

Indent markers Small markers (two triangles and one square) on the horizontal ruler that indicate the indent settings for the selected text.

Insertion point A blinking vertical line that indicates where the next character will appear when text is entered in a text placeholder in PowerPoint.

Integrate To incorporate a document and parts of a document created in one program into another program; for example, to incorporate an Excel chart into a PowerPoint slide, or an Access table into a Word document.

Interface The look and feel of a program; for example, the appearance of commands and the way they are organized in the program window.

.jpg The file extension for the JPEG (Joint Photographic Experts Group) file format.

Kiosk A freestanding booth that can contain a computer used to display information, usually situated in a public area.

Laser pointer A pointer you use in Slide Show view to highlight parts of the slide.

Launch To open or start a program on your computer.

Leading The spacing between lines of text in a text object within the same paragraph.

Legend Text that provides information about the data series in a chart.

Link A connection between a source file and a destination file, which when the source file is updated, the destination file can also be updated. Can also refer to a hyperlink. *See also* Hyperlink.

Live Preview A feature that lets you point to a choice in a gallery or palette and see the results in the document without actually clicking the choice.

Macro An action or a set of actions that you use to automate tasks.

Major gridlines Identify major units on a chart axis.

Margin The distance between the edge of the text and the edge of the text box.

Master view A specific view in a presentation that stores information about font styles, text placeholders, and color schemes. There are three master views: Slide Master view, Handout Master view, and Notes Master view.

Masters One of three views (Slide Master view, Handout Master view, and Notes Master view) that stores information about the presentation theme, fonts, placeholders, and other background objects.

Metadata Another name for document properties that includes the author name, the document subject, the document title, and other personal information.

Microsoft Graph A program that creates a chart to graphically depict numerical information when you don't have access to Microsoft Excel.

Mini toolbar A small toolbar that appears next to selected text that contains basic text-formatting commands.

Minor gridlines Identify minor units on a chart axis.

Narration A voice recording you make using a microphone on one or more slides. Narrations play during a slide show.

Normal view The primary view that you use to write, edit, and design your presentation. Normal view is divided into three areas: Slides or Outline tab, Slide pane, and Notes pane.

Notes master view The master view for Notes Page view.

Notes Page view A presentation view that displays a reduced image of the current slide above a large text box where you can type notes.

Notes pane The area in Normal view that shows speaker notes for the current slide; also in Notes Page view, the area below the slide image that contains speaker notes.

Object An item you place or draw on a slide that can be modified. Examples of objects include drawn lines and shapes, text, clip art, and imported pictures.

Office Web App Versions of the Microsoft Office applications with limited functionality that are available online from Windows Live SkyDrive. Users can view documents online and then edit them in the browser using a selection of functions. Office Web Apps are available for Word, PowerPoint, Excel, and One Note.

Online collaboration The ability to incorporate feedback or share information across the Internet or a company network or intranet.

Outline tab The section in Normal view that displays your presentation text in the form of an outline, without graphics.

Pane A section of the PowerPoint window, such as the Slide or Notes pane.

Paragraph spacing The space before and after paragraph text.

Photo album A type of presentation that displays photographs.

Picture A digital photograph, piece of line art, or clip art that is created in another program and is inserted into PowerPoint.

Placeholder A dashed line box where you place text or objects.

PowerPoint Viewer A special application designed to run a PowerPoint slide show on any compatible computer that does not have PowerPoint installed.

PowerPoint window A window that contains the running PowerPoint application. The PowerPoint window includes the Ribbon, panes, and Presentation window.

Presentation software A software program used to organize and present information.

Presenter view A special view that permits you to run a presentation through two monitors.

Previewing Prior to printing, seeing onscreen exactly how the printed document will look.

Quick Access toolbar A small toolbar at the top of the PowerPoint window that contains buttons for commonly used commands such as Save and Undo.

Quick Style Determines how fonts, colors, and effects of the theme are combined and which color, font, and effect is dominant. A Quick Style can be applied to shapes or text.

Reading view A view you use to review your presentation or present a slide show to someone on a computer monitor.

Read-only A file that can't be edited or modified.

Ribbon A wide (toolbar-like) band that runs across the PowerPoint window that organizes primary commands into tabs; each tab has buttons organized into groups.

Rotate handle A green circular handle at the top of a selected object that you can drag to rotate the selected object.

Row heading The gray box containing the row number to the left of the row in a worksheet.

Scale To change the size of a graphic to a specific percentage of its original size.

Screen capture An electronic snapshot of your screen, as if you took a picture of it with a camera, which you can paste into a document.

Screenshot A static picture you take of an open program window and insert on a slide.

Selection box A dashed border that appears around a text object or placeholder, indicating that it is ready to accept text.

Series in Columns The data in the datasheet columns is plotted on the y-axis, and the row axis labels are shown in the legend. The column axis labels are plotted on the x-axis.

Series in Rows The data in the datasheet rows is plotted on the y-axis, and the row axis labels are shown on the x-axis.

Sizing handles The small circles and squares that appear around a selected object. Dragging a sizing handle resizes the object.

SkyDrive An online storage and file sharing service. Access to SkyDrive is through a Windows Live account. Up to 25 GB of data can be stored in a personal SkyDrive, with each file a maximum size of 50 MB.

Slide layout This determines how all of the elements on a slide are arranged, including text and content placeholders.

Slide Library A folder where you store presentation slides for others to access, modify, or use.

Slide pane The section of Normal view that contains the current slide.

Slide Show view A view that shows a presentation as an electronic slide show; each slide fills the screen.

Slide Sorter view A view that displays a thumbnail of all slides in the order in which they appear in a presentation; used to rearrange slides and add special effects.

Slide timing The amount of time a slide is visible on the screen during a slide show.

Slide transition The special effect that moves one slide off the screen and the next slide on the screen during a slide show. Each slide can have its own transition effect.

Slides tab The section in Normal view that displays the slides of your presentation as small thumbnails.

SmartArt A professional quality graphic diagram that visually illustrates text.

SmartArt Style A pre-set combination of formatting options that follows the design theme that you can apply to a SmartArt graphic.

SmartArt text pane A small text pane attached to a SmartArt graphic where you can enter and edit text.

Source file Where an object you create with the source program is saved.

Source program The program in which a file was created.

Status bar The bar at the bottom of the PowerPoint window that contains messages about what you are doing and seeing in PowerPoint, such as the current slide number or the current theme.

Subtitle text placeholder A box on the title slide reserved for subpoint text.

Suite A group of programs that are bundled together and share a similar interface, making it easy to transfer skills and program content among them.

Tab A section of the Ribbon that identifies groups of commands like the Home tab.

Tab selector Icon on the horizontal ruler that cycles through the four tab alignment options.

Task pane A separate pane that contains sets of menus, lists, options, and hyperlinks such as the Animation task pane that are used to customize objects.

Template A type of presentation that contains custom design information made to the slide master, slide layouts, and theme.

Text label A text box you create using the Text Box button, where the text does not automatically wrap inside the box. Text box text does not appear in the Outline tab.

Text placeholder A box with a dotted border and text that you replace with your own text.

Theme A set of colors, fonts, and effects that you apply to a presentation from the Themes Gallery.

Theme colors The set of 12 coordinated colors that make up a PowerPoint presentation; a color scheme assigns colors for text, lines, fills, accents, hyperlinks, and background.

Theme effects The set of effects for lines and fills.

Theme fonts The set of fonts for titles and other text.

Thumbnail A small image of a slide. Thumbnails are visible on the Slides tab and in Slide Sorter view.

Tick mark A small line of measurement that intersects an axis and identifies the categories, values or series of a chart.

Timing *See* Slide timing.

Title The first line or heading on a slide.

Title placeholder A box on a slide reserved for the title of a presentation or slide.

Title slide The first slide in a presentation.

Trendline A graphical representation of an upward or downward movement in a data series, used to predict future tendencies.

User interface A collective term for all the ways you interact with a software program.

Value axis The vertical axis in a chart.

View A way of displaying a presentation, such as Normal view, Reading View, Notes Page view, Slide Sorter view, and Slide Show view.

View Shortcuts The buttons at the bottom of the PowerPoint window on the status bar that you click to switch among views.

Web server A computer that hosts Web pages.

Windows Live A collection of services and Web applications that people can access through a login. Windows Live services include access to e-mail and instant messaging, storage of files on SkyDrive, sharing and storage of photos, networking with people, downloading software, and interfacing with a mobile device.

WordArt A set of decorative styles or text effects that is applied to text.

Word processing box A text box you create using the Text Box button, where the text automatically wraps inside the box.

Worksheet Where the numerical data is stored for a chart.

XML Acronym that stands for eXtensible Markup Language, which is a language used to structure, store, and send information.

Zooming in A feature that makes a document appear larger but shows less of it on screen at once; does not affect actual document size.

Zooming out A feature that shows more of a document on screen at once but at a reduced size; does not affect actual document size.

Zoom slider A feature that allows you to change the zoom percentage of a slide. Located in the status bar.

Index